Classroom 15

Classroom 15

How the Hoover FBI Censored the Dreams of Innocent Oregon Fourth Graders

Editor & Introduction: Peter Laufer, PhD

Foreword: Ann Curry

Managing Editor: Julia Mueller

A

ANTHEM PRESS

Anthem Press
An imprint of Wimbledon Publishing Company
www.anthempress.com

This edition first published in UK and USA 2021
by ANTHEM PRESS
75–76 Blackfriars Road, London SE1 8HA, UK
or PO Box 9779, London SW19 7ZG, UK
and
244 Madison Ave #116, New York, NY 10016, USA

British Library Cataloguing-in-Publication Data
A catalogue record for this book is available from the British Library.

Library of Congress Control Number: 2020951574

ISBN-13: 978-1-78527-597-5 (Hbk)
ISBN-10: 1-78527-597-6 (Hbk)

Cover image: From the McFetridge family collection

This title is also available as an e-book.

CONTENTS

FOREWORD

by Ann Curry

The former NBC News Correspondent is a graduate of Ashland High School in Ashland, Oregon, a couple of hours south of Roseburg. She received an honorary doctorate in journalism from Southern Oregon University in Ashland. She earned her B.A. at the University of Oregon School of Journalism and Communication, where she has served as a member of the board of trustees and endowed the Ann Curry Scholarship for journalism students.

A good story can get into your bones. For a time, it can almost feel a part of you, eliciting surprise and delight and a drive to discover what happened next.

This story, about what happened in an America embroiled by McCarthyism during the Cold War—when curious elementary school children tried to communicate with children in Russia—was compelling enough when it was first reported, including in *The New York Times*. But it has never been so riveting as it is now, finally fully told.

The surprise is in its newly uncovered nuances. The delight is in its mysteries revealed. The story of what happened next covers 60 years of developments in America and in Russia, the involvement of the FBI and the unlikely discovery of a box of letters.

The team of intrepid reporters that uncovered all of this, through persistence, investigative journalism, as well as shoe-leather reporting, proves there is great value in doing what is too rarely done: following up on stories and being open to wherever they take you.

This good story now before you reflects the true adventure of pure journalism. It is an example of why truth is both hard to find and worth the effort. Plus, it includes an old recipe for Apple Butter Spice Cake, which I for one, am eager to taste.

INTRODUCTION

by Peter Laufer

As the talented cohort of journalism students at the University of Oregon was completing this book, I realized that *Classroom 15* is not the first such communal project to originate on our bucolic campus. In 1990, Penguin Books published *Caverns*, by O.U. Levon, with an introduction by Oregon alumnus Ken Kesey. Thirteen authors are credited for the work, students in Kesey's UO creative writing course (consider the author of record's name backward—O.U. Levon—to reveal the not-so-secret message: Novel U.O.). Response from critics was mixed. *Publisher's Weekly* was wary regarding a stable of fiction writers working together. "Eccentric characters and entertaining incidents boost the pace of this novel but cannot camouflage the strain imposed by the collective voice of 13 writing students," the trade magazine sniffed. But at *Library Journal* the work received enthusiastic praise. "With the notable exception of the Bible (which, after all, is in a class by itself)," its reviewer began, setting quite the high standard for comparison, "few good books have been written by committee. This novel is a rare exception." The *Los Angeles Times* checked in with "the result can't by any stretch of the imagination be called great literature, but it's an entertaining story of great inventiveness." And the *Washington Post* noted that "*Caverns* must have required an immense amount of writing and rewriting by its 13 authors to become a single, unified work."

During the final editing process for *Classroom 15*, I reread Kesey's introduction to *Levon*. I was seeking inspiration from what I figured was a fellow traveler down the rugged trail of rounding up and corralling disparate student points of view into a coherent unified story. "A few months into the first term," Kesey wrote, "we had the plot blocked out and I began assigning sections—write 'em at home then read 'em aloud to the class. The trouble was, I quickly saw, that the prose being brought in was going rapidly purple. When we tried to sew these pieces together we came up with a monstrosity that only Mary Shelley could love." Kesey's solution: The authors would write only during class and read their words aloud to the group for immediate peer review. Fueled by coffee and Cabernet, Kesey reported, the collective strategy worked.

But *Classroom 15* is no novel. It's nonfiction and a work of investigative journalism. Our writers fanned out across time and place to research, report and finally write an untold story of the Red Scare as it played out in rural Oregon, an important and often entertaining story that resonates still. Their datelines range from Roseburg to Washington, DC, from our campus library to remote Russian villages. Their characters include sweet schoolchildren and J. Edgar Hoover, Senator Joseph McCarthy and an innovating small-town elementary school teacher. Securing credible, reliable sources required filing Freedom of Information Act requests, combing through archives, convincing players in the drama to speak on the record—and patience. Lots of patience combined with arduous creativity.

The rigors of this type of in-depth news reporting forced the authors to work alone or in pairs. In order to conquer the tasks on their to-do list the group needed to divide the ever-growing workload. The authors came together twice a week during their scheduled Reporting II class time to compare notes, organize the story development and exchange ideas as the content grew in complexity and importance.

"Nobody missed much class," Kesey wrote about his students, "you couldn't afford to." The same was the case with the Reporting II authors of *Classroom 15*. And when the term was over but the reporting was not finished, the class elected unanimously to continue to meet the next term. And the next. How could they not? They're journalists, journalists telling breaking, fascinating and important news. They don't go running to recess when the bell rings.

Once the elements of the story became clear, chapters were assigned to the reporters. But rather than seek a unified voice for the book, the challenge of one story with many authors was met by embracing the distinct writing styles of the reporters and giving them license to tell the piece of the story they were assigned to probe and to write it in a manner they figured worked best to tell the tale.

Winter term at the University of Oregon sometimes feels like a grind. I'm convinced weather is the villain. The days in the Pacific Northwest darken. The sun rises late, sets early. And more often than not, the ceiling in the Willamette Valley hangs low with gray. If it's not a bone-chilling steady rain, it's a cold low, wet fog—day after day, often week after week, punctuated by periodic snowfall. Temperatures hover around freezing. It's a slog to weather the weather and hang on waiting for glorious spring, a season that teases with early crocus pushing through that snow but which might well not fully blossom until June. Students with eight o'clock classes head for campus in the pitch-black dark.

Or as a Kesey character points out in *Sometimes a Great Notion*, "… you got to go through a rainy season or so to get some idee." It's not for nothing that our sports teams are called Ducks.

As a professor teaching journalism, I look to punctuate the syllabus with opportunities for students to experience the thrills of journalism: digging up news important to tell, finding sources and convincing them to share experiences and documents, making use of public record files, and finally crafting that raw material into compelling stories. Ours is an always-changing and exciting profession to practice, a profession crucial to a healthy society.

So, on one of those bleak winter term days, I regaled my Reporting II class with a clipping from *The New York Times*, a brief clipping that featured an event that occurred an hour's drive south of our Eugene campus, in Roseburg, and featured a protagonist who was 10 years old back in 1960. The assignment for the day was simple: Find that girl (now well into her years of eligibility to collect Social Security). The classroom came alive with the thrill of the search; it turned into a newsroom with students divvying up duties. And before the bleak day was over, a surprised and delighted cry of "I found her, I found her!" filled the room and was so loud it probably echoed into neighboring Allen Hall classes. A week later, our Reporting II team finally connected with Janice Boyle on the telephone—alive and well (and ready to talk).

The successful exercise sparked the students' journalism flame. When they returned for the next class meeting none wanted just finding Janice Boyle to be the end of their investigative work on *The New York Times* brief mention of the schoolgirl. They realized that they had stumbled on an untold story that was not just history but a parable for their own generation and its crises. And they realized that they were not just studying journalism, they were practicing it, and that journalism was great fun. They renamed their Reporting II course Janice 101 and kept working long after the course concluded. This was no longer a classroom of students, Janice 101 had morphed into a newsroom of journalists—newshounds on the hunt.

That hunt sent Janice 101 reporting teams down to Douglas County, over the Cascades to the mountain hideaway of Sisters, Oregon, and on to the glitz of Las Vegas. It sent its researchers deep into the papers of an infamous Oregon congressman and the records of the FBI in the National Archives. It kept its writers and editors up late night after night, draft after draft. And as the year-long effort to tell this important story was nearing its conclusion, the crew realized that in order for the work to be complete, one crucial dateline was missing: It became clear that a Janice 101 globe-trotting reporter must be dispatched from our sleepy college town to the heartland of Russia. So on a chilly Oregon winter morning, Zack Demars climbed into a plane in Eugene holding a ticket to Moscow.

What these now-seasoned journalists accomplished—and share in these pages with readers—is a stark reminder of how important it is to learn from history's mistakes. The research, reporting and writing that came out of the Janice 101 newsroom exposes a fascinating footnote to the Cold War that offers contemporary lessons for us all, lessons from a period of our history often as bleak as an Oregon winter day, lessons we'll do well to pay attention to so we can work together toward a future as bright as the Oregon springtime.

DRAMATIS PERSONAE

Janice (Boyle) Hall: Fourth-grade student at Riverside Elementary School in Roseburg, Oregon, in 1960 and retiree in Henderson, Nevada.

Ray McFetridge: Fourth-grade teacher at Riverside Elementary School in Roseburg, Oregon in 1960.

Charles O. Porter: US Representative for Oregon's 4th congressional district (1957–1961).

Beverly Zehner: Widow of Ray McFetridge.

Linda Priest: Daughter of Ray and Beverly (Zehner) McFetridge.

John F. Kennedy: US President (1961–1963).

Fidel Castro: First Secretary of the Communist Party, Prime Minister and President of Cuba (1961–2011).

Nikita Khrushchev: First Secretary of the Communist Party and Premier of the Soviet Union (1953–1964).

William B. Macomber, Jr.: Assistant Secretary for Legislative Affairs, US State Department (1957–1961 and 1967–1969).

J. Edgar Hoover: Director of the FBI (1935–1972).

Charles Taylor Adams: Retired advertising executive who wrote to Janice Boyle under the pen name Charles Pemberton.

Roy Crain: Principal of Riverside Elementary School in Roseburg, Oregon, in 1960.

Mahlon Cloyd Deller: Superintendent of Roseburg, Oregon, schools in 1960.

Leo B. App, Jr.: Former FBI special agent.

Mitchell Palmer: US Attorney General (1919–1921).

Joseph Stalin: General Secretary of the Soviet Union and Premier of the Soviet Union (1924–1953).

Joseph McCarthy: US Senator from Wisconsin (1947–1957).

Edward R. Murrow: CBS News correspondent and CBS network vice president (1935–1958).

Lyndon B. Johnson: US President (1963–1969)

Nicholas Kristof: *The New York Times* columnist.

Arthur Flemming: University of Oregon President (1961–1968).

Peter DeFazio: US Representative for Oregon's 4th congressional district.

Genee Parr: Fourth-grade student at Riverside Elementary School in Roseburg, Oregon, in 1960.

Richard Nixon: US Vice President (1953–1961) and US President (1969–1974).

Diana Fast: Yoncalla, Oregon, elementary school teacher.

Chapter One

CHILDREN AS VICTIMS, CHILDREN AS PEACEMAKERS

by Zack Demars

In which student journalist Zack Demars opens the scene from a present-day visit to Russia in an attempt to ignite the pen pal relationship originally sought.

On a freezing December night in Moscow, over the course of about twenty minutes, I watched 12 different people—couples, tourists, locals—filter through a park, pass through wrought-iron gates and gaze upon a brass monument for a few moments at a time. While I was visiting the park specifically to observe the monument, most visitors used the spot only as a short detour on an evening stroll. But a few lingered longer, braving the dark night's chill to take in the message offered by the monument's 15 statues. Around the outside of a large granite platform, 13 black figures took on a mix of animal and human—a man with a bird's beak, a woman with a frog's head. Underneath each, small gold text offered English translations to the Russian words above, naming the figures for what they represented: *War. Alcoholism. Child labor. Propaganda of violence.*

The 13 sleek black symbols all faced inward to the center of the platform where, on a pedestal, they could see the targets of the ills they represented: In gold brass, two young children, a boy and a girl, laugh and play with a ball and books on the ground—but blindfolded, oblivious to the dangerous, evil, dark and black world that awaits them outside the reaches of their playful youth. The two children looked gleeful, and the vices ready to pounce.

That brisk night, one visitor to the park—which sits on an island in the middle of the Moskva River—lingered for about ten minutes. I quietly observed from outside the monument's gates as he looked upon each figure of the monument, then on the monument as a whole, and then walked around the back face of it. When he'd taken in its message, he walked back toward the park's green beyond the black gates of the monument's pavilion. Before he got there, though, he stopped and read a statement by artist Mikhail Shemyakin printed in four languages on a white placard:

> For many years it was affirmed and pathetically explained "children are our future!" However, to list the crimes of today's society children [sic] would need volumes. I, as an artist, call on this work to look around, hear and see the sorrows and horrors that children are experiencing today. And it's not too late for sensible and honest people to think about it. Do not be indifferent, fight, do everything to save the future of Russia.

Statues of children play unsuspectingly in front of 13 representations of "adult vices." The children are blindfolded, preventing them from noticing the ills that plague their world like alcoholism, indifference, ignorance, irresponsible science, war and more.

After reading, the man in the black coat left the monument, titled "Children are the Victims of Adult Vices." As he walked away, the figures appeared to gaze upon the children. Standing slightly to the left of center was the statue of a man dressed as a jester, with a long double-breasted coat and a court jester's scepter in one hand—and the head of an ass atop his body. *Ignorance.*

Perhaps, as he walked away having viewed the monument, the man who'd stared at it for so long was a little less susceptible to this vice. Perhaps he'd go home wanting to seek out connections with people he doesn't know before passing judgment on them. Perhaps, for the sake of children and the future of Russia (and maybe the world), he'll go on to strive to overcome ignorance. What is certain though, is that children have been its victim. Just ask a 1960 group of American fourth graders who wanted to make friends in the farthest away place they could imagine—or a group of Russian fourth graders who tried the same thing 60 years later.

***

The students were very eager to receive responses to their letters, according to Tatyana Kornilova, principal of Gimnazium 14, a primary and secondary school in the south of Russia. And she was right. At Kornilova's school, the fourth grade (or the "fourth form," in the Russian colloquialism—in other words, about 80 nine- and ten-year-old students) had just written pen pal letters to similarly aged peers in Yoncalla, Oregon. After this exercise, they were excited to get something back from their new "correspondees" and to make friends. In addition, Kornilova and the school's other teachers were excited to have the students practice their English skills. Gimnazium 14 is a "special school," as one of its staff members told me. Not only does the curricula in the Russian city of around a million include intensive study of the English language beginning in the third grade, but it also asks students to pick up a third language, in addition to English and Russian, beginning in their fifth year of study. Even after only a year of reading, hearing and speaking English, the students' abilities were already impressive to the native-English ear. It gave them a greater ability to be curious about the world around them, about someone from cultures unlike their own, to ask questions, to talk about themselves—and to sing.

"There's nothing better in the world than a good friend. Except perhaps a good song about friendship," a young boy said, introducing a group of about a dozen fourth-grade students ready to sing in Gimnazium 14's auditorium. The rest of the class sat and watched, waiting to pepper the school's guest that day with probing questions about his very American, and not-at-all-Russian, life. "The more we get together (together, together), the happier we'll be!" the performers, clad in their brown and gray school uniforms, admonished in shout-like singing voices.

With their songs, their motives were clear, for they'd laid out their hopes in a poem: to share, and to make friends. "I want to live and not to die, I want to laugh and not to cry! I want to feel the summer sun, I want to think that life is fun. I want fly into the blue, I want to swim as fishes do. I want to stretch out friendly hands to all the young of other lands. I want to laugh and not to cry, I want to live and not to die."

Now, by this point, an argument could be made that these weren't really the wishes of the students, that they were simply doing what they were instructed by their teachers, that the opportunity was just one more for the "special school" students to practice their English in front of a native speaker. Their teachers had, after all, indicated at every discussion that chances for cultural exchange—international visits, pen pal friendships and whatever communication could be cooked up in the age of social media—were opportunities for students to practice what they've learned of the language of global society in a setting where there's "no way out," as one put it.

But, no matter for what reason the teachers in the school had gotten on board with the idea of an intercultural interface, it quickly became clear that the students' intentions were genuine. As part of their presentations, several students shared about themselves—again in nearly perfect academic English.

"My name is Mary. I am ten. I am a pupil of the fourth form," one student introduced herself. "My hobby is reading and my favorite lessons at school are reading, English and math."

"I have a very big family," said another, Daniel. "I have a mom, dad, three brothers and three sisters. I like to play football and basketball."

Fourth-grade students share poetry and songs about friendship, along with short introductions about themselves in English.

After I introduced myself in a similar way (though, an English teacher would later mention, in only "good" English, compared to the "perfect" English of my translator and guide, a former student of the school), it was time for students to ask questions about me. In some ways, we could not have been more different—I was a 20-year-old university journalism student from the west coast of the United States wearing jeans and a sweater, they were nine-year-old English students from the south of Russia wearing uniform dresses, blouses, ties and jackets. Regardless, they were curious: What is my favorite season? What is Oregon like? What do I do in my free time? Do I live in a house or in a flat? Do I like Billie Eilish? What about Ariana Grande?

Almost as if asking questions right out of an English textbook—quite similar to the ones they'd answered about themselves in their earlier presentations—the enthusiastic students engaged every tool in their English toolbox to learn about the life of the stranger in front of them. It's impossible to hide a child's curiosity and argue that it is merely a result of their desire to perfect their English. When a girl's eyes became glassy in the face of a new friend from afar, when a class full of hands sprang straight to the air to offer their inquiries, when young ones squirmed in their seats because of how badly they wanted to know about my brother—that is the curiosity of a child. That is seeking to understand the unknown instead of fearing it. That is being blindfolded to the vices all around.

✻✻✻

Asking questions to a visiting foreigner is not, of course, the only tool in a person's toolbox to understand the world around them. Gimnazium 14 had, in years past, engaged in another method of combating cultural ignorance. In 1989, with the help of funding from a program of the USSR's President Mikhail Gorbachev aptly titled *Children as Peacemakers*, two teachers, two school administrators and ten students spent two weeks in the United States, staying in the homes of the families of American peers. After time in the States, two students—one from Russia, and the other from the United States—would return to Rostov and spend two weeks living together in Russia. The next year, then-teacher and now-principal Kornilova would join the exchange trip as it traveled to Mobile, Alabama, and Baton Rouge, Louisiana.

THE CITY HALL

The program of our visit was varied & fascinating. One day we payed an "official visit" to the local city hall situated in the downtown. we were conquered by the hospitality of the mayor of the city of mobile — michael Dow. he really liked cossack songs...

A scrapbook page memorializes the class trip to Mobile, Ala. (Courtesy Gimnazium 14.)

Our group:

Teachers: Pelts Elena Yurievna, Kornilova Tatyana Albertovna.

Students: Nina Parzyan, Anna Popova, Karina Chobanyan, Andrei Alaverdyan, Edic Kasyan, Karina Valentseva, Vladislav Minko, Nina Novikova + Lena Emelyanenko, Sasha Khalyn.

Another scrapbook page memorializes the Rostov-on-Don students who traveled abroad. (Courtesy Gimnazium 14.)

The program went on for a few years after that. Even during the fall of the Soviet Union, the program was sending students back-and-forth between the two cold-warring countries—yes, literally *during* the fall of the Soviet Union. Students and teachers from Gimnazium 14 were in the airport on their way home when they learned of the USSR's August, 1991 dissolution. "We knew nothing about future life, what could happen to everybody," remembered Olga Tenyakova, who was a teacher during the trip and still teaches at the school. "There were a lot of reporters—journalists and TV tried to torture us to death, asking us what should be done. From morning till dawn. Surely it was a tragedy for us because we were afraid, we knew nothing about our future."

But, in spite of the opportunity the US government provided them to stay in the States instead of return to a nation whose future was uncertain at best, each of the Gimnazium 14 students and teachers returned from the trip (albeit after extensive delays at the airport). Maria Petrosyan, who now teaches English at Gimnazium 14, was a student on that particular trip and remembered the value that it had to her education.

"I was really willing to communicate, to participate and all those things. We were dancing, singing songs, whatnot together. American children as well," Petrosyan said of the exchange. "It was really interesting that we were different in different ways. It showed us what is all this learning English for. At that time, it was really difficult to communicate, there was no internet or other sources. So it helped a lot, to tell the truth."

When they talked about the value of the exchanges with American students, Gimnazium 14's English teachers tended to focus on what might be expected—how activities of this kind help students learn English. Understandably, total emersion in a language forces a student to become used to it and allows them to take their fourth-grade academic ability to the conversational ability displayed by the school's eleventh graders. But a project of that scale—to cross the ocean to make American friends—must have bigger implications than to just offer English practice. It must satisfy curiosity—it must strive to overcome ignorance with curiosity.

"Children are children everywhere. Children are all the same, and they have common interests ..." another teacher interrupted, adding "music, sport" to the list of common interests among children "... of their own. Maybe a little bit different, but still."

"... But they are not interested in politics," added the teacher who'd interrupted previously.

"They are interested in communication, in the world around them, in different events," a third said of her students.

A few years after they began, Gimnazium 14 had to give up the US–Russia cultural exchanges it had started. As government funding dried up, the trips became prohibitively expensive for students. And after the September 11 attacks, Petrosyan thinks, both the Russian and US governments were unsure about the safety of such trips with groups of students. So, those governments filled their uncertainty with fear, and ended their support of the programs.

Now, Gimnazium 14's English teachers want to have cultural exchanges again. "The pupils of the eleventh form ask, 'Why don't we have some such contacts? When will you organize our trip to America?' And they would like to receive students form America here in our families," said Vera Shilkina, an eleventh-grade English teacher. "We are ready," said another. But they recognize that it will be a process before such exchanges can be rebuilt. And it starts, they say, with small connections.

"Letters, pen pals—it's the first step," noted Kornilova.

✳ ✳ ✳

Adults have a voice in politics. In propaganda. In assumptions. In fear about what they do not know—or in the words of the artist Shemyakin, to ignorance. Often, adults will pass on these vices to their children through media or religion or dinner-table talks—but for every child, there is a period wherein they're free from these vices. It's a period when they are ignorant about much of the world around them, yes, but instead of accounting for this ignorance with fear, they account for it with curiosity.

In 1960, a class of Oregon fourth graders had that period of curiosity-filled ignorance when they wanted to send letters to Russian peers. In 2019, a class of Russian fourth graders who'd filled a Russian flag-adorned gift bag full of letters was in the midst of that period when they bombarded an American student with questions— "Do you have a pet?" (yes) "Are you a sportsman?" (no) and "Do you have a wife?" (we didn't get into it).

For both groups of students, the questions weren't complex—but the ask was big. The hopes for foreign friends had to span three continents and an ocean, run through six decades, circumnavigate a language barrier, survive the fall of Communism in Russia and witness the rise of digital technology and methods of communication which far outpace snail mail. In other words, what began as a fairly innocuous hope ballooned into a bureaucratic denial, a blip in a class's memory, a foray into international politics, and, in light of modern international relations, another curious question about what would happen this time, 60 years later, if a group of kids tried to do what they do best: to make friends.

Chapter Two

JANICE 101

by Maddie Moore

In which serendipity plays a role for student journalist Maddie Moore's quest to interview Janice Boyle in person. Moore's previously scheduled sorority spring break trip calls for a week of rest and relaxation on the Las Vegas Strip—sun and fun poolside, just a few miles from Janice's Nevada home. She leaves Oregon not only with a bathing suit and sun block but also recording equipment and her reporter's notebook.

The year was 1959. At 4 feet 2 inches, with thick red cat-eye glasses and a few freshly lost teeth, nine-year-old Janice Boyle was as unassuming as any small-town schoolgirl, her life for the most part unfazed by the Red Scare closing in around 1960s America. Janice was secretary of her fourth-grade class at Riverside School in Roseburg, Oregon, where she lived with her father, mother, and two sisters. In school, Janice was a curious student, whose inquisitive chatter would earn her hallway time-outs from her teachers. At home, Janice spent most of her time outside, playing with her neighbors and sisters until their mother would call them in for dinner, a brief interlude before she went back outside to play until the sun went down.

The city of Roseburg, where Janice spent her elementary school days, is nestled in the Douglas fir forests of southern Oregon along the I-5 corridor, unsuspecting and pastoral. The "Timber Capital of the Nation" was known throughout the mid-twentieth century for its booming logging industry, though not much else. In Janice's youth, Roseburg had a quaint downtown wherein most businesses, including Janice's father's jewelry shop, welcomed the heavy foot traffic. The nearby forests were mottled with walking and hiking trails. The winters were cold and the summers were hot. Janice's childhood in Roseburg was ordinary. Ordinary, that is, until a seemingly straightforward class project propelled her into the national news cycle. Ordinary until what Janice would later dub her "15 minutes of fame."

In the fall of 1959, Janice's fourth-grade class was working through a geography unit on "How People Work Together." The teacher, an innovator named Ray McFetridge, helped the class initiate a pen pal project: They'd write back-and-forth with schoolchildren in another country, learning about different ways of life. The class chose Russia—then the Union of Soviet Socialist Republics—which was as far from Oregon as the group of American schoolchildren could imagine. Unsure of how to facilitate the project themselves but eager to pursue it, Ray McFetridge and his class drafted a letter to their congressman, Charles O. Porter, asking for his help in connecting them with a group of schoolchildren in a Russian town similar in size to Roseburg.

In the late 1950s and early 1960s, America was in the thick of the Red Scare—and the fear of a communist threat, particularly that of the empire-building USSR, was peaking. International political tensions were rising between the United States and the Soviet Union. Competition bristled in combative propaganda, the space race, and the nuclear arms race.

These political factors, surely at the forefront of any state department's concerns at the time, collided with the students' request for assistance in finding new friends. The students' request was denied by the US State Department in late 1959, but just the simple request was enough for the FBI, stateside communist sympathizers and major news publications to become concerned by and involved with a seemingly innocuous fourth-grade class geography project.

Nearly 60 years later, Janice looks back on her atypical elementary school experience. Chatting in her Henderson, Nevada, home—where she lives with her husband, Tom, and three dogs—Janice is happy at the chance to tell her story. Not just happy—elated. She is an avid record-keeper and still has an array of yellowed newspaper clippings that her grandmother labeled and dated from the pen pal incident of her youth. She's kept boxes of old school photos. She even has a copy of her fourth-grade class picture: a portrait of a young, beaming Janice from the year of her "How People Work Together" class lesson. She remembers the more mundane details of elementary-school life, like who her boyfriend was at the time (he was pictured next to her in the photo accompanying the newspaper articles covering the incident), but she also remembers the time she was called into the principal's office to discuss the news coverage of her class's pen pal project—and the FBI's interest in it. Janice's memories illuminate the until-now buried story of how US–USSR relations, propaganda, McCarthyism, and political fear led to an FBI intervention in the lives of 1960s Oregon schoolchildren who couldn't yet locate the Soviet Union on a map.

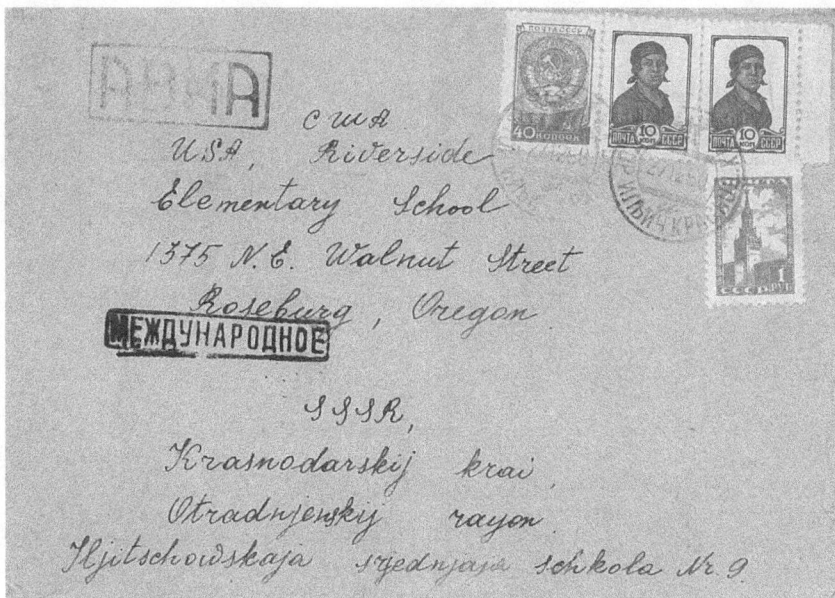

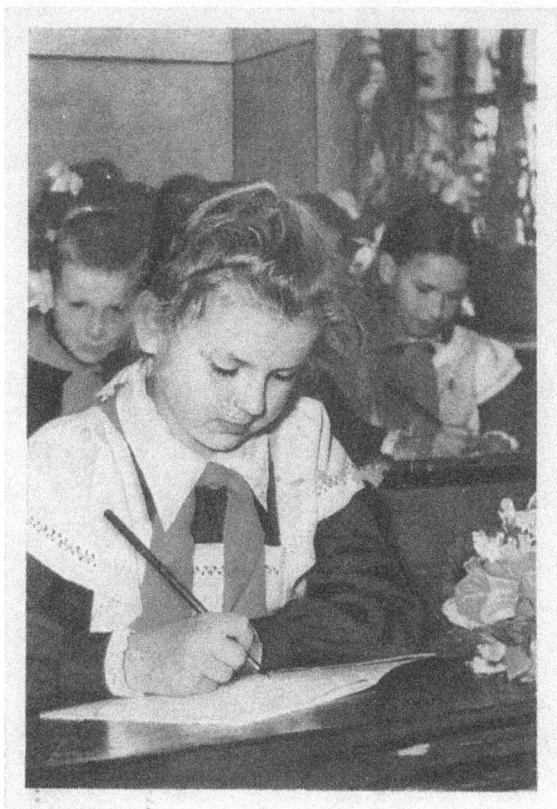

Correspondence flowed from the Soviet Union to Roseburg.

Дорогой друг!
Я очень благодарю тебя за открытки. Я думаю, что скоро мы станем хорошими друзьями.
    Твой друг
    Гучкова Таня

Дорогой друг.
Меня зовут Таня Гучкова. Я благодарю тебя за твоё письмо и за открытки, которые ты прислала нам. Я учусь в 4 классе в Дугнинской средней школе. Нашу учительницу зовут Наталия Ипполитовна Перевозчикова. Твой друг Гучкова Таня.

МЕЖДУНАРОДНОЕ   Международное

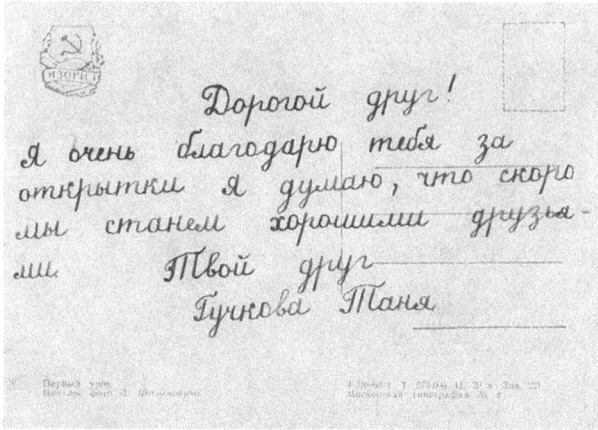

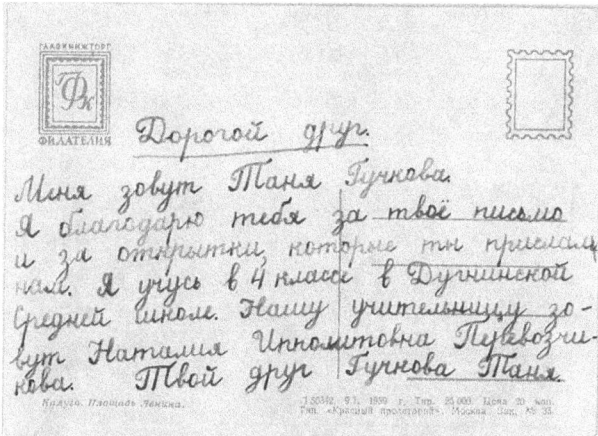

More from the pile of cards and letters found in the McFetridge family cedar chest. Note: The lower postcard is reproduced in its glorious Soviet color on the cover of this book.

United States Post Office
ROSEBURG, OREGON

_____April 4_____ 1960

Principal

Riverside School

It has been determined that the

enclosed letter originating in the USSR

is intended for Janis Boyle, a pupil in

your school

CLYDE W. CARSTENS
Postmaster

U. S. GOVERNMENT PRINTING OFFICE   6—17522

Neither rain, nor sleet, nor snow nor hail kept the United States Post Office from delivering the letters to Riverside Elementary.

✳✳✳

When our cohort of University of Oregon reporters first contacted Janice and assured her that, no, we weren't soliciting donations for some charity she had never heard of or offering to restructure her student loans, a flood of memories came rushing back to her. Janice hadn't been too hard to find—her affinity for tracking her family's genealogy records online and her "classmates. com" membership led us to her contact information quickly. She was delighted to hear from students at a university less than 60 miles from the city in which she had spent much of her childhood. When we first got to talking about the incident, we had to politely ask her to slow down so we could keep pace with what she calls her "excited storytelling voice." The initial contact with Janice

was made as a simple journalism school exercise, a lesson in locating interview subjects and verifying their identity. But it became evident as soon as she
started talking that she had a fascinating tale to tell. By the second phone call,
travel plans to Las Vegas were in the works.

Fast-forward nearly two months after our first phone call and Janice is
sitting in front of the computer in her home, sharing her firsthand account
of the pen pal story while Bentley (her five-month old Cocker Spaniel-Poodle
mix puppy with an easily excitable tail) threatens to steal her spotlight. She
makes small talk for a while. She had recently set out to find out more about
her family history and ancestry. When she starts to talk about what happened
that winter of 1960, her eyes brighten as she recalls the excitement she felt
reading her name in the headlines of the local newspapers.

Janice recalls that the pen pal endeavor started out as nothing more than
a typical class geography exercise wherein the students set out to each write a
letter to USSR elementary schoolers. During the pre-internet days of 1960,
they decided that they would need some help getting into contact with their
would-be pen pals. Janice was selected to write a letter on behalf of the class
to their congressman.

"Everyone was supposed to write one of the letters to the Russian students,"
said Janice. "I was class secretary for that term. It just fell into my lap, so
I wrote the letter we sent to Congressman Porter." After everyone in the class
had written their own letters to anonymous peers, Janice wrote, in collaboration with the class, a letter to Congressman Porter, seeking his help in finding
and contacting a class of Russian fourth graders to whom they could send their
pen pal notes. Mr. McFetridge (the class teacher was known to the students
with a formal salutation) forwarded the letter to Porter. Janice said that, even
after sending the request, the class all but forgot about the assignment. They
moved on to studying other subjects. But then, to their surprise, they received
a response from the congressman.

To Janice, the pen pal project was—before the headlines hit the presses,
that is—just another class exercise. She was unaware of the political tensions
between the United States and the Soviet Union. Janice and her younger sister
both recall that their family didn't discuss politics at home and her classmates
didn't discuss politics at school, so she couldn't have been expected to have
much political awareness.

"I didn't understand the weight of this matter, of this issue. I couldn't. I was
just a kid," Janice said. Even now, though, she doesn't believe there was an
ulterior motive behind teacher Ray McFetridge assigning the project. Though
the choice of the Soviet Union seemed intentionally controversial to some, it
was just a simple school project to Janice and her classmates.

A few weeks after the initial request was sent to their congressman, the class received a response that would change the trajectory of their project and further complicate their attempts to carry out their pen pal plan. Congressman Porter explained that he supported the class's efforts but had referred their request to the State Department. What came next was more definitive: Porter's bid to the Eisenhower administration for guidance putting the children in contact with Soviet citizens was denied. The administration's point of view did not mirror Porter's support of the project, and Porter's final reply to Janice included a letter from the State Department that effectively denied Janice and her classmates government help gaining access to Russian elementary school students.

The justification for the State Department's denial was fear that Janice and her classmates would be propagandized and influenced by the Soviet Union. The State Department explained to Porter that they feared anything written to the American students could be subject to the influence of Soviet teachers, the Soviet school administration, Communist Party officials or parents toeing the Communist Party line. Because of this, the State Department told Roseburg's representative it could not verify whether the letters from Russian students would be genuine voices of the children. The State Department worried that the project would be used as a political tool to further the USSR's political agenda and the USSR's goal of spreading communism.

The federal government's refusal to fulfill this small-town class's request brought the problematic pen pal project to the front page of the Roseburg's *The News-Review*. Within days of Porter's response letter, the story was covered by news outlets throughout Oregon, and it was not long before international media outlets like the Associated Press and *The New York Times* were sharing the story that was gaining momentum as an issue of censorship and fear. Though there were some instances of errors—like the *Times*'s article about "Janis" rather than Janice—and confusion over the content of the initial letter, the State Department's rejection of an elementary school geography project was covered by newspapers and broadcast programs across the country.

At just nine years old, Janice was elated to find her name plastered across the front page of *The News-Review*. "I remember coming home from school, and the evening paper was there, and my name was on the front. I called my mom shouting, 'Mommy! Mommy! I'm in the newspaper!' and I was just so excited about that that I never really thought of anything else." Anything else, to Janice, includes how and why her class exercise was canceled or that she was not about to meet a class of Russian pen pals.

U. S. Bars a Girl's Plea For Russian Pen Pals

WASHINGTON, Jan. 28 (AP)—A schoolgirl in Rose-burg, Ore., was advised today that the State Department opposed allowing her and her friends to write letters to Russian children.

Janis Boyle had asked for a list of names so that she and her classmates in the fourth grade at Riverside School could make friends with some Russian pen pals.

But her Congressman, Representative Charles O. Porter, a Democrat, advised her that Assistant Secretary of State William B. Macomber Jr. had refused, fearing Soviet censorship and propaganda.

Mr. Porter said he planned to try to get some names for Janis and her friends from the Russian Ambassador, if necessary.

Conceding that the Russians practice censorship and engage in propaganda, Mr. Porter said:

"This is like telling your kids never to walk across the street because some people get hit by cars."

The New York Times
Published: January 29, 1960
Copyright © The New York Times

An example of the splash Janice Boyle made in the national news.

Janice, who was too young and politically unaware to understand the big deal being made about their attempted correspondence with young citizens of the Soviet Union, remembers more about the media coverage surrounding her class pen pal project than the project's actual implications. There was never an opinion imparted on her by her parents, teacher or peers, she said from her Nevada home, that influenced her thinking of the whole ordeal as "good" or "bad"—although the two o'clock in the morning wake-up tele- phone call from *The New York Times* to the Boyle family home looking to verify the story certainly made for one angry Mrs. Boyle. Still, Janice didn't think much about the pen pal project's implications beyond how great her name looked printed in the Times New Roman typeface in newspapers across the country. For nine-year-old Janice and her friends, this news coverage meant nothing more than some local notoriety.

Janice remembers thinking mainly about the significance of the contro- versy as it contributed to her moment in the spotlight. Nonetheless, before the class even had the chance to send a letter back to Porter, Janice had already received mail about the project—though not the kind of mail she'd been expecting. Because of the story's national coverage, Janice learned that she received a pile of letters from the American public, both hate mail and letters of support. While most of the correspondence was kept by the school admin- istration, Janice fondly remembers receiving a letter from another young girl, also named Janice Boyle, who lived in Kentucky. She was delighted to have made a friend across the country who shared her name.

Janice recalled feeling no more important or special than her classmates simply because she was the main subject in most of the news stories, and she said she never let the fame go to her young girl's head, despite how excited she was to be featured in the news.

"At the end of the day," she said, "it was my 15 minutes of fame. My name being in the paper was the biggest deal of it all to me. I still didn't really realize why the response was such a big deal to everyone else, I just thought, 'Oh well, they said no,' and I moved on."

The most important mail of all, though, arrived at Riverside School soon after the story was published in national newspapers, and it arrived in a suspicious-looking packet. Amidst both the fan mail and criticism, the school received, on behalf of Janice and Ray McFetridge's class, a small packet of letters from schoolchildren in the USSR, who reached out to the American class to try to communicate. Looking back, Janice figures that these letters must have been written following national coverage by *The New York Times* and the Associated Press, which had brought the story to the Soviet Union's radar. Though she has little memory of the letters themselves or the content within them, Janice remembers the class being excited that they had succeeded in connecting with similarly aged children abroad. Because the letters were written in Russian, the class contacted a translator from the University of Oregon to interpret the letters into English for the McFetridge's fourth graders.

Janice remembers being called into her principal's office after the pen pal story gained some notoriety. The summons came early one morning, shortly after the bus dropped her off at school. She found this odd; she was typically a well-behaved student who rarely got into trouble. But with the frenzy of attention she and her classmates were getting about the project, she assumed the principal was calling her in to talk about something related to it, and she quickly made her way to the office.

As Janice remembers it, the principal sat Janice down and told her that the "authorities" had come to the school and taken all the letters, both the letters that the class had written and the letters they had received from the Soviet Union and the United States. Janice said the principal offered little explanation as to why they had done so, or why it even mattered, and too-quickly tried to brush it off, as if she needn't question the adults in charge. Though she was young and ill-informed about the sociopolitical influences at play, she thought it strange how quickly such a seemingly important —or, at least, exciting— story could be dismissed and never spoken of again.

Janice's class soon forgot about the letters and the project. Shortly after she had been called into the principal's office, Mr. McFetridge announced to the class that they would no longer be pursuing pen pals. Janice vividly remembers the ease with which the students accepted this outcome and continued with their usual routine, as if the project hadn't been suggested or even attempted. Her only problem with this announcement was that it meant she wouldn't be allowed to keep the letters sent to her from her new acquaintances across the country. She remembers being worried she would have nothing left to commemorate her brief moment of fame.

Nevertheless, Janice accepted the fate of their failed pen pal project and resumed life as a typical fourth grader. She rarely thought about the incident for the rest of her childhood years.

The story, while dramatic in the weeks surrounding Congressman Porter's involvement, was ultimately short-lived, and it received next to no attention after its initial publication. There was no more media coverage following the first round of stories published, and no one involved was interviewed about the project again. The Roseburg class never talked about it again either, nor did Janice's friends and family.

✹✹✹

On January 29, 2019, *The New York Times* ran its usual page-two "On This Day in History" column, highlighting that day a story they had written exactly

59 years prior, titled "U.S. Bars a Girl's Plea For Russian Pen Pals." The column briefly told of nine-year-old "Janis" Boyle and her request for a list of Russian names with whom she and her classmates could communicate. Only an hour's drive north of where the story originally occurred, our reporting class at the University of Oregon School of Journalism and Communication in Eugene was assigned to find out what we could about what was, for us, a local story. Confused at first by the *Times'* use of what we soon figured out to be a misspelled version of Janice's name, we continued our quest for the story.

When we finally got in contact with Janice and found out that she was willing to talk to us, we started to think about the contemporary potential of this story. As we learned more and more about the story through background reporting, like looking up other classmates from her fourth-grade class and seeing how many related newspaper articles we could find, the story seemed increasingly interesting, important and viable for us to pursue. Once we discovered that Janice lived in Las Vegas—and one of our reporters just happened to be visiting Las Vegas in a few months—we knew we had a story that we wanted to pursue.

What made the story even more compelling was the access to related documents and media we were able to find and analyze. Through Freedom of Information Act requests, we were able to locate the documents sent from Porter and the State Department to Janice, including the notes that stated their opinions on the project. We were also able to locate the numerous letters from American citizens across the country who wrote to Janice supporting the class and the project, as well as the packet of letters that had been sent to Janice and Mr. McFetridge's class from the Russian school children. These documents, in conjunction with the interviews and research we conducted about Roseburg and its inhabitants at the time, illuminate a fascinating historical narrative of continued import to our current era.

Given the context of Russian–American relations now, Janice's 1960s pen pal story provides a compelling comparison between the two time periods: Though Russia is no longer a communist state, it still is a US adversary. This look back at the complexities of mid-twentieth century communication provides an example of a time when most people relied on letters, envelopes and stamps to connect with one another, though they operated with the same importance and urgency of communication as we see in our high-tech modern world. It also serves as a reminder of how deep into American society the Red Scare penetrated, and how it had influence beyond just the bureaucracy and the politicians in Washington, DC.

Though it may not have meant much to Janice beyond the media coverage she received, the fear of communism was so entrenched that it interfered with an elementary school geography project, which is important in contextualizing the United States' relationship with Russia, both then and now. The

US government has a similarly fearmongering and forceful tone against its enemies and adversaries regarding contemporary issues as its anti-communist propagandizing of the 1960s, and so it is important that these stories are told, to remind us how it was then, how it is now and the effects that these governmental decisions have on our world.

✳✳✳

Janice, 2019, holds onto Janice, 1960.

Sixty years after the attempted pen pal project, Janice recalled details of this childhood story with a nostalgic smile on her face. Though her red cat-eye glasses have been replaced with a more sophisticated black-rimmed pair, her hair's been cropped much shorter and toned a vibrant red, and she's had over half a century to learn more about the political implications of America's complex historical relationship with Russia, she is still the same talkative, vibrant person she was as a little girl. Her eyes sparkled as she told stories of her life: how she got to interview Dean Martin for a high school journalism class, the joy she felt when she gave birth to her daughter, or how her early retirement allowed for her to pursue her many hobbies and activities.

Now that she is old enough to grasp the gravity of her old class's fleeting role in Cold War politics and the forces at play in the government's decision not to put her and them in contact with Soviet Union children, Janice understands why the State Department made the decision that they did, though she still is not sure that she agrees with it.

"I never really sat and thought about it then," she said, "but I think our government overreacted, looking back on it now as an adult. We were just kids, and it's not like we had an agenda. When they said things like 'communism,' I didn't even know what they were talking about!" She laughed as she recalled her childish ignorance. She supposes Russia could've been using the situation to advance a sense of innocence, though she still doesn't think they were trying to propagandize a class of nine-year-olds for any sort of political gain. "I do think Russia was trying to use the situation to their advantage, to say 'See? We're sending these children letters, and we're not doing anything wrong,' so," she added, "I think it was probably more to their advantage than it was to ours." Janice speculated that the Soviet Union was trying to make a goodwill statement by responding to the letters in a positive, non-political way despite the apparent fear of communism propaganda from the American government. It was good public relations and made the United States seem over-reactive and fearful.

When asked if she thinks this situation would've played out differently had it happened in the Trump-Putin era she now finds herself amid in 2019, Janice shook her head and laughed, exclaiming, "Can you imagine if we had the technology we have now when this happened?" It would be much easier for a group of kids to get in contact with kids in a different country in this age of Facebook and its offspring. The government would never need to get involved to facilitate these communications. Though the Soviet Union no longer exists and Russia is no longer a communist nation, the internet facilitates Russian propaganda's successes. Janice figured contemporary US relations with Russia would make a re-creation of this project intriguing, particularly in light of President Trump's relationship with Russian President Putin and Russia's meddling in the 2016 US presidential election. Laughing, Janice daydreamed, "Can you imagine if we had Facebook back then?"

Though she maintained that the story didn't drastically affect the course of her life, Janice recognizes now, after the project, that it means more than just the "15 minutes of fame" she had previously considered it to be. It gave her an early look into how government and bureaucracy work, as well as the power of journalism and the effect that reporting and storytelling have on the events that happen in the world. She said that her involvement in the tumultuous class assignment serves as a fond memory of her childhood days. Since we first contacted her about the story, Janice reports that she has spent much more time through online genealogy databases and websites trying to learn about her family and friends' histories. She has also done her own background research on the pen pal project attempt, digging up as many newspaper clippings and letters related to the event as she could find from her overflowing boxes of family memories. She has a more complete account of the story now than she ever had before.

Whether directly or indirectly, the incident had one profound effect on Janice's life: It introduced her to journalism. Shortly after her class's "How People Work Together" project, Janice and her family moved from rural Roseburg, Oregon, to Las Vegas, Nevada. As soon as she enrolled in high school, she took a keen interest in journalism and worked as a reporter for the school newspaper. It was at this job that she interviewed stars from the Strip, learned how to be a reporter, and first appreciated the importance of fair and unbiased journalism. She said these experiences made her absolutely fall in love with reporting and journalism and, though she never pursued it as a career because "life got in the way," she maintained her writing skills and made use of them throughout her professional career and still reads the newspaper and watches television newscasts every day.

And these decades after her first flush of fame, she's delighted to be back in the spotlight for a second 15 minutes—or more.

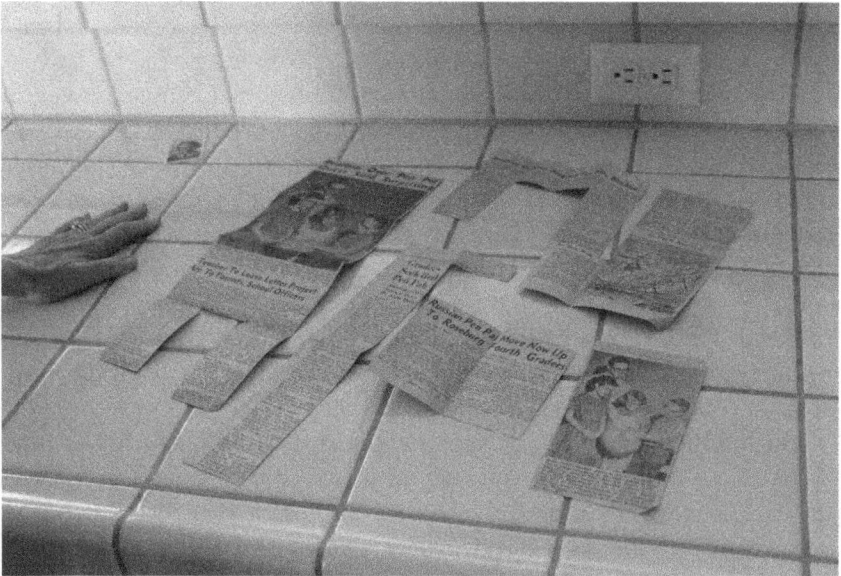

In her Las Vegas kitchen, Janice enjoys the yellowing clips from her fifteen minutes of Warholian fame.

Chapter Three

HOOVER'S G-MEN COME
TO TOWN—SORT OF

by Zack Demars

In which student journalist Zack Demars efficiently uses the Freedom of Information Act to undercover long forgotten evidence of how the FBI became involved in an innocent fourth-grade project and how public-school officials conspired to censor correspondence from Russia to Janice.

✺✺✺

"...such correspondence is frequently used as a vehicle for the dissemination of communist propaganda."

*– William B. Macomber, Jr., Assistant Secretary of State for Legislative Affairs, in a letter
to Representative Charles O. Porter, January 1960*

✺✺✺

William B. Macomber, Jr. was the assistant secretary for legislative affairs in the US State Department of 1960. He was a lifelong diplomat and, in January of that year, his Washington, D.C., desk at the State Department nearly 3,000 miles away from Roseburg became the final stopping point for Janice and her co-conspirators. With musings about the dissemination of communist propaganda, he added his voice to the crowd—and a letter to the growing historical record documenting a rural Oregon town's strange foray into international intrigue.

Macomber's file now sits in the National Archives, the number 105-82823-3 hand-scrawled across the top by an FBI bureaucrat of the past. The file tells a winding story of letters and memos to and from government officials and school superintendents. Above all, it tells the story of J. Edgar Hoover's FBI smelling communism in Classroom 15 of the Riverside School in Roseburg and beginning their offensive.

The letter from Assistant Secretary Macomber marked the procedural death of the class's requests for the assistance of its own government in locating a Russian school with which to correspond. Because of Macomber's letter, there would be no Russian pen pals—or at least no government help securing them. Rejection came, however, not directly from the State Department. Instead, the underwhelming refusal came to Roseburg from Macomber by way of the class's biggest ally: their home congressman Charles O. Porter.

Months before the request's untimely end in State Department offices in Washington, DC, on October 28, 1959, Janice Boyle's letter was picked, or so goes one account of the story, out of the crowded field volleying for the attention of representatives. Each of the excited students in Ray McFetridge's fourth-grade class had written a letter, and, after McFetridge performed his teacherly duty by correcting each submission, Janice's message was chosen as the sole representative of the class's wishes. From there, McFetridge duly forwarded the letter to Congressman Porter, who considered the logistical and political viability of the students' request. Porter then contacted the State Department in hopes that it would provide the students with the requested Russian names and addresses. But swayed as Porter may have been by the youngsters' request, Macomber was not similarly persuaded.

Instead, Macomber informed Porter on January 15, 1960 that his department would be of no assistance. "Information available to the Department indicates that correspondence between Americans and citizens of the Soviet Union is subject to censorship by the Soviet Government," Macomber wrote. "This is particularly true in the case of students. Their replies might well be inspired by their instructors, and, in some cases local Communist Party functionaries might even review the letters before mailing," he warned.

Macomber went on to describe other avenues to international friendships that the students might pursue—correspondence with what he deemed "free world countries," as facilitated by a nationwide pen pal organization. What Janice was explicitly requesting was—in contrast to "free world countries"— what most capitalism-loving US State Department officials would likely tremble at the thought of in the midst of Cold War 1960: Interaction with countries behind the Iron Curtain, giving Soviet actors the opportunity to invade small-town America (the gateway to mainstream America, of course) and spread the dangerous message of communism to the minds of young, malleable fourth graders.

Some 60 years later, though, the historical record is clear about Macomber's fears: They were misguided, misplaced and misdirected. It is important to note that the State Department did not—and could not—forbid an exchange of letters between the two countries. Rather, what the department did was offer no assistance establishing contact with Russian students, stalling the project in a world without the ease of getting in contact via the internet. Today, the National Archives file that tells this story isn't the file of a young political deviant named Janice, or the file of a pair of conspiratorial parents, or even the file of a closeted communist teacher. Instead, the 27 scanned pages of the Roseburg story are just one small portion of a much larger file, one that the National Archives records archivist said would take over two years to compile and release in response to a Freedom of Information Act request.

The propaganda that Macomber feared would infiltrate from the USSR sits instead in the FBI file of an American: Charles Pemberton. The New York City advertising executive was, according to FBI investigators, an American citizen and "prolific letter writer" who sought to share his critical view of the US government with the young Janice Boyle he saw grace national headlines.

***

"A girl as intelligent as you deserves to be well informed."

– Charles Pemberton, "prolific letter writer," in a letter to Janice, February 1960

***

Upon the State Department's rejection of Janice's request for contact with a class of Russian friends, the Oregon elementary schoolers' efforts began to attract broader attention. *The News-Review* in Roseburg followed the saga and, on January 28, 1960, ran the story of the students' rejection by the State Department on their front page, headlined "'Pen Pal' Plan Denied Youngsters: School Class Gets Support of Porter." The next day, the story hit the Associated Press newswire and ran as far as *The New York Times*, telling readers around the nation that "U.S. Bars a Girl's Plea for Russian Pen Pals." That girl was Janis Boyle—yes, *Janis* was the AP's off-the-mark way of spelling "Janice," a reporting error which was reproduced by other newspapers, letters sent by the public, and even by Porter and Macomber, and which now confuses the aging historical record as it sits in archive.

Janice and her Classroom 15 co-conspirators had hit their moment of notoriety, and with fame comes fan mail. With her name—albeit misspelled—published in papers far and wide, the young secretary of Riverside School's fourth-grade class received her fair share of that mail.

Charles Taylor Adams was a retired advertising executive living in New York City in February 1960. Charles Taylor Adams, said an archivist from the

National Archives, sometimes went by the truncated pen name Taylor Adams in some of his correspondence. But on February 24, 1960, the man (who was concretely identified as Charles Taylor Adams in his 1981 obituary) signed a letter with yet another name: Charles Pemberton. He wrote to Janice mainly to decry what he found to be censorship on the part of the American government. He opened his letter by telling Janice how he heard of her story through the press—not the American press, like *The New York Times*, but the Russian weekly *New Times*.

"My dear Janis," Pemberton began, "I have just read in the Russian weekly magazine 'New Times' that our State Department has forbidden you to correspond with children of your own age in Russia, in order to learn their ways and to teach them our ways." From the remainder of Pemberton's file, it was clear which of these goals was of far greater interest to him: to convince Janice and her peers of "their ways."

Pemberton continued to lament. "I am not surprised at this: I could give you many such examples of the fear and suspicion and hate which our leaders are trying to create and sustain in the American people." Pemberton offered suggestion upon suggestion for Janice, if she sought to further learn *Russian ways*. From where, though, did Pemberton's ire for American censorship come? The memos to and from FBI functionaries (which just happened to be pressed into the same lengthy file as Janice's correspondence) leave the historical record with brief clues about Pemberton and his tendencies—and his proclivity to write.

One of those clues came in December 1959 when the clerk of a Massachusetts county court in Boston, one Mr. Thomas Dorgan, wrote his own letter. This one had nothing to do with Roseburg or a class of fourth graders, but everything to do with Russians. That letter, says the FBI's memo, eventually made its way to the presses at the *Boston Herald*, as a defense of the late Senator Joseph McCarthy, the ostensibly America-loving (or free-speech-hating, depending on who you ask) leader of the fight against domestic communism. After Dorgan's letter appeared in the *Herald*, he received a response (this one criticizing McCarthy's work) from none other than Charles Pemberton. As was evidently the trend at the time, his letter to Dorgan drew the attention of the FBI.

The exchange between Dorgan and Pemberton was neatly summarized in a memo sent almost four months later to the Bureau's headquarters, as a response to a call to field offices for any and all Pemberton-related interactions after his letter to Janice. The New York FBI office, aside from recounting that exchange, wrote about Pemberton's contacts with the Soviet UN delegation. In the end, the office decided, because of his frequent activities, that any further investigation of Pemberton would prove fruitless:

It appears from the information at hand that
PEMBERTON is an individual who chronically engages in writing
letters regarding various controversial issues, and in view
of this, NY is not conducting any further investigation.

The New York office draws its conclusion about Pemberton.

In the winter of 1960, Pemberton picked a controversial issue to write about in excess and frequently sent his opinion to Oregon. In his letter to Janice, Pemberton sought to encourage Janice to research communist *ways*, particularly those of the Chinese. Pemberton, it seems, was a good propagandist—he knew his audience. His message was carefully tailored to a young girl still growing in her understanding of the world around her and her social position as a woman. He wrote at length about the quality of women's rights in China and Russia when compared to the United States. "Just think of that," he implored Janice at the suggestion of equal access to educational facilities.

He also understood a young child's need for visual, tangible aids, so he included some in his message as well—pages from the August 1959 edition of *China Reconstructs,* a collection of articles and pages from an "unidentified magazine" and three photographs of Chinese girls in school or working happily at a tractor station. Many of the resources he provided touched on one of the main themes of his letter: the centrality of women's rights and freedoms in communist nations. It was almost as if Pemberton had expected Assistant Secretary Macomber's objections to students learning about non- "free world countries," and sought to prove the freedom he perceived in Russia and China. One of the clips he chose to send to young Janice discussed an all-women's army company.

"I was somewhat impressed. 'They are all right,' I thought," the company's male battalion leader wrote in the magazine in support of the women's ability on display. Another told the story of a female radio announcer, with the article's male author going so far in the name of freedom as to write, "It would not be so difficult if I were asked to write about an engineering project, but to write about Pan Chieh as a radio announcer, wife and mother of our two children—I've never done anything like that before." The article's male author went on, in one of the clips' few lines which actually concerned women's rights in communist China, "Well, men are always pleased if their wives are good housekeepers. Pan Chieh is not bad at that. But that's not the only thing on her mind. She loves her work very much, too. Like all of us in China, she is well aware that she is working to build a happier life for others and for herself."

Yin Wai-chen, Director of the Huangtukang People's
Commune near Peking makes a present of bean noo-
dles produced by the commune to the delegation.

The Red Army's All-Women Company

YANG YEN-CHU

IT happened some 26 years ago, yet the impression the women's company in the Red Army made on me is still fresh.

"A hundred and twenty."

"So many!" I thought to myself. "If there were fewer they would be easier to handle. Most

A small sampling of the clippings from communist magazines sent by Charles Pemberton to Janice.

In light of this propagandizing letter, it seems that Assistant Secretary Macomber truly missed the mark in his decision to reject aid to the young students—his curt message through Congressman Porter to the students spiraled outward to the public through the press, ending in Pemberton's contribution of communist clippings to Janice and her compatriots. Pemberton's efforts to help Janice become "better informed of their ways" did not end with the clippings, though, as he had much more to offer a malleable young mind such as that of our enthusiastic young protagonist.

"There are several firms," Pemberton wrote, describing options in New York, London, Peking, and Moscow, "through which you can get books, magazines, newspapers and pamphlets on every phase of Russian and Chinese life." Pemberton could attest to the success of these firms, having taken more than a hundred of the "wonderfully interesting" resources over the past year, according to the fading typewritten text on the correspondence.

Pemberton was no stranger to the struggles of a nine-year-old girl grasping to understand the vast complexities of communism and "Russian ways"— for he had, he informed Janice, a 10-year-old daughter of his own. His daughter's wish, he wrote, was to go to a school in Russia, the virtues of which he extolled: namely, their openness to both women and men at the time. All professions and institutions in Russian society, it seemed from Pemberton's excited description, were prime examples of communism's respect for the equality of men and women.

"In no other land on earth do women have such opportunities," he wrote, attempting to connect with, inspire and persuade this young girl, only barely beginning to understand her own place in the world, much less the gendered inequality around her. Under the assumption that she had some understanding of the inequality which existed between men and women, Pemberton shared with Janice statistics he hoped would impress her with the successes of communism: that half of Russia's doctors and a third of its engineers were women. Admittedly, if true, Pemberton's statistics prove the benefits of communism for women's entry into health and science professions, as only about 7 percent of US medical school applicants and 1 percent of US engineers were women in 1960.[1]

Of course, as any good educator—propagandist, informer, Soviet functionary, or whatever term to apply to him—Pemberton not only gave Janice information to educate her, but also encouraged her to seek more. As the letter rambled down the page, the final lines abutting the bottom edge of Pemberton's letterhead and interrupted by his curlicue signature, he extended an offer. If she wished, he would be more than happy to share more examples of literature the nine-year-old might enjoy, as well as the most exciting thing a fourth grader could wish for: a *list* of those firms—presumably the aforementioned ones in New York and London and Peking and Moscow—with even more resources to offer.

If you would like me to send you some examples of these Russian and Chinese newspapers, magazines and books, and a list of the firms where you can get them, please let me know and I will send them. A girl as intelligent as you deserves to be well informed.

Pemberton closes with an offer to share more communist literature.

To aid in Janice's efforts in pursuing further indoctrination, Pemberton also offered guidance about the dangers of her own government. As if with Assistant Secretary Macomber in mind, he warned Janice that she must persist in her requests to receive news and literature from China. Otherwise, Pemberton warned, the post office would prevent her from receiving Chinese mail, and American censorship laws would necessarily prevent her from getting true accounts of China from China rather than the "false and misleading" reports in American newspapers. The policy of the Postal Service, until it was struck down by the Supreme Court on First Amendment grounds in 1965 was, in fact, to hold any mail containing communist propaganda unless specifically requested by the recipient. Interestingly, the Postal Service's policy was ended at the hands of a lawsuit brought by then-ACLU Director Corliss Lamont. The American Civil Liberties Union (ACLU) is a nonprofit, nonpartisan organization which, since 1920, has been providing aid to defend legal and constitutional rights, often in unpopular or controversial cases. Lamont received a message from the Postal Service about his communist mail—a copy of *Peking Review,* mail he hadn't even intended to receive—being withheld by the agency under the regulation unless he specifically asked for it. So Lamont, another "staunch socialist" who'd had his moment before the House Un-American Activities Committee according to a Forbes article recollecting his work, did what civil libertarians do best: He sued the government. Lamont's legal argument was that citizens should not be required to go out of their way in order to access their mail, and they shouldn't have to put themselves on the agency's list of people who wanted to receive communist-looking mail pieces (as was the Postal Service's practice at one time).

Education, which was the express purpose of Charles Pemberton's message to Janice, was high on the mind of both Lamont—a former Columbia University philosophy professor—and Supreme Court Justice William Douglas, who wrote the Court's opinion overturning the procedure of reading and holding mail with communist sentiments. "Public officials, like school teachers who have no tenure, might think they would invite disaster if they read what the Federal Government says contains the seeds of treason," Douglas wrote of the policy, as if with the young residents of Oregon (and their school teacher) in mind.

Despite Justice Douglas's affection for the possibility of education, government censorship—even if not from the Postal Service—is exactly what the town of Roseburg saw a few years before that 1965 decision.

✹✹✹

"Mr. Deller stated that he considers this letter to be full of Communist propaganda and believed it to be of interest to the Bureau."

– *Memo from Portland Field Office, Federal Bureau of Investigation, March 1960*

✱✱✱

Pemberton's attempt at the radicalization of Janice and her classmates—as did many things in 1960—sounded alarm bells in the southern Oregon timber town of only 11,000 residents. Prior to Congressman Porter's response to Janice and Assistant Secretary Macomber's rejection of her request—the curious assignment of Ray McFetridge's fourth-grade class flew relatively under the radar of the school's principal and district administrators. In fact, the project itself didn't raise the attention of the school's principal or the district's superintendent until the public became aware of the students' diplomatic debacle in January. Upon the magnification of the issue in national papers, however, administrators began to take notice of the potentially subversive efforts in Classroom 15.

At that time, Patricia Boyle, mother of Janice, had given the school's principal permission, in light of the nationwide press coverage, to open "any and all mail that might come" to the Riverside School addressed to Janice. "Any and all mail," the historical record shows, included Charles Pemberton's offer and enclosures to Janice. It was at this point—the attempt by Pemberton to keep Janice and her classmates, who were just beginning their academic careers and the process of lifelong learning, "well informed of Russian ways"—that district administrators' attention to their students' activities turned into concern for the purity of their long-engrained American capitalist ideology. So, the district administrators did what other good, freedom-loving Americans might do: They forwarded the letter to the FBI, instead of to Janice and her classmates, the letter's intended recipients.

Janice only read the words intended for her 58 years later. Pemberton, it seems, had been correct in his prediction of censorship, but it wasn't the Post Office doing the censoring, and it wasn't the Chinese doing the mailing: It was Pemberton's own propaganda-filled correspondence censored at the hands of school district bureaucrats. Pemberton's goal was to expose the youngsters to a variety of perspectives, ways of being, and methods of "How People Work Together." But the conductors of Roseburg's educational machine, in a fit of McCarthy-fueled fear, decided instead that that discourse should not proceed with the young students, ending what seems like a poignant current-events teaching moment.

The concern rose up the ranks. From the mailbox, the letter found itself in the hands of duly appointed mail-reader (and elementary school principal)

Roy Crain and, later, the desk of superintendent Mahlon Cloyd Deller. Deller, upon reading the letter, found that it was similar to many things thought evil in 1960s America: communist propaganda. And so further up the ranks Pemberton's letter went, this time to the FBI. Instead of the hands of a curious child, the letter from New York's prolific letter writer would wind up in a file about its author, sitting untouched for 58 years without so much of a hint of its existence to the rightful owner of the letter: Janice Boyle.

Today, the FBI's website lauds its own work during the Cold War in managing internal threats to American democracy. In a biography of the bureau's notorious former director, J. Edgar Hoover, the agency's website describes the support it provided in the war against communism by investigating the backgrounds of applicants to government jobs to prevent infiltration and sabotage. Hoover was the founding director of the Federal Bureau of Investigation and led that law enforcement agency from 1935 until his death in 1972. Among his top priorities was fighting against communism, and the posthumous profile even mentions the "headlines garnered" under Hoover's reign by the intelligence agency's "staunch efforts" to combat communist espionage. The profile goes on to describe how Hoover's anti-espionage efforts continued into the sixties and seventies, even as "political violence" drew on many of the Bureau's resources (though the site isn't clear if that "violence" refers to the Civil Rights Movement, protests against the Vietnam War, or something else). What the six-paragraph recounting of the director's 48-year career neglects to include, however—aside from his counterintelligence efforts to disrupt the work and personal life of Martin Luther King, Jr. and other civil rights activists of the day—was any form of counter-propaganda effort in American classrooms.

Regardless of how the agency remembers the career of its longest-serving director and whether or not it acknowledges it, the fact remains that the Bureau did partake in that classroom counter-propaganda effort, bringing the heat of the Cold War to southern Oregon's all-American Roseburg. Or, it could be argued instead, Roseburg brought that heat when the superintendent sent the letters addressed to Janice more than a couple of hundred miles up what would years later become Interstate 5, to the regional headquarters of the FBI. Having had his communist-propaganda alarm bell rung by Janice and her compatriots, McFetridge's *dangerous* project, and Pemberton's attempt to mold the young minds, Principal Crain made that journey himself to Portland in March of 1960, knocking on the door of the nation's top law enforcement investigators. Despite Assistant Secretary Macomber's best efforts to quell a possible bureaucratic and diplomatic nightmare, it was too late. The federal government was faced with an attempt to inject communism into small-town America.

Years before, a man named Leo B. App, Jr., had fought a battle much greater. During the Second World War, App served in the US Army Air Corps, fighting this time in concert with the Soviets against Nazism and the Axis powers. For 30 years after the war's conclusion, App served his country as a special agent for the FBI, working in Washington DC, Los Angeles, and, finally, in Portland. Portland was the last stop in his professional journey, and there he worked as a firearms specialist, training agents and police officers in the ways of the craft. Today, after his death in 2014, App's name adorns an award, the *Leo B. App Top Shooter Award*, which recognizes graduates of Oregon's police officer training program for their leadership and teamwork skills, as well as their proficiency with firearms. In 1960, though, after his service fighting threats abroad and outside of the specialization which gave him stature as an award-name-worthy marksman, App had new orders for the protection of his country: the investigation of a man from New York and of the fourth-grade class to which Charles Pemberton mailed a letter.

To that end, Roseburg Superintendent Deller brought the letter from Pemberton to Portland, where he was interviewed by Special Agent App. In that office, Deller spilled all he knew: how the class had sought to become pen pals with Russian peers, how administrators had been in the dark until the arrival of Pemberton's letter, and how fearful Deller was that the letter had been "full of communist propaganda and of interest to the Bureau." Clearly, the seven-paragraph letter and 19 pages of literature and photos had been sufficiently of interest to the Bureau, as they took the pages and left them, for nearly 60 years, in Pemberton's file. As a result of App and Deller's conversation about the past five months' events, the FBI's Portland office began to turn the bureaucratic wheels, crafting a six-page memo to its headquarters describing those suspicious months. Typewritten and, all these years later, scrawled upon by any number of functionaries busy pushing them from folder to folder and file to file, the documents sat and collected dust in the depths of the National Archives' campus in College Park, Maryland. That memo—the only point of the federal government's involvement in the Roseburg pen pal project other than Congressman Porter and Assistant Secretary Macomber's correspondence and diplomatic denial—provides the official account, as filtered through Deller and, later, App, of what went on in Classroom 15. That historical record, and the lack of any others, shows that, contrary to Janice's original memory, there was no "raid" of Riverside School or the Boyle home, by Hoover's G-Men. In fact, in spite of Janice's memory of her parents having been interviewed at work by agents, the historical record—built upon 12 sets of letters and emails from government agency recordkeepers, 11 of which concluded with some form of "therefore, your request is being closed"— shows no evidence that those G-Men ever even came to town.

Note

1   Medical school applicants: Jolly, Paul. "Medical Education In The United States, 1960–1987." *Health Affairs* 7, no. suppl 2 (1988): 144–57 (154). https://doi.org/10.1377/hlthaff.7.2.144. Engineers: Hill, Catherine, Christianne Corbett, and Andresse St. Rose. "Why So Few? Women in Science, Technology, Engineering, and Mathematics." AAUW, 2010. https://www.aauw.org/files/2013/02/Why-So-Few-Women-in-Science-Technology-Engineering-and-Mathematics.pdf.

Chapter Four

JANICE'S TEACHER

by Amelia Salzman

In which student journalist Amelia Salzman learns previously unreported details about the role Janice's teacher Ray McFetridge played in international affairs from his post in typical small-town America. Following a lead from a source, Salzman travels up and over the Cascades to Sisters, Oregon, where she discovers physical evidence of Classroom 15's global reach.

The letters were in a simple paper sack, slipped into the corner of a cedar chest. The bag's crumples and wrinkles had flattened, pressed rigid from years untouched. The chest holding the letters was a wedding gift to 17-year-old Beverly from her husband, Ray McFetridge. It traveled with their family as they moved around Oregon, keeping sentimental items, memories, and a bundle of cards and letters from Russian children preserved. The family heirloom now belongs to Linda Priest, Beverly's youngest daughter.

Today, the yellowing letters from the cedar chest cover Linda Priest's kitchen table, in her house tucked inside a grove of Ponderosa pines. Deer linger across the road with little notice of cars or passerby. A retired nurse now living in Sisters, Oregon, Linda had never given much thought to the correspondence except as a reminder of her father's time as a teacher in Roseburg.

"Without all of this paperwork, I wouldn't really know much about the pen pal project. I don't remember it being a super big deal. Although, he did save all of these," she muses, pulling the letters out of the bag, one by one. Protected in cedar for decades, each letter holds a story, delicate and preserved. Barely touched, even by curious members of the family, each letter and postcard beams with color. Illustrations look vibrant and youthful, suggesting the energy and enthusiasm of the children who sent them. Holding the postcards and stationery some 60 years after they were sent, it's easy to feel their age. Pressed flat from storage, the folded edges frayed, the typewriter ink lightly faded. The letters were written with care—the penmanship is precise—by Russian school children studying in different places in Russia: cities like Dugna, 140 miles outside Moscow with just 2,000 residents, and Ilyich, a city in southern Russia near the Black Sea. The authors read about the failed attempt by American schoolchildren to connect with Russian pen pals and offered to initiate such relationships.

But the Eisenhower administration State Department looked at the Roseburg project and saw the potential for propaganda, not innocent friendship, to be transmitted through this pen pal effort. After the *Associated Press* story about the school project was published in newspapers worldwide, the Soviet newspaper *Pravda* (whose name means "truth" in Russian) printed the story. The tri-weekly paper was the official publication of the Communist Party and was distributed throughout the Soviet Union. Established in 1912, *Pravda* claimed at its peak to reach 11 million readers, and it shaped the narrative of official information in the Union of Soviet Socialist Republics (USSR).

Because of the paper's wide circulation, many Russians read the story of the McFetridge project. Some of them reached out in support—and this support is now memorialized in the McFetridge family's cedar chest. These letters are a glimpse of what the project could have created if political concerns, both from the State Department and the Roseburg school, had not quashed it.

Decades before his daughter opened the chest, when these Soviet letters were fresh from the post, Ray McFetridge showed them to his students in Classroom 15.

The Russian envelopes were embellished with bright colors and layers of postage marking their miles of travel through the international mail, with three, four, and sometimes five stamps lined up carefully above the straight-forward American address: *Riverside Elementary School, Roseburg, Oregon*. But instead of stamps depicting American flags, bald eagles, and the country's leaders, these showed factory workers and the hammer-and-sickle symbol of the Soviet Union.

Russian students ranging in age from nine to 13 wrote about their lives and their excitement about the idea of connecting with other students in the United States.

The Russian letters were filled with warm greetings. They wished the Roseburg children a happy New Year and described their own lives in the bit-terly cold winter in rural Russia. The letters were devoid of political tensions. As Janice recalls, the American school children expressed little interest in the Cold War, and these letters imply that Russian schoolchildren shared the same lack of interest.

After teacher McFetridge failed to gain State Department support for the project and the FBI became involved, the case was lost to history, but in keeping these USSR letters, McFetridge preserved a part of the story that could have easily landed in school secretaries' wastebaskets or added to the government files filled with otherwise lost papers and stories.

"He was quiet, calm and very kind," says Genee Parr, who was a student alongside Janice Boyle in McFetridge's class in 1959–60. "Like, when I fell, he picked me up." She remembers her teacher's warmhearted reasoning behind starting the project: "He thought each of us should get a pen pal in Russia and then explain what we did as children and hear what they did as children. He just kind of thought we probably did about the same things."

Hello dear friends!

Greeting you is fourth-grade student Gouchkova Tatyana. Dear friends, I would like to be your pen-pal very much. Dugna's school students have also established mail connections with many countries. I live in Dugna. Our surroundings are beautiful. The forest and the river create beautiful conditions for medical treatment. In Dugna there are two libraries, parks, three schools and two community centers. The Oka River flows nearby. There is an open-pit mine on one of the banks of the river, our town is on another.

Dear friends, I congratulate you with the beginning of a new school year!

Respectfully yours,

Gouchkova Tanya.

Translated to English from Russian, this letter is one of many written to "dear friends" or "my American friend." Although these children were across the globe from each other, they all spent their childhood nestled among the trees, rivers and forests, enjoying their childhoods, oblivious to or despite the tensions of international politics. In this sense, Roseburg doesn't seem so far from this town surrounded by the mountains of Russia.

One young student wrote to the Riverside School students:

Dear American friend!

My name is Nadya Serkina. I am 14 years old. I am a seventh-grade student.

I would like to be your pen-pal.

With warmest greetings, Nadya.

02/27/60

They wrote not only to send greetings and solidarity to their American peers, but to directly request a pen-pal exchange:

Dear American friend!

My name is Vera Migulina.

I am 12 years old. I am a sixth-grade student.

I would like to be your pen-pal.

Friendly greetings, Vera.

Because of the curious worldwide following for the fourth-grade class's adventure in a sleepy Oregon town, McFetridge was on the receiving end of dozens of letters—the equivalent of a contemporary Facebook jammed with comments—each one either praising or condemning the project in Classroom 15 at Riverside Elementary in Roseburg.

Although most of these letters came from children, one was written by a Russian school teacher. This letter spoke directly to McFetridge's goal of connecting students with one another and teaching them about the world they shared.

Stripped away from Cold War politics and government fear mongering, this letter suggests a like-minded fellow teacher who wanted to teach peace. Its sentiment moves beyond the immediate benefits of connecting children globally and looks toward a possible future world of peace.

To Ray Mak Fetridge, teacher.

Dear colleague!

I congratulate you for the 1961 New Year, wishing you and your family complete well-being and the fulfilment of all your wishes.

Your letter and American kids' postcards have brought us sincere joy.

Let's hope they will live during more peaceful times for mankind and would be able to keep the peace for centuries to come.

We would like to continue our conversation on a more regular basis.

It will help not only to develop good feelings, but will also help to learn about our respective people's lives in better detail.

Our school is located in the Caucasus Mountains, our students are mostly collective farm workers' kids.

Once again my greetings and congratulations to you.

M. Lozhkin, school principal.

1960, 12/25

U.S.S.R.,

Krasnodarskiy Kray,

Khutor Ilyich, Otradnenskoye District,

Secondary school #9

Hoping to "live during more peaceful times for mankind" is a vision that is exemplary of the goals and dreams of educators, spending their lives committing themselves to the generations beyond themselves. Failed attempts to communicate across borders like this one force people on both sides to question solidarity and unity, and make them susceptible to fear and division.

✳✳✳

Beverly McFetridge, now Beverly Zehner after remarrying following her husband's death in the late '70s, is 86 years old when we meet. She lives in a small, cheery neighborhood in McMinnville, Oregon, with a lap dog companion she calls Big Rig. Her home is located among the rolling hills and blooming fields off the I-5 corridor, a three-hour drive north of Roseburg. She is a self-taught painter and her work hangs throughout her house, mostly landscapes showing rich colors and seasons. Alongside her paintings, old family photos cover the walls—young smiles growing older between each frame. The photos show the arc of overlapping lifetimes.

Beverly and Ray McFetridge had five children together and were married for almost 30 years. To this day, Beverly remembers the ease and comfort she had in her marriage to Ray.

Beverly is quick to correct her late husband's name. He was Bud to the family, and only Ray to his coworkers and those who didn't know him well. This tight-knit family is excited to talk about Bud; he remains a comfort for and influence on each of them, and they share memories of Bud's life and the class project as if it all happened yesterday.

The story goes like this: As a baby, McFetridge was small enough to fit in a shoe box. Born with a congenital heart condition, McFetridge was rejected by the Navy before being drafted into the Army at the beginning of the Korean War. He tested high enough on military aptitude tests to qualify for officer training. This took newly-married Bud and Beverly to Fort Benning, Georgia.

"They would do everything possible to make you give up," Beverly recounts about those days in training. "They would get him in the middle of the night to do five-mile runs. But his heart held up and he did it." He became a US Army officer.

The young couple was living in Georgia during the 1950s, a time and place of overt racial discrimination and racist attitudes and actions, and this didn't go unnoticed by the McFetridge family. After years in Oregon, Beverly recalls experiencing extreme culture shock as she tried to acclimate to the Deep South. Though Oregon faced its own issues of racism and income inequity, they were not as explicit. She remembers families living in houses with dirt floors, and signs directing people to segregated restrooms, building entrances and drinking fountains.

Living in Georgia during the emergence of the Civil Rights movement, Beverly and Bud were on the front lines of American history. While they lived their lives like many Americans did and still do—school, jobs, raising children—their lives were unfolding while the country was growing and changing. They watched as, after President Franklin Roosevelt's death shortly before the end of World War II, Harry Truman became the first in a long line of Cold War presidents. They lived in the South as Martin Luther King fought Jim Crow laws. Car radios blasted out the music of Chuck Berry, Elvis Presley and Patsy Cline, songs about love and heartbreak. "It seemed like the world was changing," remembers Beverly. "My life was certainly changing."

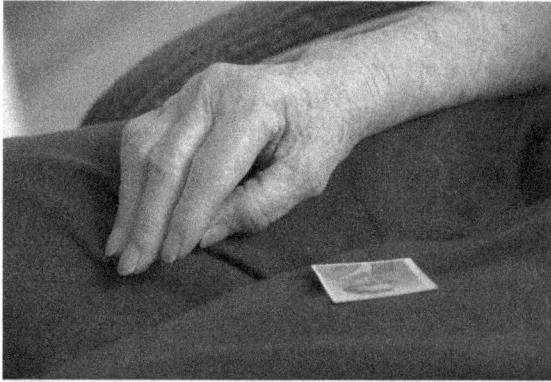

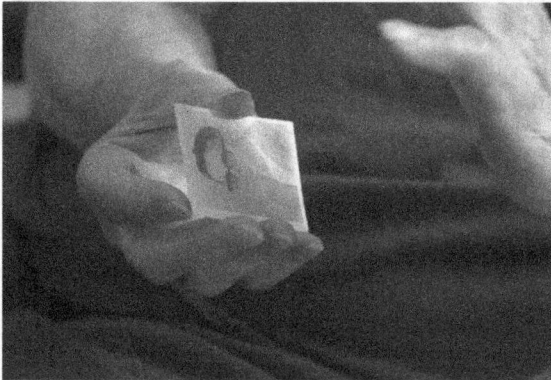

Beverly shows a photograph of Ray.

After three military years served in the South, Bud and Beverly returned to Oregon, the place they both considered home. Bud began working at a newspaper, selling classified ads, then a stint selling insurance door-to-door. This wasn't a good fit for him. Ultimately, he realized he wanted to teach.

By the time Bud fixed on teaching as a career, Oregon was desperate for new, energetic voices in classrooms. In the late '50s and early '60s, Oregon suffered a scarcity of teachers and this scarcity allowed for a fast-track to a new career: Go back to school for two semesters and get an emergency teaching certificate. After getting a steady job as a teacher in the Roseburg school district, Bud continued to attend education courses at Oregon State University during the summers. McFetridge and his growing family spent summers in Corvallis student housing.

"They had all these little houses that ran by the railroad tracks, and you could rent them. At the time there were six of us, all crammed into this little house." Bud's daughter Linda laughs at the memory. "Graduate students from all over the world lived there. We were these little McFetridge kids that didn't really know anything."

This was the beginning of her father's lifelong teaching career. During the school year, the family lived in small, sleepy Roseburg, in a house near a lumber mill. The Roseburg lumber mills operated wood waste burners, known as beehive burners, used to dispose of wood scraps and sawdust. The smoke from these burners left an earthy, musty smell in the air. The tannins released from cutting the wood added a chemical edge to the smoke. The cone-shaped burners would release huge amounts of smoke into the Roseburg atmosphere and the beehives were not equipped with scrubbing or filtering devices. Their smoke produced Roseburg smog, often sending ash and cinders into the kids' hair when they played outside. These years spent in Roseburg became formative for the family as they learned both how to cope with the environmental side effects of living in a timber town and how to live off of a teacher's relatively meager salary.

The McFetridge family made the best of this less-than-ideal lifestyle and looks back on the years fondly. The McFetridge clan were family-oriented and spent most of their free time together. Theirs was a household built on board games and old stories. The family treat was stovetop popcorn—Bud's favorite snack. Beverly made a conscious decision to devote herself to raising her family, taking them to church on Sunday and leading Campfire Girls groups.

During his time at Riverside School, Bud devoted himself to the school. "He put a lot of time into his classes. He would go to school really, really early. He would also walk out to the school just for the exercise," Beverly recalls. "It's a long way. And then he would stay late most nights. He really dedicated himself to his classes."

Former student Julie Davie, who was also a friend of the McFetridges' oldest, Janet, remembers Ray as both a teacher and a friend. She has not forgotten hiking with Ray and Janet, getting to know the family as well as his teaching. "He was very even-tempered, I can't think of anything negative."

Today, Janet is a retired teacher and immigration activist living just a few miles south of the Canadian border in New York. She has become a severe critic of Trump-era immigration policies.

"My father's life was about teaching. He felt strongly that reaching out to others is a great thing that bonds us as humans," Janet says, confident that he would approve of her volunteer work at the border.

During the winter of 1960, Janet was a student at the elementary school where her father taught. She was shy and timid. "She was so shy and would get so nervous," Beverly recalls. "Janet wouldn't ride on the merry-go-round at recess because she was so shy and she thought that she would be late for her next class."

Today, Janet McFetridge's voice is exuberant and outgoing. The oldest of the McFetridge children, she remembers the famed pen pal project well. "Of course I remember my parents talking about it. But I was more scared that he was going to get arrested," she says. "You know how kids are. It was at the height of the Cold War. We were doing duck-and-cover drills under our desks. I don't think anyone realized how much heat my father was getting from outside sources like the school board and reporters."

Duck-and-cover drills were common at the time, in schools across the United States. School children, from kindergarten to high school, learned the basics of how to prepare for a nuclear attack, as per the government's recommendations. They were shown cartoons starring Bert the Turtle avoiding a stick of dynamite to teach children about danger. Children were taught to cower under a desk or table, as if avoiding broken window glass from a nuclear blast would compensate for radioactive fallout. These drills were less about practical safety and more about bringing awareness of nuclear danger to America's young citizens, and they also served propaganda purposes. The drills brought the Cold War conflict and Cold War fear into classrooms. They reinforced the role of the Soviet Union as an adversary.

Janet kept her duck-and-cover-fueled worries to herself. Beverly didn't find out about her daughter's concerns for her father's safety until Janet was an adult. Raising a young family through the Cold War, Beverly and Bud didn't spend much time dwelling on fear about global conflict.

"I had four little kids, and the oldest was only seven. I never had really any fear." But reminders of potential atomic disaster kept penetrating her nuclear family. "A few years later, the government sent out pamphlets on making the basement safe in case of nuclear attack and that was a little scary."

The arms race between the Soviet Union and the United States led to arms testing. Above-ground tests increased public awareness of radioactive fallout. During the 1950s and into the 1960s, talk about home bomb shelters became commonplace throughout the country. Reading material on building shelters and preparing for an attack became widespread.

Ray McFetridge started the pen pal project with intentions of teaching geography and social studies. Instead, his class assignment became a footnote in the Cold War. Many of McFetridge's students remember the USSR being chosen for the project because it was the farthest place from Roseburg that they could think of; McFetridge's wife, though, remembers he chose Russia because of its news value. Still, McFetridge never imagined that the project would become a controversy that led his fourth-grade class into the local and international spotlight. He saw the project as something that went beyond simple politics. He wanted to push his students to think about people on a human level.

"It was always in the news; they were the so-called 'enemy,'" says Beverly. "He wanted American children to realize that the Russian children were just like they were, that they didn't need to be afraid of them. He was a real conservative. He was a Republican. We both were. But he also hated the McCarthy stuff. He felt McCarthyism was really bad."

The following year, McFetridge would move his family north to Salem, Oregon. There, he would accept a teaching job at McKinley Elementary school teaching fourth grade. In a phone call with Nancy Hadely, one of McFetridge's former students who was in his fourth-grade McKinley class in 1962, she remembered her parents talking about how the McFetridge family was middle-class, hardworking and respected. She remembers her community of the time, recalling a much smaller, simpler Salem. As early as the fourth grade, she walked to school without a worry. McKinley was a small school at the time. Nancy recalls only two fourth-grade classes, and hers had just 20 students.

Nancy remembers the fear she had during the Cold War. "Well, I remember hiding under our desks, not for earthquakes but for bombs." She had grown up with the then recent history of World War II and she recalled her parents telling her the story of Pearl Harbor.

In 1963, Nancy was working in her lunch room as a ticket taker when the news came in about President John F. Kennedy's assassination. Classes were dismissed and Nancy felt a panic shared by most Americans. "I ran all the way home looking up at the sky. I was sure there was going to be a bomb." This thought crossing the mind of a child gives a glimpse into the mindset of the country during that uncertain time.

Still, Nancy looks back on her days as a student of Ray McFetridge fondly. "Well, it's funny the things kids remember. I remember our play, we did it on the weather, I was the thermometer and I played on the slide flute, and he was just the kindest. I would have to say he was probably the teacher who got me interested in science." Nancy paints an image of fourth graders wiggling and dancing their way across school auditorium stages, paper cutouts and home-made costumes filling young—probably first-time—performers with nerves and excitement.

McFetridge was also Nancy's first male teacher. She remembers that most teachers were women, and describes McFetridge as being a big deal for the time period. "I even remember the desk I was sitting in and where it was in the class." A hint of excitement enters her voice at recalling such clear memories from all those years ago. "He came up and put his hand on my shoulder and asked if I was okay. I wasn't really looking well and he recognized it without me saying anything. He quietly helped me out of the class room before I got sick. He was just so sweet like that."

Nancy remembers all the care that McFetridge put into his students. "He was maybe a little bit serious but I think it was because he was so dedicated."

***

Back in her house in the pines, McFetridge's daughter Linda leans over the letters, scrutinizing them. "I think he was shocked that people cared about fourth graders talking to each other. He could have chosen anywhere, but he did choose Russia. Probably because of the political situation. He was always doing things like this."

Removed as the modern world is from the time of the Cold War and in the contemporary world of email and text, it's difficult to imagine struggling to find and connect with new acquaintances around the world. The grounds for refusing to help the students given by the State Department were the fear that "such correspondence would be censored and some might be used for propaganda."[1]

McFetridge made a public statement to *The News-Review* stating he would leave the fate of the project up to the parents of the class but would no longer pursue the letters personally. According to his wife Beverly, this was McFetridge's attempt to protect his class from the public spectacle, a spectacle that was picking up steam.

On a regular, likely gray and rainy Oregon morning, Linda says FBI agents arrived at Riverside School. McFetridge was among the few they talked to about the pen pal project.

"He told me the FBI came and talked with him," says Beverly. "He said he didn't want anything to do with the project. He really didn't want his students to be worried or concerned. So he had to shut it down as fast as he could."

Beverly remembers calls from all over the country swarming the McFetridge house. "There wasn't too much involvement in our home. But I got lots of phone calls from across the country from newspapers for days."

McFetridge's class had experienced a brief moment in the public spotlight. Following the failed pen pal project and the FBI investigation, life went back to the usual math and reading curricula found in most elementary school classrooms. But in the days and weeks following the news stories, letters from all over the country and the world arrived in Roseburg.

During the initial research for this book, these letters were unaccounted for and assumed to be lost, much like the letters destined for Russia written by Janice Boyle and her classmates. However, somewhere between the letters arriving at the school and the shutdown of the project, McFetridge must have secretly removed the letters out of Riverside School and into his home. There they were placed in Beverly's cedar chest without much thought, beginning their long-term hibernation.

McFetridge continued teaching and never shied away from pushing his students to think big. His family recalls him as a teacher who was engaging and excited to learn as much as he taught. According to them, the 1960 pen pal project was just one of many unique school projects that he initiated during his career as a teacher.

Life for the McFetridge family continued without national attention. Just a year after the pen pal project, Bud began teaching junior high science in Salem, Oregon. The family settled down, and Bud and Beverly welcomed one more child into their family, a baby boy named Scott. They bought a larger house in Salem, one that the kids laughingly remember being haunted by a friendly ghost.

One of the foremost memories the family shares is a road trip across the country to Washington, DC: One goal of the journey was to see as many of the states as possible.

"We liked history; we liked our country. We wanted to see everything we could of our country. The boys were a bit young, but Bud and I decided that was where we wanted to go," recalls Beverly. "I remember getting chills when I saw the Washington Monument. It was so beautiful."

They camped, rain or shine, living out of their Impala station wagon along the way. It was always referred to as The Trip by the family, one more example of the way they viewed America and their place in it. Even after an FBI investigation and public accusations of condoning communist propaganda, Bud and Beverly stayed true to their core beliefs and kept loyal to their deep-rooted love for their country. They admired the country in which they had grown up, served, and raised their family.

Beverly and Bud were a part of a larger narrative. They were witnesses to monumental moments in American history, moments they traversed with a close-knit family, and which left them with a greater understanding of what the world could be.

As the years passed and the McFetridge children grew older, Beverly returned to school. She began taking classes. She discovered a love of art, particularly landscape painting, the proof of which now hangs on the walls of her home. Bud continued teaching, though he suffered from a lifelong heart condition and endured a few medical crises over the years.

Early one morning, Beverly was pulled out of class for a phone call. She felt she knew instantly what the call was about, and her fears were confirmed: Ray McFetridge died in his classroom one early morning while preparing for his day. He was 49 years old.

It was an incredible life, Beverly remembers, and she keeps her husband's memory alive through stories.

One of her favorite stories is that of Saturday nights: While the household was sleeping, Bud stayed up, blacking out windows and developing his own photographs. He captured the smiling, toothless grins of his children. He developed images of landscapes and wildlife, many of the Pacific Northwest. McFetridge was an Oregon native and felt a deep connection to the state.

Bud McFetridge with his first grandson.

The oldest McFetridge daughter, Janet, is confident her father would approve of her work. The family is quick to say that Bud would be right alongside her.

Linda Priest, McFetridge's youngest daughter, became a nurse and head of the Cancer Outreach department in her hospital. She raised a family while working and saving lives throughout her career.

Steve worked at a company that sold and installed newspaper inserting machines, installing the devices and training local newspaper employees to use them.

Tim, who lives close to the family home and looks after Beverly, has worked for many years as an engineer with the Oregon Department of Environmental Quality.

The youngest of the children, Scott, became a journalist and works as an editor for the Associated Press.

The McFetridge children are a lasting tribute to the impact that Bud had on the world. McFetridge taught his children and his students to be kind and dedicated in their work, and to reach out to others. Through them, the legacy of the teacher lives on.

Note

1 *The News Review* January 28, 1960.

Chapter Five

ROSEBURG THEN AND NOW

by Carol Kress

In which student journalist Carol Kress takes readers on a stroll down memory lane to revisit life in the Roseburg, Oregon, '50s.

On the chilly morning of January 27, 1960, nine-year-old Genee Parr got ready for school.[1] She wore a striped dress and leather saddle shoes, her usual school attire. Her dark hair was pulled back into a ponytail, her bangs curled forward. She might have had some pancakes made with Albers Flapjack Mix (only 39 cents for a 4-lb bag!), paired, of course, with Morrel's Pride Bacon Slabs (33 cents a pound!) and syrup (now only 59 cents!).[2] She would then ride the bus to school and arrive for class with her fourth-grade teacher, Mr. Ray McFetridge, as she did every school day.

That morning, however, was different than her routine school day. That day, a photographer from the local paper, *The News-Review*, had come to Riverside School to take her picture.

Genee, along with two of her classmates, Janice Boyle and Mark Wilborn, were led to a corner of the classroom with their teacher, Mr. McFetridge. Janice was handed a globe and placed in the middle of their small group, the photograph was taken, and the reporters left.

On a typical weekday like that one, Genee would have gone home and eaten dinner with her family. Maybe she watched some of "Uncle Bill's Cartoons" or "Cartoon Circus." She would've gone to sleep thinking little of the reporters that had visited her classroom that day.[3]

The next morning, January 29, 1960, Genee was in the paper.

"Reaction over 'Pen Pal' Quest Said Surprising," the headline read.[4] In the black-and-white image accompanying the picture, Genee was taller than her peers, but all three children were looking at the globe and pointing to Russia. The caption read:

Pupils Seek Pen Pals—Genee Parr, Janice Boyle and Mark Wilborn (left to right), members of Ray McFetridge's (standing) fourth grade class at Riverside School point to a spot on the map of Russia. They want to correspond with a class of children from a town similar in size to Roseburg in that Communist nation "to learn their way of life … and we would like to make friends."

ROSEBURG, ORE.   FRIDAY, JANUARY 29, 1960   ★ ★ 23-60   PRICE 5c

Reaction Over 'Pen Pal' Quest Said Surprising

PUPILS SEEK PEN PALS — Genee Porr, Janice Boyle and Mark Wilbarn (left to right), members of Ray McFetridge's (standing) fourth grade class at Riverside School point to a spot on the map of Russia. They want to correspond with a class of children from a town similar in size to Roseburg in that Communist nation "to learn their way of life … and we would like to make friends." (Paul Jenkins)

Teacher To Leave Letter Project Up To Parents, School Officers

Fans, Opponents Of Castro Riot

African Tribes Honor British Prime Minister

Genee, Janice, and Mark cradle the globe under the approving eyes of their teacher, Ray McFetridge.

***

Looking back, Genee said that those days, the days of her childhood in Roseburg, she lived in "la la land" and for her, that was the end of the story. She was unaware of the kind of fallout their news story would receive and the attention it would bring to the small town where she grew up.

For Genee, Roseburg was the place she called home. It was where she played with her sisters after school, and where she would grow up, meet her husband, get married, and retire.

But although Roseburg was a small town, not even the *News-Review* could avoid the fear that permeated throughout the country.

Headlines screamed:

**"Anti-Red Demonstration of Students Marks Opening
of Soviet Exhibit in Cuba"**
(February 6, 1960) Havana[5]
"High Court Defers Action on 3 Cases of Communism"
(February 6, 1960) Washington[6]
"Communist Nations Fight U.S.–Japan Security Treaty"
(February 1, 1960) Tokyo[7]
"Red Chinese Taking New Tack in Peace Diplomacy"
(January 29, 1960) Washington[8]
**"Khrushchev Seen Scheming to Build New Berlin Crisis
to Weaken Western Allies"**
(February 9, 1960) Washington[9]

These stories from around the world filled the pages of the *News-Review* during Genee and Janice's childhoods. As of January 28, 1960, however, Roseburg had its own story to fuel the fires of the Red Scare. A tale of a far-away terror—communism—reaching all the way to a small town in Oregon, to innocent nine-year-olds.

In 1960, the population of Roseburg was about 12,000, less than 1 percent of the population of the whole state of Oregon, but this was, surprisingly, not the first time in the past year Roseburg had made national papers.[10] On Aug. 7, 1959—just a few months before the pen pal project picked up—at around 1 in the morning, Janice Boyle and her younger sister, Jodi, were fast asleep in their childhood home. It was the peak of summer, so the young sisters were on top of their blankets, with only their nightgowns to cover them. Their bed was pushed against an open window.

A man named George Rutherford had parked his truck outside a store downtown for the night. The driver was only passing through town, but his truck carried dangerous cargo: two tons of dynamite and over four tons of ammonium nitrate.[11]

Janice still vividly remembers the moment she woke up to the curtains on the girls' bedroom window blowing straight up, perpendicular to her bed, as if on a hinge, as a mushroom cloud from the explosion downtown reached her home. The sisters remember watching the cloud and thinking about how, if their windows had been closed, the glass would have shattered—sending shards all over them as they slept.

They remember hearing their father shout, running outside in only a T-shirt and underwear, no doubt thinking about the jewelry store he owned, located in the heart of The Blast.

The Blast was felt from up to seven miles away, and reportedly could be heard from as far as Eugene, the bigger college town an hour up the road.[12]

Known throughout Roseburg and the rest of Oregon as simply "The Blast," the disaster remains a tragic event of Oregon history. It resulted in what newspapers then reported as 14 deaths, over 120 injuries[13] and at least 10 million dollars in damages.[14] Looking back on the tragedy in a 2009 article, the *Oregonian* reported, "Roseburg, then a town of 12,000, made worldwide news. Lawmakers rewrote the rules about how explosives are handled, the federal government issued a damning report and the city tried to rebuild. Investigations piled up and lawsuits flew."[15]

At the time, some Roseburg residents, unaware of what had caused The Blast, first thought that an atomic bomb had been dropped by the Soviet Union.[16] Such a conclusion was understandable in a time when propaganda and warnings of Russia testing weapons were weaved into newspaper headlines, posters, political debates, and presidential speeches.

It would take years for Roseburg to recover from the downtown destruction caused by the explosion. Janice and Jodi Boyle remember their father telling them about the painstaking process he went through, picking through the glass wreckage of the blast for days after, searching for diamonds from his store's window display.

In 2019, all that remains of The Blast is a stone monument in downtown Roseburg with a metal plaque that reads: "This is the site of the explosion which occurred in the early morning of August 7, 1959, resulting in fourteen deaths and injuring fifty-seven persons. A fire in a lumberyard detonated a truck loaded with explosives and caused property losses estimated at more than twelve million dollars."[17]

***

The News-Review
Tues., Feb. 2, 1960

Pet Skunk Still Away from Home

Petunia, the skunk still is missing.

Her owners, the John LeDuc family of 615 SE Terrace Ave., Roseburg, feel their pet may have headed for the hills behind the LeDuc home.

Petunia, whose nickname has been Pete since the family learned "she" is a "he," is described by LeDuc as friendly.

How does one tell Petunia, a pleasant creature minus the body odor characteristics that often mar human-skunk relationships, distinguished from his less favorably endowed brethren?

"It's hard to tell," LeDuc admits. "By the time you found out, it might be too late." Petunia looks like any other skunk, according to LeDuc, but he feels sure he can tell his pet from the others."[18]

✳✳✳

Cinched waists, full skirts, and white socks were the outfit of choice for most schoolgirls in the early 1960s.[19] Adult women might have looked up to fashion icons like Jackie Kennedy (looks she wore to accompany her husband on the presidential campaign trail of 1960 became timeless haute couture), Audrey Hepburn, or Twiggy.

Roseburg businessmen wore suits or button up polo shirts. Colorful clothing was coming into style, replacing the darker neutrals of the 1950s with brighter hues. Men's pants became tighter, and a Sears catalog from the sixties dubbed the style "Low Riding, skinny, and very popular." From that collection, a pair of olive green, heavy cotton, twill slacks would have cost $3.77.[20]

On January 26, 1960, $3.77 could also afford a Bulky Knit Orlon sweater at the Newberry's Leap Year Sale, according to an ad in the *News-Review*.[21]

Children, like Genee and Janice, would often wear the leather saddle shoes that Genee remembers wearing to Riverside School. They were durable and could last an entire school year. In the Parr family, Genee and her siblings were given two pairs of fancy shoes a year: black patent leather ones for Christmas, and white ones for Easter. One day, for a class party, Genee remembers being allowed to wear her black leather shoes to school. She called them her "slippy-shoes," and the sleek leather lived up to its nickname. The soles became skates on the school floor, causing little Genee to slip and cut her head open behind her ear. Mr. McFetridge was the one who came to her rescue, picking up the crying child, holding her head to stop it from bleeding.

✻✻✻

The News-Review
Feb. 17, 1960

COMMUNITY NEWS BRIEFS

Ray Barnhart of 1324 NE Malheur Ave attended the Oregon Conference on Pesticides at Corvallis last week. He represents the Aaarbee Control Service in Roseburg. The conference dealt with the importance and proper use of agricultural chemicals.

Reedy Berg, son-in-law of Mr. and Mrs. Archie Amorde of this city has just returned to his home in Sunnyvale, Calif., following a business trip to Kansas City, New York and Atlantic City. While in Atlantic City he saw pictures in various places of his wife, the former JoAnn Amorde, who was Miss Oregon of 1947 and who placed fifth in the Miss America contest in Atlantic City that year. The Bergs are parents of three children. Berg is a lumber broker.

Mrs. William Wishart, who suffered a fractured right arm in a fall at her home on SE Reservoir Avenue last week, is able to be out.

Jack Smith, Clyde Manning and John Patton drove to Portland Saturday to see the boat show.

Friends and relatives are invited to attend an open house honoring Mrs. Elizabeth Galdabini on her 80th birthday Sunday, Feb. 21, at the home of Mrs. Len Brown in Analuf on Buck Creek Road. The open house will be held from 1:30 to 5pm. Cards would be appreciated. Relatives and friends have been requested not to bring gifts.[22]

✻✻✻

Daydreaming in class, fourth- and fifth-grade students of Riverside School might stare aimlessly out the window across the street at the lumber yard that burned sawdust, which could be smelled like a campfire even from the classroom across the street, remembers Genee.

For outsiders, "Timber-town" might seem like an odd name to promote so proudly. Driving down the I-5 freeway however, on the road to Roseburg, it's common to pass a truck laden with logs—then another, then another. Then come the lumber mills, then the lumber yards, and so it becomes easy in the tree-studded landscape to understand why Roseburg so proudly wears the badge of "Timber-town."

Timber was a booming industry and Roseburg was at the front of the line. In the Disaster Recovery Plan for Roseburg following The Blast of 1959, architect Richard J. Neutra encouraged Roseburg to use the foundation of timber to help rebuild the town:

"Wood is an extremely warm, sympathetic building material compared with the synthetic building supplies which characterize our age," he wrote, "and wood is not only old, but new—its applications and the engineering ingenuity devoted to it have made branches of the wood products industry take the national lead, and Roseburg is in the middle of the area in which the wood industries have their seat."[23]

There are two main types of timber from Douglas County: Douglas Fir and Western Hemlock. Douglas Fir trees ready-for-harvest range from 200 to 250 feet tall and stand strong, sturdy, and proud. When cut, the trees are a light color, typically used in construction.[24] Western Hemlock is a slightly smaller tree in general, and used for boxes, pallets and crates.[25] Both types of trees are often cut—when the right size—for living rooms, used for Christmas trees. But although the Douglas fir tree is popular in Douglas County, the county was named after a US senator, Stephen A. Douglas from Illinois, who was an early proponent of bringing Oregon into the Union.[26]

✳✳✳

The News-Review
Fri. Sept 23, 1960

Hungry Burglar Hits Drive-In

It was a hungry burglar who entered Rudy's Drive In Café at 1022 NE Stephens St. in Roseburg Wednesday night.

The burglary was not discovered until late morning Thursday, and an investigation showed he had taken 85 pounds of hamburger patties and some silver from the cash register.

Investigating sheriff's deputies said entry had been made by prying a door open with a screwdriver. The investigation is continuing.

Also Burglarized Wednesday night were Joseph Lane Junior High School, Western Distributors Inc. and two cars in Roseburg motels.[27]

✳✳✳

While the children of Ray McFetridge's fourth-grade class were campaigning to write letters to children across the world, Republican Vice President Richard Nixon and Democratic Senator John F. Kennedy were each campaigning for the presidency during the pivotal election of 1960. Eisenhower's right-hand man for eight years, Nixon was presented by the Republican Party as the best choice for president. He centered his campaign on his experience—ready to lead America through the Cold War.

This was the era of the Civil Rights Movement – of the boycott to end racial segregation on the busses of Montgomery, Alabama, and of the 1954 *Brown v. Topeka Board of Education* Supreme Court ruling that segregation in public schools was unconstitutional, a ruling designed to end the "separate but equal" doctrine that had previously allowed schools to exclude students on the basis of their race.[28]

Nixon's presidential hopes were dashed by John F. Kennedy. The Massachusetts senator had the televised-debate glamour and the endorsement of a cast of show-business celebrities. He came from a powerful family and had his charismatic wife, Jackie, at his side. However, JFK was young and a Catholic, two factors that alienated some southern Protestant voters and led to a tight primary race. At the start of the campaigns, it didn't seem as if Nixon had much to fear. In large part because of Kennedy's religion, the primary elections divided the Democratic Party in two: northern Catholics eager to have one of their own faith in the White House, and southern Protestants who feared the change and much preferred the Democratic alternative, Senator Lyndon B. Johnson. Kennedy united the Democratic Party by selecting Johnson as his vice president. Now the only person in his way was Nixon.

❋❋❋

The News-Review
Thur., Nov. 10, 1960

ELECTION NOTES

By Charles V. Stanton

A newspaper office on election night is a mighty busy place. Operators take reports from precinct workers all over the country. Tabulators keep precinct-by-precinct totals and prepare the tables that are to appear later in the newspaper. Two radio stations occupied the newsroom Tuesday and relayed precinct reports to listeners as rapidly as information came in. Reporters telephoned to The Associated Press, while gathering news for their stories. Candidates, their managers and political observers kept rushing in and out to get the latest news. Following an all-night job, many of the election crew stayed on throughout the Wednesday daylight shift.

It is surprising how a night crew working on election news can put away food. Dozens of sandwiches were on hand Tuesday night, together with cakes, potato chips, and various other items of food. To top it off, Chuck Brundage sent in several dozen fresh doughnuts from Weber's Bakery—and, boy, how they disappeared![29]

***

Kennedy won by a hair. Nixon won 26 states to Kennedy's 23, but Kennedy's states boasted more Electoral College votes. Kennedy won the popular vote—though the margin was less than 1 percent.[30]

Although Oregon was a majority Republican state and cast its six electoral votes for the Republican Party candidate, Douglas County and Roseburg were in favor of the Democrat.[31]

The technological advancements of the 1950s and 1960s allowed for a never-before-seen campaign event: televised debates. This was a key factor that pushed the election in Kennedy's favor. Families all over the country could see the candidates live on their Zeniths. They could watch the debates and feel more connected to their would-be presidents. Nixon tried to reach the population by promising to visit all 50 states in person, but all that did was run him ragged. A simple knee injury became infected, putting Nixon in the hospital for two weeks and rendering him ill for the first-ever televised presidential debate on September 26, 1960. Kennedy bided his time and prepared for the debate that would reach the living rooms of more Americans than Nixon ever could on the physical campaign trail.

The historic debate was one of four between the presidential candidates. Now, families like the Boyles or the Parrs in small-town America could see what their candidates were like in real time. They could build trust and associate a voice and a face to the news they had been reading in the paper or listening to on the radio.

The first televised debate was produced and directed by Don Hewitt, a CBS News executive who would later create the network's popular magazine show "60 Minutes." A common analysis was that Nixon won over those listening on the radio, but those watching on television gave the debate to Kennedy. The Democrat's persona, body language, and preparation all led him to be more visually impressive than his opponent who, by comparison, appeared sickly, unprepared, and meek. According to Hewitt in an interview, Kennedy triumphed due to appearances: "Kennedy, looking tan and fit. This guy was a matinee idol." Nixon, on the other hand, looked, said Hewitt, like "death warmed over."[32]

The election broke records as having one of the highest television audiences of the century, and small towns like Roseburg in Douglas County played critical roles in reaching those numbers. An article in the *News-Review* on election day 1960 noted, "More Oregon voters cast their ballots early today than ever before in history. From county after county came reports of a record turnout. At Grants Pass one woman telephoned the *Daily Courier* for help. She wanted to vote early but couldn't go until she had learned the birth date of Sen. John F. Kennedy. (He was born under the sign of Gemini)."[33]

The voter turnout could have been affected by the sunny weather, the televised debates, or the divided opinions on who should lead the country, but whatever the reason, the election made history and was an epoch-defining decision for 1960.

✸✸✸

The News-Review
Sat., Dec. 10, 1960

Reader Opinions

Armed Forces Service Said Duty, Not Right

To The Editor:

It seems to me that your recent correspondent on integration is putting the Constitution not only beside the point but off the map. Democracy, after all, is more than the rule of the majority. It also contains an intelligent recognition of the rights of minority groups, any one of which might someday include ourselves. It becomes therefore a matter of simple justice to all citizens of the United States.

I would question whether paying taxes or serving in the armed forces is a right. It appears to me that it is more a duty or responsibility in return for the privilege of being a full-fledged citizen. Therefore, common logic would seem to dictate that where privileges are denied, responsibilities be omitted. Southern justice, unfortunately, does not go so far.

As for your school integration, perhaps if your child had to acquire his education in a shed, drink water out of the nearest ditch, and go four blocks to find a restroom, you too would feel a little more strongly on this matter of equality.

It is amazing that anyone should consider the white man as being the chief custodian and author of human rights. Surely God, who uses all colors with such gorgeous impartiality in nature, has not relinquished His prerogatives nor restricted His favors to only the white of the human race.

Years ago, I read a haunting story of a woman who coldly refused the shelter of her boarding house to a negro couple, despite their desperate pleas. And then in the morning after, the luminous Christmas morning, she found out too late that Joseph and Mary had been abroad once again and that she had turned away a tiny, adorable, black Christ Child from her door. Actually, we have no proof that Jesus was white and I have more than a suspicion that He was one of those "coffee-colored" people mentioned so disparagingly by this same correspondent.

I also wish to state that I really have no qualms at all about having a negro governor in my state, a negro pastor in my church, or little black children going to school with mine. It seems sad that the prestige we so painfully and annually purchase with three or four million dollars spread around the globe can evaporate so swiftly in the flare of racial violence. If we can't be more moral, for heaven's sake, let's at least be economical!

Mrs. Roger (Gretchen) Reeder

624 NE Chestnut Street

Roseburg, Oregon.[34]

***

Although the Civil Rights Movement most famously took place in the south and in Washington, DC, Oregon's relationship with civil rights is also tumultuous, and the state did not escape the search for freedom and integration in the new decade.

Roseburg, Oregon was not, and still is not, a diverse place. In 2017, Roseburg's population was almost 92 percent white—and less than one percent of the population was black.[35] Although the Civil Rights Movement was being pushed to every corner of the nation, places like Roseburg experienced the brunt of the activism and conflict secondhand, through the news media.

The *News-Review* published many articles in 1960 about the Civil Rights Movement; however, they were almost entirely Associated Press articles filed by the wire service's reporters from distant places.

Portland's chapter of the NAACP was actively engaged in fighting prejudice across the country. The Roseburg's *The News-Review* published a letter in December of 1960 from reader Joseph B. Hulse who wrote, "As the white man gave him all these rights, is not the white man entitled to say just where those rights stop? Does the white man wish to remain dominant in the U.S.? Marriage of mixed colors is bound to occur. Do negroes or white want a race of coffee-colored people? We should be frank with ourselves and see just what we do want."[36]

Students in Douglas County at the time connected integration and the Civil Rights Movement to the other big issue of the day: The Cold War with the Soviet Union. In January 1959, a survey of high schoolers at Riddle High School in Douglas County showed that nearly 100 percent of the school agreed that the conflict between white and black Americans was terrific propaganda for Russia.[37]

***

The News-Review
Thurs., Oct. 1, 1959

Winter Dessert Round Up

May as well accustom ourselves to the idea, winter has settled for a spell.

What to do about it? Why enjoy it of course. While the wind whistles outdoors, we'll be testing our culinary skills on a bevy of desserts best appreciated this time of year.

Fragrant apple butter spice cake, like many deserts, has extra appeal when served still warm from the oven. The sugar-nut topping baked both inside and on top of the cake contrasts temptingly with the feathery texture sour cream imparts.

Apple Butter Spice Cake

½ cup brown sugar
1 teaspoon cinnamon
½ teaspoon nutmeg
½ cup chopped nutmeats
2 cups sifted flour
1 teaspoon baking powder
1 teaspoon soda
½ teaspoon salt
½ cup butter or margarine
1 cup sugar
2 eggs
¾ cup apple butter
1 teaspoon vanilla flavoring
½ cup whole bran cereal
1 cup sour cream

To make topping: Combine brown sugar, cinnamon, nutmeg and chopped nutmeats, set aside.

Sift together flour, baking powder, soda and salt. Blend butter and sugar. Add eggs; beat well, stir in apple butter, vanilla and whole bran cereal. Add sifted dry ingredients alternately with sour cream, blending well after each addition (begin and end with dry ingredients). Spread ½ the batter into greased 13 x 9-inch pan. Sprinkle with half of topping. Spoon remaining topping. Bake in a moderate oven (350 degree F.) about 40 minutes. Cut into squares and serve warm or cold, plain or with whipped cream, if desired.

Yield: 12 3-inch squares.[38]

✳✳✳

But amid all this turmoil, Americans who were children in the 1960s remember worrying more about what was for dinner and what entertainment was on TV that night than big issues like elections, or even pen pal requests.

When the children of Ray McFetridge's fourth-grade class were juniors in high school, President Lyndon B. Johnson signed the Child Nutrition Act.[39] This set aside money to give free lunches to children in need. Kids in the 1960s might have had burgers or pizza for lunch on special occasions, but most days had some kind of main protein (beef goulash, oven-fried chicken, or tuna and noodle casserole were a few choices) paired with a fruit and vegetable. Every meal also came with bread and butter and milk.[40]

Once the Great Depression and World War II had run their course, households' increased food security allowed families to leave rationing behind. Fast food restaurants like McDonalds, Burger King, and Wendy's became more popular. As the television set became a common household appliance, commercials for restaurants and fast-food places encouraged people to go out for lunch or dinner.

If dinner was at home, however, the choices were seemingly endless. Popular meals from the era included meatloaf, casseroles, and Jell-O encasings.[41] Advertisements also highlighted treats like frozen pizza bites that could be made in the oven, Lipton onion soup mix, and instant coffee were advertised in those pre-Starbucks days as tasting the same as a freshly-percolated cup of joe.[42]

***

The News-Review
Tues., July 31, 1956

Roseburg Woman's Jottings Get Around

Word from pen pals really gets around, Mrs. Arthur Marsh, Roseburg, has discovered.

The story she relates goes this way:

Mrs. Elizabeth Chambers, Glasgow, Scotland, sent a clipping from the overseas corner of the Glasgow newspaper to her Walla Walla Wash., pen-pal. The clipping was signed by Mrs. Wallace M Brisbin, a native of Scotland, who now lives in Roseburg.

Mrs. Brisbin, told of visiting Highlands Inn on Monterey Peninsula, Calif., which is decorated in a Scottish motif. She sent the item to Glasgow. The clipping was sent from Walla Walla to Mrs. Marsh here.

Mrs. Marsh returned this week from a meeting of the board of directors of the 'round the world friendship circle of Pen Pals being promoted by the Pacific Cooperator Women with headquarters in Walla Walla.

Meeting with the Pacific Women's Council was Mrs. Lillian Heard, vice president of the Women's Guild of England and Wales. She urged participation in the pen pal movement as a means of furthering friendly relations with foreign countries. She spent several weeks touring Canada and visiting Canadian Guilds. Mrs. Heard also toured Northwest farms and coops. She has been associated with the cooperative movement in England and Wales for the past 30 years.[43]

**

While the concept of writing to children in Russia seemed revolutionary and threatening to some State Department officials at the time, the concept of pen pals was far from original. Letter-writing was, of course, a predominant form of communication, but the more systemized practice of linking up with a stranger to start a get-to-know-you correspondence seem to have developed in the early twentieth century. Schools across the nation facilitated "pen friends" programs as class projects to increase literacy, to encourage empathy, and (like Mr. McFetridge's goal) to help children understand different cultures and people who lived differently than they did.

Programs like International Pen Friends started as early as 1920 but became popular in the 1960s. International Pen Friends in particular was used at the 1964 New York World's Fair to promote the theme "Peace through Understanding." They collaborated with the People-to-People Foundation, initiated by former President Dwight D. Eisenhower. The program expanded throughout the 1960s and 1970s and was adopted and reinvented by different smaller organizations across the country. Popular participants were children and housewives.[44]

Roseburg, although their plan of sending letters to Russian children was unsuccessful, was no exception to the national popularity of pen pals. An article in the *News-Review* published July 20, 1957 reports on 350 women in the Pacific Northwest who were participating in pen pal programs. "The main purpose of the moment is to further friendly relations among the women of the world." Women distributed handkerchiefs with their names and addresses embroidered on them and people across the globe wrote back.[45]

Across the city from Janice, students from Roseburg High School would write over a hundred letters to students in places like France, Switzerland, and Germany. A piece, published just one year after Janice's pen pal project was stymied, praised students for helping encourage Roseburg commerce by building relationships with other children: "A number of youngsters in Roseburg schools have become pen pals with boys and girls of like age throughout various parts of the United States. In becoming pen pals, they are making themselves Roseburg Chamber of Commerce boosters. They are important cogs in a unique and successful advertising program."[46]

Students from across the country would write to the Roseburg Chamber of Commerce, who would then write the return address on an empty envelope and pass the open envelopes, along with some information on the students, to the local elementary schools. All the students had to do was write the letter, seal the envelope, and, just like that, lifelong friendships were created.

Even students from Ray McFetridge's class would be successful in later pen pal initiatives, Genee Parr says. She herself had a pen pal whom she found via a notice in a copy of *Highlights* children's magazine that she was reading at her doctor's office.

***

The News-Review
Tues., April 26, 1960

Jeralee, Eifert Given Honors

Jeralee Bunnell and Joe Eifert have been named Girl and Boy of the month for March at Glide High School.

Jeralee, a junior, was chosen for her work during March on the junior-senior prom scheduled for April 30 at the Gold Room of the Hotel Umpqua. She is also a member of the National Honor Society.

Eifert, a senior, was chosen for his many activities in the Glide High band, of which he is vice president, an honor band member, and was selected to play in the All-State Band in Portland during spring vacation.

Talent Show Slated

A Talent Show will be held at the Camas Valley school Friday.

The deadline for entries is Wednesday. Those desiring to enter my contact Carol Hill or Gary Baker, student Masters of Ceremonies.

Three first place prizes will be given for acting, singing, and instrument playing. Second place winners will also receive an award. A grand prize will be given the [sic] "Sweepstatkes" winner.[47]

***

The News-Review
Fri., Jan 29, 1960

Lunch Party Is Enjoyed

One of the most delightful and enjoyable parties of the season took place Thursday, when Mrs. John Doering entertained a group of friends at a 1 o'clock luncheon at the Elk's Club in compliment to Douglas County's well-known author, Mrs. Norman (Gladys) Workman, who has also acclaimed for her work in ceramics, as a toastmistress at ceramics and hobby shows and for her work among handicapped persons.

The luncheon tables were placed in the form of a large U with the decorations being beautifully carried out in daffodils, acacia, red tulips and yellow tapers.

Coming with Mrs. Workman to the party besides her nephew, Norman Jackson of Scottsburg; Mrs. Paul Jackson and Mrs. Mae Vanetta of Scottsburg; Mrs. Walter Palmer of Elkton and Mrs. Hertha Anderson of Reedsport. Also at the party from out-of-town included Mrs. Charles Geazy of Eugene.

Mrs. Workman is no stranger to residents of Roseburg, having worked in the ceramics field for the last several years. Her ceramics business grew to such proportions size so many other ceramics were made on her time, that she sold the business and kept only sufficient parts of the business to run her work with handicapped persons and other classes in ceramics.

Known throughout the country for her first book, "Only When I Laugh," Gladys Workman will soon have her second book off the press and which her many friends are anticipating with much pleasure. Mrs. Workman was featured in Ralph Edwards "This Is Your Life" and her nephew, Normal Jackson, showed the sound film of the program, much to the delight and enjoyment of the guests.

Glady's Workman has the great talent for drawing people to her, for holding them in turn the greatest possible enjoyment. Friends here are looking forward to seeing and hearing her early in February when she is the guest speaker at the Roseburg Woman's Club.[48]

***

Today, the population of Roseburg has doubled since 1960—from about 12,000 to its current 24,000.[49] The school where Ray McFetridge taught, Riverside School, closed some years after he died and was later badly damaged in a fire. The gymnasium and cafeteria have been replaced by a church, the first- through third-grade classrooms are a parking lot, and the red building that housed Janice's fourth-grade classroom has become an office building.

The view has changed out of the old schoolhouse windows. Where students used to daydream and look at the glowing red sawmill across the street, there is an AT&T Store, Waldron's Outdoor Sports, and a Jiffy Lube.

But of course, in some Roseburg households, meatloaf, casseroles, and various things encased in Jell-O still grace the dining room table.

Notes

1 "The Weather: Airport Records" *The News-Review*, January 28, 1960, p. 1.
2 "Get Both Here! Food Quality and Savings!" *The News-Review*, March 21, 1960, p. 9.
3 "Radio and TV Programs" *The News-Review*, January 28, 1960, p. 10.
4 "Reaction Over 'Pen-Pal' Request Said Surprising" *The News-Review*, January 29, 1960, p. 1.
5 "Anti-Red Demonstration of Students Marks Opening of Soviet Exhibit in Cuba" *The News-Review*, The Associated Press. February 6, 1960, p. 2.
6 "High Court Defers Action on 3 Cases of Communism" *The News-Review*, The Associated Press. February 6, 1960, p. 2.
7 "Communist Nations Fight U.S. - Japan Security Treaty" *The News-Review*, The Associated Press. February 1, 1960, p. 14.
8 "Red Chinese Taking New Tack in Peace Diplomacy" *The News-Review*, The Associated Press. January 29, 1960, p. 4.
9 Hightower, John M. "Khrushchev Seen Scheming to Build New Berlin Crisis to Weaken Western Allies" *The News-Review*, The Associated Press. February 9, 1960, p. 12.
10 "Roseburg, Oregon Population 2019" *World Population Review*, World Population Review, http://worldpopulationreview.com/us-cities/roseburg-or-population/. "Oregon Population 2019 (Demographics, Maps, Graphs)" *World Population Review*, World Population Review, http://worldpopulationreview.com/states/oregon-population/.
11 LaLande, Jeff. "Roseburg Blast." *The Oregon Encyclopedia*, https://oregonencyclopedia.org/articles/roseburg_blast/#.XQXk-dNKjOQ
12 *Ibid.*
13 *Ibid.*
14 "Toll heavy as blast strike downtown Roseburg" *The News-Review*. August 7, 1959, p. 1.
15 "The blast that ripped apart Roseburg, Oregon, and the psyche of a man who was held responsible" Walth, Brent, August 29, 2009. *The Oregonian*.
16 *ROSEBURG BLAST: A Catastrophe and Its Heroes*. Produced by Greg Frederick, Narrated by Barry Serafin, Southern Oregon Public Television, 2004. SOPTV.org. http://www.soptv.org/roseburg-blast-a-catastrophe-its-heroes/.
17 The plaque reads 57 injuries, though the number of injuries reported in the papers was much higher; "Roseburg Blast monument." *360 cities*, William L, January 6, 2019, https://www.360cities.net/image/roseburg.
18 "Pet Skunk Still Away from Home" *The News-Review*, February 2, 1960, p. 2.
19 Reddy, Karina "Fashion History Timeline: 1960–1969" *Fashion History*. Fashion Institute of Technology, August 11, 2019. https://fashionhistory.fitnyc.edu/1960-1969/

20   Sears. "Low riding, skinny and very popular." 1965.

21   "Leap Year Sale 9" *The News-Review*, January 26, 1960, p. 7.

22   "Community News Briefs" *The News-Review*, February 17, 1960, p. 11.

23   "Architect Sees Disaster Recovery Plan for the City" *The News-Review*, November 11, 1959, p. 1.

24   United States, Department of Agriculture, Natural Resources Conservation Service. "Plant Fact Sheet" *Douglas Fir*, February 5, 2002, https://plants.usda.gov/factsheet/pdf/fs_psme.pdf

25   United States, Department of Agriculture, Natural Resources Conservation Service. "Plant Guide" *Western Hemlock*, Prepared by Lincoln M. Moore, June 19, 2002, https://plants.usda.gov/plantguide/pdf/cs_tshe.pdf

26   "Douglas County Overview" *Douglas County, Oregon*, Douglas County Information Technology, August 27, 2018. http://www.co.douglas.or.us/overview.asp

27   "Hungry Burglar Hits Drive-In" *The News-Review*, September 23, 1960, p. 1.

28   *Brown v. Board of Education*, 347 U.S. 483.

29   Stanton, Charles. "Election Notes." *The News-Review*, November 10, 1960, p. 4.

30   "1960 Presidential Election Interactive Map." *270 to Win*, Electoral Ventures, 2019, https://www.270towin.com/1960_Election/interactive_map

31   "1960 Presidential Election Results." *1960 Presidential Election Results | JFK Library*, https://www.jfklibrary.org/learn/about-jfk/life-of-john-f-kennedy/fast-facts-john-f-kennedy/1960-presidential-election-results

32   *Don Hewitt*. Performance by Don Hewitt, Archive of American Television. https://interviews.televisionacademy.com/interviews/don-hewitt#people-clips

33   "Douglas County Voters Join State, Nation in Trend to Record Onslaught at Polls" *The News-Review*, November 8, 1960, p. 1.

34   "Reader Opinions: Armed Forces Service Said Duty, Not Right" *The News-Review*, December 10, 1960, p. 4.

35   "Quick Facts: Roseburg city, Oregon." *United States Census Bureau*, 2017, https://www.census.gov/quickfacts/roseburgcityoregon.

36   Hulse, Joseph B. "Constitution Not Issue in Integration Hassle." *The News-Review*, December 6, 1960, p. 4.

37   *Russian Propaganda Helped by Integration Issue, Says Riddle High School Student Body*. January 19, 1959.

38   "Winter Dessert Round Up" *The News-Review*, October 1, 1959, p. 17.

39   Child Nutrition Act of 1966. Public Law 89–642, Enacted October 11, 1966. https://legcounsel.house.gov/Comps/Child%20Nutrition%20Act%20Of%201966.pdf

40   "School Lunch Menus" *Ypsilanti Press*, May 3, 1965.

41   "1950s Cookbooks: Recipes From a Decade of Hope and Regret." *Flashbak*, January 12, 2016. https://flashbak.com/1950s-cookbooks-recipes-from-a-decade-of-hope-and-regret-51243/

42   Classic Commercials. "43 Classic Retro Snacks, Food & Treats Commercials." *YouTube*, January 21, 2014. https://www.youtube.com/watch?v=eIDl8IbCfRA

43   "Roseburg Woman's Jottings Get Around" *The News-Review*, July 31, 1956, p. 2.

44   "The History of the International Pen friends Program" *International Pen Friends*. http://www.internationalpenfriends.com/History.html

45   "Co-op Pen Pal Plan Continued" *The News-Review*, July 20, 1957, p. 4.

46 Stanton, Charles V. "Pen Pal Boosters." *The News-Review*, April 8, 1961, p. 4.

47 "Jeralee, Eifert Given Honors" *The News-Review*, April 26, 1960, p. 6.

48 "Lunch Party is Enjoyed" *The News-Review*, January 29, 1960, p. 17.

49 "Oregon Population 2019 (Demographics, Maps, Graphs)" *World Population Review*, World Population Review, http://worldpopulationreview.com/states/oregon-population/.

Chapter Six

A TIME OF FEAR

by Madie Eidam

In which student journalist Madie Eidam tackles pivotal twentieth century historical events in US–Soviet and US–Russian relations—news events that led to the heated political climate Janice and her classmates naively entered while believing they were simply seeking pen pals.

The mid-twentieth century was transformative for America—kids growing up in the '50s could feel it. Music, art and media were changing. A new American sound reflected new American attitudes: The music made space to go against the grain and to think critically about American culture and the decisions made by people in power. The birth of rock 'n' roll, for one, altered the future of American music and helped establish a sense of revolution in a generation. Fats Domino, one of the founding fathers of the genre, explained in a television interview, "Rock 'n' roll is nothing but rhythm & blues."[1] To the youth of the '50s, rhythm and blues was an intoxicating sound that incited free movement and self-expression for many Americans. The music's revolutionary messages spread, adding fuel to already-burning ideological fires. The acceptance of a diversifying culture through music added momentum to a young generation dedicated to an evolving country.

Another medium that had become an equally powerful force (if not more powerful) in popular culture began its influential reign in the '50s. Between 1950 and 1960, the percentage of households owning televisions jumped from around 10 percent to close to 100 percent.[2] The '50s ushered in the Golden Age of Television. TV screens across the country featured "I Love Lucy," "Gunsmoke," and "Leave It to Beaver." Sitcoms depicted an idealized American life, showcasing stereotypical models for women and men; at the same time, variety programs like "Your Show of Shows" and cartoons like "Bullwinkle" and "The Flintstones" provided comic relief and a welcome escape from tensions at home and abroad. The comforting routine of Saturday cartoons babysat. The sobering reflections of the evening news were embraced by families gathered around the television set at the end of the day with a TV dinner—a classic favorite was roast turkey with stuffing, whipped potatoes and an apple-cranberry cake cobbler. Whether watching "Dragnet," "Looney Tunes" or Walter Cronkite reporting world events, figures of television shaped Americans' understanding of the rapidly changing world around them.

With only three news networks and a few local stations to choose from, news anchors became distinguished and lasting figures in the American political landscape. Cronkite was the anchor of the CBS Evening News broadcast from 1962 to 1981 and Chet Huntley and David Brinkley co-anchored their eponymous newscast on NBC from 1956 to 1970. For the first time in US history, rather than hearing the happenings of the world through word of mouth, radio, still photographs or the written word, Americans could see with their own eyes what was happening in other parts of their country and the world—often live. They witnessed excessive police force during chaotic civil rights protests in the South that led to civilian harm and arrests. In 1963, millions of people watched as thousands of Americans protested racial discrimination with Martin Luther King, Jr. during the March on Washington.

And so, in spite of sociopolitical conflict and racial tensions that still permeated the country, a new and lasting chapter of American life began. Emerging out of the Great Depression and World War II, America sought to rebuild a society that was thriving, prosperous and safe. With that vision in mind, there was a strong cultural push to conform to societal norms and expectations. Suburbia became aspirational: quiet nights, a backyard, and open space for kids to roam their neighborhood freely. People wanted to feel safe and secure after such unsure and trying times. Nuclear families—a family typically comprised of a breadwinning father, a stay-at-home mother, and two children—became a professed cultural cornerstone of normalcy.

Janice Boyle grew up in a post-Depression era, a typical Baby Boomer in many ways. Hers was a childhood of freedom: staying out until dark, playing with the neighborhood kids, biking all over town, and walking to the community pool. It was a time of simplicity for Boomer kids. Life, for many, seemed good—at least the "Ozzie and Harriet" version of life. But in actuality, inequity and discrimination were the painful reality that people of color, women, the poor and other struggling communities experienced every day. These marginalized citizens faced challenges getting the jobs that they wanted, buying the homes that they wanted or attending the schools that they wanted. Living in blissful ignorance was not a luxury most Americans could afford.

Civil rights activists such as Rosa Parks, Martin Luther King, Jr. and Thurgood Marshall helped define a decade in which ordinary citizens and activists alike united to effect monumental changes to the course of American history. And with civil rights as with rock 'n' roll, young people were a driving force of revolution. College students led sit-ins on campuses, on buses and at lunch counters in the South in protest of segregation. They created art and poetry in support of social change. And they oriented themselves firmly against the looming Cold War developing between the United States and the Soviet Union.

**

Decades before these dramatic social transitions shook the United States, nations in Eastern Europe and Central Asia experienced even larger, more violent political changes. For nearly 200 years, a succession of monarchs called "czars" had governed the Russian Empire which covered vast areas of Europe, Asia and beyond. Russia also claimed land in North America from Alaska to California, including parts of the Oregon Territory.

In 1917, Bolshevik revolutionaries began an armed insurrection to over-throw the Russian imperial government. This subjugation led to the brutal murders of the royal family, a civil war and, in 1922, the creation of the USSR. After World War II, with the Communist Party having taken total control of most of Eastern Europe, the Soviet Union was viewed by many in the United States as the antithesis of democratic, free-market capitalism. The clash of their competing economic ideologies—capitalism and communism—set these two powers on a collision course. Each used scare tactics to frighten their respective populations.

The first Red Scare in the United States occurred in the 1920s. Alleged leftists and anarchists were accused of conducting bomb attacks against government officials and business owners. Federal agents engaged in a series of dragnet operations known as the Palmer Raids, named after US Attorney General Mitchell Palmer and commanded by future FBI Director J. Edgar Hoover. In search of leftist radicals and anarchist immigrants, the raids resulted in the arrest, prosecution and deportation of supposed communist threats. In an effort to stoke fear, distrust and ignorance, government officials warned citizens to beware of communists lurking around any and every corner disguised as educators, labor organizers, journalists and artists.

Meanwhile, life in the USSR grew more menacing under the totalitarian regime of Joseph Stalin. Stalin's predecessor and the first leader of the Soviet Union, Vladimir Lenin, did not believe that Stalin should lead the rapidly evolving country. But after Lenin's death in 1924, Stalin maneuvered his way to power and executed political enemies. He notoriously ruled the Soviet Union from 1924 to 1953 through systematic intimidation, exile and murder.

World War II brought the adversaries together as allies to fight against their common enemies: Germany, Japan and Italy. But after the war, the Soviet-American alliance collapsed. What followed was the Cold War—nearly five decades during which anti-capitalist doctrine dominated the USSR, and anti-communist dogma shaped US policy.

The US Senate resolution condemning Senator Joseph McCarthy.

A further Red Scare in the United States flared up in the 1950s and was showcased in Congress by televised hearings. The House Un-American Activities Committee investigated the supposed influence of communism on the entertainment industry. As a result, writers, actors and directors—many having inconsequential or no communist ties—were blacklisted and rendered unable to work.

In the other chamber, Joseph McCarthy, the junior senator from Wisconsin, spearheaded a similar campaign. He falsely accused Americans within the government of disloyalty. The eponymous term "McCarthyism" came to be equated with this type of defamation. McCarthy ultimately was widely denounced for his misdeeds and for the careers and lives his demagoguery ruined.

Among those who condemned McCarthy was Edward R. Murrow, the radio and television reporter for CBS News already famous for his on-the-scene World War II reporting. At the height of his career, Murrow took on McCarthy and exposed his flagrantly demagogic tactics.

The Senate voted overwhelmingly to censure McCarthy in 1954. He died three years later at age 48.

***

As Janice studied her fourth-grade lessons at Riverside School, the country was gripped by the fear of war, nuclear destruction and communism. Americans had been warned relentlessly to brace for nuclear disaster at any moment. The iconic 1964 political advertisement, "Daisy," was produced by the election campaign for President Lyndon B. Johnson and exemplifies the intensity of messages Americans were receiving during the Cold War.[3] The ad was broadcast only once during a primetime movie on the NBC television network. It was subsequently discussed and criticized, but then canceled because of its inflammatory suggestion that Republican presidential candidate Barry Goldwater, if elected, might be more likely than Johnson to use nuclear weapons. Between the one showing and the subsequent critical attention, viewers absorbed its potent message: A young girl, looking no older than four, is counting flower petals in a field when a menacing countdown interrupts her peaceful moment. On the count of a booming "one!" an atomic bomb obliterates the screen and—as the campaign producers hope we will deduce—the innocent girl. The grim voice of President Johnson fills the moment of silence declaring, "These are the stakes. To make a world in which all of God's children can live, or to go into the dark. We must either love each other, or we must die." Then an announcer's voice states, "Vote for President Johnson on November 3rd. The stakes are too high for you to stay home."

"Daisy" was certainly not the first or only fear-mongering message produced for television in the '50s. In 1957, CBS showed a half-hour program titled "The Day Called 'X'" that took place not too far from Roseburg in Portland, Oregon. CBS, one of the three networks available on televisions at the time (alongside NBC and ABC), was producing comedies, dramas and Westerns to fill its evening schedule. Given the limited variety of programs available, many Americans across the country had little choice but to tune in to one of the three or simply turn off their televisions.

"The Day Called 'X'" opens with sirens and a notice from a wearied and stoic man informing the public that enemy planes are approaching—and a nuclear attack will ensue shortly. Throughout the film, there is a recurring notice along the bottom of the screen, assuring viewers that a nuclear attack is not actually taking place. They can relax (for now). Narrator Glenn Ford, a popular actor of the era, briefly appears on the screen to emphasize that this could indeed happen. The drama slowly unravels, beginning with an average day in Portland, only three hours away from Roseburg. Babies are born. Breakfast is made. The newspaper is read, though the front page is skipped because of "scare headlines." It is worth noting this detail in the script, put together by CBS and the Federal Civil Defense Administration, which acknowledges an awareness within the media itself of the its role in inciting fear in viewers.

Church services are held throughout Portland. City council meetings occur. "An average day in an average American city," Ford reminds us. The modern viewer of "The Day Called 'X'" is able to witness what life was like in classrooms just like Janice's in the '60s.

The story continues. At 10:32 a.m., December 8, 1957, a day "which began in such an ordinary way" is disrupted by a siren and an alert that unnamed enemy aircraft are 3 hours and 15 minutes away from Portland. The message is calmly passed along to the then-mayor of Portland, Terry Schrunk, despite Ford's voiceover suggesting the likely possibility of these planes carrying "an H-bomb or two." Sitting behind a desk during a city council meeting, Schrunk announces the arrival of enemy planes and that the council will be immediately reconvening in the Emergency Operation Center.

During a montage of firefighters, policemen and other rescuers assembling for action, Ford explains that there are 99 major cities across the country that are considered "critical targets" and Portland is only one of them. As diners and classrooms are evacuated, Ford emphasizes the different kinds of reactions people may have—some people "naively" continue about their day while others, like electrical grid dispatchers, cannot leave their position despite the imminent danger. However, these sacrifices are worthwhile, Ford says, since some "men are expendable." With time to spare, the city of Portland undergoes a well-organized evacuation plan. Older kids are depicted flooding out of their high schools, heading home in a mass of bicycles. The participation of known public figures, such as the actual mayor of Portland, lends the film further legitimacy and credibility.

In search of greater viewership and higher ratings, the media processed the American fear of communism as a trend in the contemporary environment and exploited that fear just as the government did. Adults and children alike were inundated with messages that communism and war were real threats to every single American's health and safety. These messages came at a time when more than 70 percent of the public trusted the government to do the right thing.[4] As of June of 2019, that number is at 17 percent—neither the press nor the public in Janice's youth were nearly as skeptical of their governing bodies as they would become in later generations.

✳✳✳

Nicholas Kristof of *The New York Times* is a journalist who focuses on human rights and global affairs. He was born in Chicago but grew up in Yamhill, Oregon, not far from where Ray McFetridge's widow, Beverly, lives. In a September 4, 2010 column entitled "America's History of Fear," Kristof writes, "Suspicion of outsiders, of people who behave or worship differently, may be an ingrained element of the human condition, a survival instinct from our caveman days." Kristof says these fears trigger something primal in our brains. A threat to our way of life leads our minds to seek answers and to find solutions to that potential threat. When a trusted leader tells people that there is an abstract threat to an abstract facet of their life, people will listen in search of any grain of logic that will calm their anxieties. Kristof reminds us, however, "that historically this distrust has led us to burn witches, intern Japanese-Americans, and turn away Jewish refugees from the Holocaust." Fear, he says, "is part of America's heritage."

✳✳✳

Many commentators reacted to the small-town Roseburg pen pal project incident as a violation of personal liberties. *The News-Review* covered not just the initial story, but its development as it built momentum across the rest of the country. On January 28, 1960 "Pen Pal Plan Denied Youngsters" is the headline story: Congressman Charles O. Porter writes a letter to Janice relaying the State Department's decision and their suggestion to write to free-world countries instead, but offers his support in connecting them with a Russian school.[5] February 3—"Riverside Class Stirs Up Hubbub with Pen Pal Quest": a photo of Janice, Genee and Mark is accompanied by an update that Porter's office has received letters and phone calls in response to the State Department's

Red Envoy Would Supply Names

Riverside Class Stirs Up Hubbub With Pen Pal Quest

A rising tide of protest was started in Washington, D. C., as the result of the U. S. State Department's decision that it won't help a fourth-grade class at Riverside School to start a "pen pal" program with Russian fourth graders.

Laura Olson, an assistant to U. S. Rep. Charles O. Porter, says Porter's office has received about 20 letters and many telephone calls protesting the decision. She said she had heard that the State Department, too, had started receiving protests.

One letter to Porter's office said, "How silly that we fear children."

Miss Olson claimed all calls and letters to Porter's office had protested the State Department's decision.

She also said that newspaper reporters in the capital had contacted the Russian embassy, which indicated it would be "very delighted" to supply names of children to which the Riverside School youngsters could write.

Names Sought

The hubbub all started early this month when young Janice Boyle, class secretary of a fourth-grade group studying a course called "How People Work Together," wrote Porter. She asked that he help them get the names of some fourth-grade children in a town about Roseburg's size in the Soviet Union so they could start writing to them.

The request was passed on to the State Department, which rejected the request on the grounds that such correspondence would be censored and some of it might be used for propaganda purposes.

Porter told the children in a letter that he would be glad to secure such names if they wished. However, Ray McFetridge, teacher of that class, said it had been decided after a discussion with Roseburg School Supt. M. C. Deiler that the project would be pursued no farther at present.

Neuberger Cleared For Re-election Try

WASHINGTON (AP) — Doctors have told Sen. Richard Neuberger (D-Ore) there is "no reason why he could not run for re-election," the senator's office here said Tuesday.

In an announcement, Neuberger's office said physicians had told the senator "his future life should be carefully regulated to avoid excessive fatigue."

Extensive and recent examinations in Portland "indicated no evidence of recurrence of the malignancy for which Neuberger underwent surgery in August of 1958, or any other serious developments," the announcement said.

It added that Neuberger had been suffering from fatigue and

Morale Of Doug Said Improved

NEW YORK (AP)—Gen. Doug-

Catholic Group To Meet Here

Officials of the Roseburg Knights of Columbus today announced they plan to promote Ray Martin of Roseburg for election to the office of state deputy of the Knights at their 52nd annual convention here May 13 to 15.

About 250 delegates of the Roman Catholic men's organization and their wives are expected to converge on Roseburg for the three-day convention. This will mark the first time in history the convention has been held here.

The state deputy's office, for which Martin will be a candidate, is the top office of the Knights of Columbus in Oregon. Martin has long been an active member of the organization and has been chairman of the local and state committee combating indecent literature.

The social highlight of the convention will be a banquet and dance in the Umpqua Hotel on May 13. The meeting portion of the convention will include election of the state deputy, committee reports of the past year's activities and a special session for financial secretaries. A fashion show for the wives of the delegates will be held on the first day of the convention.

Rod Nevue is chairman of the state convention planning committee. Committee chairmen named so far are Harvey Brown, transportation; Robert Wandling, registration and civic reception; John Puttman, publicity and housing; Harold Desbiens, facilities and arrangements; Nevue, Martin and Paul Bellendorf, entertainment; Ray Whitschick, advertising; and Mrs. Harold Desbiens, ladies' committee.

The regular convention meetings will be held at the Elks Lodge.

The Roseburg *News-Review* headline provides a classic example of the propagandistic language used on the American side.

decision. One letter expresses, "How silly that we fear children."[6] An *Oregonian* article includes Assistant Secretary of State William B. Macomber's justification stating, "Past performances indicate that if Janice and her friends were to become pen pals of children in Russia they will get back not just friendly, childish reports, but communistic propaganda inspired by their instructors." Porter "makes it plain" that he disagrees with the State Department's decision. Salem's *Statesman Journal* spoke with Janice's mother, who expressed, "Being fourth graders, they had no thought of propaganda. What they were thinking about was building good will between one little community in Russia and one little community here—in Roseburg."

One editorial piece written by New Jersey's the *Courier News* expressed their dismay with support for our problematic pen pals in an article entitled "Pink Pens." While the publication agreed that infiltration by the Russian government is likely, they ultimately believed that it was the right of American children and their parents to figure out for themselves "whether they are being made dupes."[7]

They go on, "It is well that we all realize that a war on propaganda is going on; the Reds will use every possible means to win it." While the publication does maintain that Russian infiltration efforts are a real threat to the United States, they continue, "[The students] must evaluate what they hear and read. No one can do it nor should do it for them." The *Courier News*'s perspective in the international dialogue that erupted following the bad news delivered from the State Department to Janice in Roseburg raises the fundamental issue that sparked such curiosity in a Reporting II class, 60 years later. To interfere with this pen pal project is contradictory to many of the values that America asserted through its music, television programs and civil rights movements.

As the *Courier News* closes their perspective piece, they wonder, why not let this "pen pal experiment" run its course? "If the Russians are trying to indoctrinate us, why not do the same? Why shouldn't our children tell the advantages of the American way of life?" Was the risk not worth the possible lessons that could have been learned? As the *Courier News* put it, "Our young letter writers should emerge … as more experienced and ultimately as wiser citizens."

***

During the summer of 1949, a little over a year before Janice was born, the Soviet Union successfully detonated its first nuclear device in Kazakhstan, marking the beginning of an intense arms race between the two most powerful countries in the world. President Harry Truman established the Federal Civil Defense Administration program, which aimed to educate the public about how ordinary citizens could protect themselves. In 1951, classrooms across the country would become quite familiar with Bert the Turtle, the cheerful cartoon character whistling a catchy tune, who introduced Americans to the famous idea of the "duck and cover" program.[8]

Duck-and-cover drills became a common occurrence throughout country with the same regularity as earthquake drills in California or tornado warnings in the Midwest today. Teachers attempted to strip away as much fear from the learning process as possible, singing songs and telling stories about how to prepare for the possibly fatal scenario. However, by 1960, the intense arms race had escalated and with it, a sense of security for many people around the world diminished.

After Stalin's death in 1953, Nikita Khrushchev prevailed in a power struggle as the USSR's new premier. The American press cultivated an image of Khrushchev as somewhat crazy and reckless, based in part on an apocryphal shoe-pounding incident: On October 12, 1960, during a plenary meeting at the UN General Assembly, the Soviet leader interrupted another delegate. To emphasize his displeasure, Khrushchev pounded his fists on the table in front of him. It was also widely reported—but without any credible evidence—that he pounded a shoe on his desk at that gathering. Nevertheless, the legend remains ingrained in popular culture.[9]

It became clear to Americans that ducking and finding shelter was no longer an adequate solution to the risk of potential annihilation. To combat the growing nuclear threat, the Federal Civil Defense Administration introduced fallout shelters to Americans through the most effective tool at the time: mass media. In the September 15, 1961 edition of *Life* magazine was a letter from President John F. Kennedy:

> "My Fellow Americans, nuclear weapons and the possibility of nuclear war are facts of life we cannot ignore today." He assured readers that the federal government was developing a program "to improve the protection afforded you in your communities through civil defense."

Suddenly, newspapers, magazines and radio stations across the country were advertising fallout shelters. One radio ad, featuring dystopian space music, grabs consumers' attention by exclaiming, "The international struggles of our world may lead to nuclear holocaust." The unsurprisingly dramatic ad reiterates the necessity of these shelters for the survival of individuals and families. The ad describes the survive-all, basement-type shelters as Civil Defense-approved for survival, made of steel and concrete that offers maximum protection to Americans.[10] However, the purpose of these fallout shelters in retrospect was more an investment in one's peace of mind than safety.

The USSR had no independent media. Two newspapers at the time—*Pravda*, meaning truth, and *Izvestia*, meaning "delivered messages" (often translated as "news" or "information")—were widely circulated. The Soviet constitution, in theory, allowed for the freedom of speech and of the press, but censorship laws significantly hindered opportunities, meaning that these publications served as official organs for the government and the Communist Party.

✳✳✳

Over a generation after the Cold War's end, what has changed and what has remained the same?

New social transformations are shaking the United States as it remains a land of constant evolution. Xenophobia is still a familiar and ever-pervasive political theme. We are no longer building backyard bomb shelters; instead, children are sent to school carrying bulletproof backpacks. Suspicion and fear are powerful motivators. Though we supported tearing down the Berlin Wall, we continue to reinforce one on our southern border.

There is no more Soviet Union, but Vladimir Putin's government invades and occupies neighboring Ukraine. The Kremlin still controls its most important mass medium: television. And it's attempting to claim control over its most prominent new medium: the internet. As did Stalin, ex-KGB agent Putin also wants to determine who votes—and who *counts* the votes.

Americans and Russians have a complicated relationship with each other; we have a complicated relationship with ourselves. Our two cultures are intertwined across time and space. Nowhere is this more evident than in Oregon, where, after English and Spanish, Russian is the most commonly spoken language.

Notes

1   Palmer, Robert. "The 50s: A Decade of Music That Changed the World." Rolling Stone, June 25, 2018, www.rollingstone.com/music/musicfeatures/the50sadecadeof musicthatchangedtheworld229924/.

2   "Television: Moving Image Section Motion Picture, Broadcasting and Recorded Sound Division." Library of Congress, memory.loc.gov/ammem/awhhtml/awmi10/ television.html.

3   Mann, Robert. "How the 'Daisy' Ad Changed Everything About Political Advertising." Smithsonian.com, Smithsonian Institution, April 13, 2016, www.smithsonianmag. com/history/how-daisy-ad-changed-everything-about-political-advertising-180958741/.

4   Research Center, Pew. "Public Trust in Government: 19582019." Pew Research Center for the People and the Press, May 29, 2019, www.peoplepress.org/2019/04/ 11/publictrustingovernment19582019/.

5   "Pen Pal Planned Denied Youngsters" *Newspapers.com*, January 28, 1960, www. newspapers.com/clip/8859986/the_newsreview/.

6   "Riverside Class Stirs Up Hubbub with Pen Pal Quest." *Newspapers.com, The News Review*, February 3, 1960, www.newspapers.com/clip/8860095/the_newsreview/.

7   "Pink Pens." The *Courier News*, February 23, 1960, p. 14—at Newspapers.com. *Newspapers.com*, www.newspapers.com/image/221863494/.

8   Rizzo, Anthony, director. *Duck and Cover. The Library of Congress*, The Library of Congress, www.loc.gov/item/mbrs01836081/.

9   "Nikita Khrushchev." Edited by History.com Editors, *History.com*, A&E Television Networks, November 9, 2009, www.history.com/topics/cold-war/nikita-sergeyevich-khrushchev#section_5.

10   Kridel, Advertising Agency. YouTube, 1961, www.youtube.com/watch?v=NQ7_0zRxF7k.

Chapter Seven

BEHIND THE CURTAIN

by Isabel Burton

In which student journalist Isabel Burton delves into the University of Oregon archives and immerses herself in the rich life of US Congressman Charles O. Porter finding documents that both championed Janice and her classmates' quest for pen pals and help unveil the depth of paranoia that plagued America during the Cold War.

"I have met many children who have learned too little, but none who have learned too much," Congressman Charles O. Porter wrote in response to a former Portland schoolteacher, Naomi Scarff, who was baffled by Porter's support for the pen pal project.[1] Porter's remarks now sit in one of hundreds of folders boxed in his archives in the University of Oregon's main library. Porter was the Oregon congressman who'd received Janice Boyle's letter on behalf of Classroom 15, requesting pen pals from Russia. He'd forwarded the request to the State Department, which declined to help the project on the premise that Janice's class would be on the receiving end of propagandistic and censoring behavior.[2]

✴✴✴

Born in Klamath Falls, Oregon, Porter moved to Eugene where his father, Frank Porter, worked as switchman on the railroad.[3] But in 1932, the bank foreclosed on the Porter family home, and 13-year-old Porter was frustrated that hard-working people like his father could so easily lose their jobs and houses to the Depression.[4] Porter's son Sam said that seeing his father lose his house to the banks because of the depression "radicalized Porter politically" and is part of the reason he evolved into a liberal FDR Democrat. At 13, Porter aspired to be in Congress—to "do his best to see that men like his Dad weren't pushed around by events over which they had no control."[5]

Porter was the editor of the Eugene High School newspaper and graduated with "top marks in his class," as he recorded in his files.[6] After delving into books by foreign correspondents, Porter decided that, to win an election in Congress, he had to achieve two things: fame and knowledge.[7] To Porter, the next logical step toward fame and knowledge meant becoming a "foreign correspondent for a big newspaper."[8] His career—from academia to Congress—was rooted in journalism.

And Porter started his career as an eighth grader, selling the Eugene, Oregon's *Register-Guard* on downtown street corners.[9] In high school, Porter worked as a sports and drama correspondent for local dailies and founded a mimeographed newspaper called the *B.A.C. Clarion*.[10] At 17, Porter found a paid job as a proofreader for the *Eugene News*, which paid 35 cents an hour— an ample wage for a student at the time.[11]

Porter became editor for his high school newspaper after arguing, through letters to the editor, that the paper's seniors-only policy should be changed and the staff opened to all students. His letters changed the policy and he was immediately hired as an editor.[12] At age 17, Porter wrote in the *Eugene High School News* advocating his support for FDR and the New Deal. "The real issue," he wrote in the paper, "is whether we go forward and tackle the social problems as they appear or mark time and procrastinate."[13] It was clear that Porter preferred the former.

Porter was beginning to maneuver into politics at 17, when he was afforded a "glass-topped desk and swivel chair" right across from the main school office as a member of Eugene High School Student Council.[14] As a member of student council, he convinced the principal to let him speak to his peers—a 900-person student body—in a gymnasium on multiple occasions.

***

An administrator of Porter's high school approached him one afternoon in 1937. "Charles, do you want to go to Harvard?" she asked—or so Porter remembers in his autobiography. Porter responded, "Sure. Just hand me the papers to fill out."[15] His college career at Harvard followed shortly after, beginning in 1941.[16]

Porter's journalistic career continued there: Porter worked as a Harvard correspondent for both *The Boston Post* and *The New York Times*. On the side, he worked waiting tables at on-campus dining halls to pay for his board.[17]

Harvard Law School followed where Porter started an anti-Nazi organization called the National Student Defense League and founded the Committee for Militant Aid to Britain. He was also the founder and president of the *Harvard Law School Record*, the first Harvard Law newspaper.[18]

In July of 1941, though, Porter was drafted into the Army as an Air Corps private in World War II. He was stationed in Europe and then in Latin America. "College and law school were parts of my plan to try to become a Member of Congress," Porter wrote in his autobiography. "But World War II was not."[19] Porter would go on to serve in the Panama jungle and as the first Caribbean-area correspondent for the army magazine *Yank*.

✱✱✱

Porter first entered into the congressional campaign as an "underdog" in 1954 and lost.[20] Just two years later, though, Porter campaigned against Republican incumbent and Roseburg native Harris Ellsworth, who served as the congressman for seven consecutive terms before Porter took his seat and served through 1961.[21] His unorthodox, internationalist agenda up against Ellsworth's domestic, routine approach to politics rendered Porter the "aspiring politician fighting an uphill battle to unseat the Republican incumbent."[22] Nonetheless, he beat out his opponent and became the first Democrat elected in southwestern Oregon in 75 years.[23]

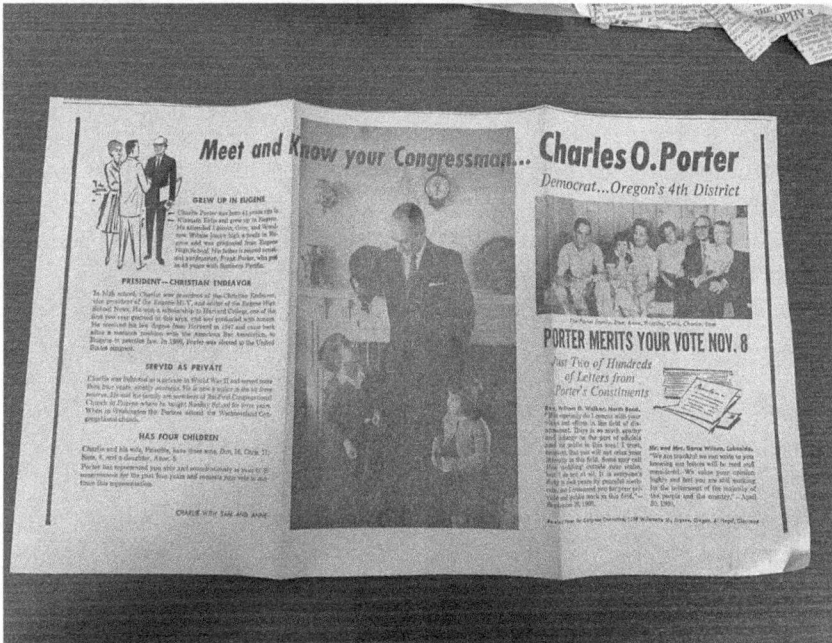

A re-election campaign advertisement presenting Porter as both the family-man and successful Congressman.

Porter's 1960 attempt at a third-term re-election was unsuccessful— in part attributed to his "entrancement"[24] in foreign affairs, which made him "vulnerable for a kind of campaign that was waged against him," or so Porter explained in a 1960 *Portland Reporter* article.[25] He lost the 1960 election, followed by five other failed attempts to win the Democratic primary—in 1964, 1966, 1972, 1976 and 1980.[26] Porter's failed attempts could be attributed to many things, as he "had a finger in almost every pie."[27]

For starters, though, Porter's critics frequently questioned his overly active role in foreign affairs, dubbing him a "self-appointed one-man State Department."[28] Porter admitted to "spreading himself thin" sometimes, although he saw it as a "virtue and a vice."[29] The Eugene *Register-Guard* resonated with his activeness: "Some may argue that Mr. Porter spent too much time on foreign soil. But it seems to us that it ought to be worthwhile to see that our congressmen get around and learn that everybody doesn't speak English and worry about gaining weight."[30]

Porter learned that being congressman was a "big salary" but one that came with "big expenses."[31] Despite scrutiny of his internationalist perspective, Porter saw his role as congressman extending outside of his district bubble. He considered his job "a matter of satisfaction of doing what you can, however little, for peace in the world," Porter said in a 1960 campaign reelection interview.[32]

✱✱✱

Even after Porter's death in 2006, Porter was most celebrated for his approach to controversy. *Register-Guard* obituary writer Greg Flint said that he "stirred pots that needed stirring and asked questions that needed asking. He pushed us to accept injustices less quietly."[33] Former state Democratic chairman, Jim Klonoski, who handled Porter's failed 1966 campaign, said, "Charlie's constituency was the world— not the 4th district."[34] But in 1976, Ron Abell, former *Willamette Week* reporter, encapsulated Porter's persona best:

> Since he's virtually impossible to describe, Charlie Porter is a man after this reporter's heart. Anybody can do an easy story, but how do you write about a guy who's brash, glib, witty, smarter than hell, younger than springtime, a political disaster, a martyr who won't stay dead, a chronic meddler, a thick-skinned egomaniac who's lovable as a puppy, persistent as a bulldog, optimistic as a bride, moral as a preacher, imaginative as a mad scientist and beneath it all, where it really counts, an authentic American hero?[35]

Porter's son, Sam, said that Porter was an idea man, not philosophically, but pragmatically. He had an "internationalist impulse early-on" and had a "cosmopolitan view much wider" than most of his fellow congressmen.

One of Porter's reelection campaign advertisements in which newspapers commended Porter for his genuineness and audacity toward local and national issues.

"He wouldn't take bullshit and, because he was a lawyer, he had leverage," Sam said. "He was undaunted by a lot, almost as if he were from another era. But most of all, he had this doggedness. He didn't back down on a whole lot of issues easily. The pen pal project is just a clear example of that."

Sam Porter saw the innocence of an international exchange like the pen pal project. The problem, he said, is that "cultures of the world know so little of each other." The unfamiliarity Americans have of other countries and worldviews creates distrust that is "ripping our society apart right now." There is no "sense of mutual understanding of each other even if we disagree." Democracies, he said, require trust and mutual understanding.

✱✱✱

In the year 1960, Porter added another controversy to his personal history: the story of Janice Boyle and the pen pal project. After State released its decision in response to Porter passing along the Classroom 15 request, Porter was flooded with letters from the public—both avid supporters and enraged opponents. Porter continued to express support for the project publicly, despite State's disagreement. He wrote to a pro-pen pal Connecticut resident in February 1960 who was "distressed" that the pen pal project was "put on ice," but he was hopeful it would "thaw out soon."[36]

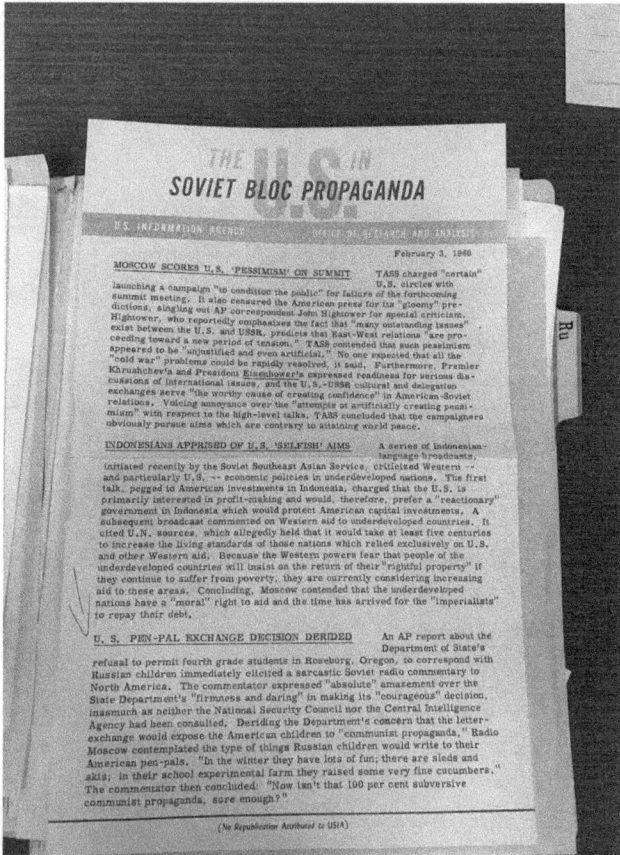

A summary of Radio Moscow's sarcastic response to the State Department refusal to help facilitate the pen pal relationship appeared in a U.S. Information Agency bulletin.

Only days later, an Associated Press report about the pen pal incident spurred Russian radio station Radio Moscow to air what the US Information Agency called a "sarcastic radio commentary" directed at North America about the project. The program mockingly acknowledged State's "daring" and "courageous" efforts.

Radio Moscow pondered the type of correspondence Russian children would exchange with their American counterparts: "In the winter they have lots of fun; there are sleds and skis; in their school experimental farm they raised some very fine cucumbers. Now isn't that 100 percent subversive propaganda?"[37]

✸✸✸

Porter proudly self-appointed himself disruptive in the subjects of "dictators, disarmament, and China."[38] He advocated for increased communication and relations with China (pushing for China's admission to the UN) to avert war and promote peaceful relations between the United States and China.[39]

"Increased communication with Communist China need not mean appeasement," Porter wrote in a December 1959 letter to the editor of *The New York Times*, who wasn't keen on Porter's disruptiveness. "What it does mean," Porter continued, "is an exchange of newsmen, members of Congress, businessmen, students and tourists; trade on the same basis we use with the Soviet Union; recognition (which doesn't mean approval or disapproval); and seating in the United Nations (where every nation, good and bad, belongs)."[40]

In June of 1959, a few months before the start of the pen pal project, Porter applied to the State Department for permission to visit China. He wanted "first-hand knowledge of Red China to help him as a legislator."[41] Assistant Secretary Macomber—the same bureaucrat who'd rejected the Classroom 15 pen pal plea—denied the application.[42] Porter wasn't happy with that response, so he sued Secretary of State Christian Herter for violating his Constitutional rights with the restriction.[43] Porter persistently fought the question of "whether the State Department can restrict this Constitutional right in the course of carrying out the nation's foreign policy," according to a 1959 UPI report found in Porter's files.[44]

In 1959, Paul Dull, a University of Oregon history and political science professor, strongly opposed "Porter's position that China should be admitted to the UN" because China wasn't ready to take on UN responsibilities, according to a *Register-Guard* article stashed in the archives.[45] "China's communist leaders 'are not in a rational state of mind,'" Dull opined.[46] But Porter's argument wasn't one of rationality—it "was that America should have a moral foreign policy—that we should communicate with dictators but not support them."[47]

✸✸✸

At the same time that Porter was trying get permission from State to go to China, and at the same time the pen pal project was beginning to surface in rural Oregon, Fidel Castro became prime minister of Cuba, on February 16, 1959. Porter's interest in Latin America began when the Eugene native and pilot Gerald Murphy disappeared and died in the Dominican Republic under "suspicious circumstances," in 1956 which began Porter's scrutinizing of the Dominican Republic and Latin American dictatorships.[48]

"It all started when our State Department tried to persuade me that my constituent, young Gerry Murphy of Eugene, got what was coming for him and I found that Trujillo felt he could give a lying explanation of Gerry's death to our government and expect it to be accepted," Porter said in a speech. "It wasn't accepted. I made sure of that."[49]

Porter's name became common in Latin American households because of his efforts to aid reform campaigns in parts of Latin America. "He is respected and admired because of the great services which he has rendered to continental democracy," Venezuelan newspaper *El Nacional* reported about him. Porter immersed himself in the "detailed study of the actual economic and social conditions of Latin America," not as an expert, but as a knowledgeable congressman and humanitarian.[50] In the 1950s, he developed working relationships with the ex-presidents of Columbia and Costa Rica, the governor of Puerto Rico, and the Dominican Republic dictator Rafael Trujillo. The former president of Costa Rica, José (Pepe) Figueres, called him the "Congressman for Latin America," because of his engagement with the region.[51]

"One of these days," Porter said in a 1959 Policies for Peace speech, "perhaps I'll write a book on how I became a hero in Latin America. It was easy. All I had to do was to make it clear I was against dictators and that I liked democratic leaders."[52]

Two years later, in 1961, Porter wrote a book about Latin America. He co-authored *The Struggle for Democracy in Latin America* with American activist Robert J. Alexander, in which they criticized governments of Latin American countries, including Cuba, for stripping citizens of their democratic rights: free elections, freedom of the press, and freedom of dissent, to name a few. Porter wrote that Castro was a "victorious guerilla leader" whose administration increasingly reflected "pro-Soviet" and "monopolistic tendencies."[53] Nonetheless, he championed the 1960 pen pal project in spite of his distrust for the communist government in the Soviet Union. To Porter, democracy meant communicating with countries like Cuba and Russia, despite rocky diplomatic relations. He summed his efforts toward establishing peaceful international relations in three words: "audacity, audacity, audacity."[54]

***

Later, in September 1963, Porter went to Cuba as a *Look* magazine journalist to visit with Castro about "securing a general amnesty" for more than 15,000 political prisoners in Cuba.[55] (This visit with Fidel Castro ultimately drove Castro to ban Porter from Cuba). *Look* never published the Porter–Castro interview. It initially was accepted by *Playboy*, but then rejected.[56] It wasn't until 1999 that the interview was released.[57]

In 1964, Porter tried to return to Cuba, again "to continue the negotiations for release of the Cuban political prisoners"[58] but ran into another passport debacle. The State Department again refused to validate Porter's passport because his correspondence with the Cuban regime would provoke misinterpretation both in the United States and Cuba. (In 1961, the State Department issued a ruling that passports would have to be endorsed by the State Department for someone to travel to Cuba.)[59] Porter was firm that he had "the right to ask questions and get answers from the Department of State."[60] But, as it was for Janice Boyle, the State Department's response was negative.

Porter pushed back. He wrote in 1964 to Senator Wayne Morse, another Oregon legend who advocated for Porter's travel, asking for the "names, addresses, occupations and other available details about each American citizen who has been allowed to visit Cuba since the break in diplomatic relations between the United States and Cuba."[61] He also wrote to the Bureau of Security and Consular Affairs inquiring, "If a magazine or a newspaper gives me an assignment to write an article requiring another trip to Cuba, will the Department of State permit me to go, as it did under similar circumstances last year?"[62] Porter didn't return to Cuba that year.[63]

❋❋❋

In the 1963 interview, Castro said to Porter, "The American government is afraid to let the truth be known. It is they who have really built a wall." The wall, as Castro referred to the growing schism between the two governments, is designed to shut out other countries. Porter offered up the idea that the US government was reticent to expose students to other countries because the US government was afraid that students would "take part in guerrilla activities and knock over rather shaky governments."

Castro assured Porter he was "ready to invite" politicians to see the work of the Revolution, and was open-minded to the flow of Cuban students into the United States. It is the American government, Castro said, "who have locked within that wall all American citizens."[64] Although Porter's negotiations with Castro were unsuccessful, the interview both illuminated the way Cuba's leader saw the US government and led to the unexpected suspension of a University of Oregon literary journal, the *Northwest Review*.

Three thousand miles away from Cuba, in Eugene, and one year after Porter's initial negotiations for authorization to travel to Cuba, former University of Oregon president Arthur Flemming was facing protests and petitions calling for his resignation after the printing of an issue of the *Northwest Review*.[65] The university's literary journal was founded in 1957 and this particular issue (Vol. 6 No. 4) included a compilation of the Porter–Castro interview, pictures of Cuba post-revolution, a radio play by Antonin Artaud, and poems by Philip Whalen.[66]

Porter, along with many others, criticized Castro for the muzzling of press freedoms under the Castro administration. ("In the early '60s, only unquestioning supporters of Castro were allowed access to radio and television," wrote Porter.)[67] In the States, in 1964, freedom of the press meant that poems like those by Philip Whalen for the *Northwestern Review*, with irreverent verses like "kissing God's ass" were published. Alongside Whalen's poems, Artaud's radio play evoked a similarly controversial message: Not only did it attack the Catholic Church, but it featured descriptions about defecation and flatulence. The combination—the "politically explosive Cuban material," Whalen's poems, and Artaud's radio play—is what spurred vociferous reactions toward the *Northwest Review* issue—both praise and outrage. The issue angered many conservatives in Eugene, which prompted protests advocating President Flemming's resignation. These reactions, in turn, inspired Whalen to write to poet Allen Ginsburg:

"SEX DEVIATIONISM HORROR DOPE SCENE DEPRAVED YOUTH &C &C GODLESS UNIVERSITY COMMUNIST ATHEIST PLOT AT TAXPAYERS' EXPENSE..."[68]

The literary fiasco caused Flemming to suspend the *Northwest Review* in 1969, the only shutdown between the journal's establishment in 1957 and its final issue in 2011.[69]

✳✳✳

Porter approached the pen pal project as an inquisitive journalist, a researching lawyer and an investigating congressman. "I think a 10-year-old has to understand that even an authority he should respect can be wrong and honestly wrong," Porter wrote in response to former Oregon school teacher Scarff.[70] "I have a great deal of respect for the Department of State and for our government generally but that does not mean I don't have the right to express my disagreement with particular policies," Porter wrote to Roseburg resident Judy Church.[71]

To Porter, the right to express disagreement epitomized the "essence of the democratic system." His position was clear: A democratic society—in accordance with the official Department of State policy—"favors person-to-person relationships even with respect to citizens of nations on the other side of the Iron Curtain," he wrote.[72]

And the press coverage continued. Porter was flooded with support letters for Classroom 15's pen pal efforts. Morton Wood, an Alaska resident who learned of the project through his local paper, congratulated Porter, writing, "It is heartening to find such evidence of sanity in the welter of nonsense, stupidity, suspicion, and childishness that seems to have motivated our foreign policy in the past 10 years. More power to you."[73]

Janice and her classmates were similarly praised for their outreach. "The desire of the Roseburg children to help destroy the artificial barriers between nations is highly commendable and should be encouraged in every way possible," a pro-pen pal Californian, Eugene Stephens, wrote to Macomber after reading a United Press International (UPI) news report about Macomber's disapproval. "Peace will come to the world only when we have completely free and unrestricted communications on a universal basis, not confined to an 'I like you because you agree with me' exchange between members of the same ideological-political group."[74]

Many of the letter writers who criticized the State Department for rejecting the project applauded Congressman Porter and Janice for their efforts. "Of all the silly notions, I think that the State Department's efforts to stop little 10-year-old Janis [sic] Boyle and her fourth-grade friends from writing to their Russian counterparts tops them all," a Connecticut resident wrote to Porter, after reading the paper one morning "more irritated than usual" with the state of the world. "It's tragic that the parochial minds continue to occupy high positions in our State Department."[75]

Californian citizen Frances Thomas wrote to Assistant Secretary Macomber:

> This seems to me the stupidest kind of policy, to discourage efforts at understanding and friendship among the children of the world. If our children are indeed so vulnerable to Russian propaganda that they might be endangered by an exchange of letters, the fault must surely lie with ourselves. I would find such an interchange a healthy and worthwhile experience for my children whom we have tried to teach by precept and example to value liberty and freedom— even the freedom to extend a hand of friendship to a child who happened to have been born behind the Iron Curtain.[76]

Thomas questioned whether the news report was an error, hoping he was misunderstanding Macomber's opposition to the pen pal project.

✳✳✳

But Macomber wasn't the only one to receive backlash. Although Porter accumulated copious amounts of fan mail, he was also criticized for disagreeing with the government. Roseburg citizen Judy Church decried Porter for disagreeing with the authority of the government and the State Department. She wrote to Porter that his facilitation of Classroom 15's pen pal project was "dangerous, foolish, and disrespectful" because State Department officials should properly utilize their knowledge and training of communist tactics, and because a "disciplined people" should strictly adhere to government authority. She also didn't hold back in her writings against Janice's teacher, Ray McFetridge, whom she called "misguided" and "ill-informed" about US–Soviet relations.[77] She asked Porter to reconsider his proposal in support of Classroom 15.

Schoolteacher Scarff, who taught nine-year-olds in Portland, thought similarly that Janice and her classmates didn't have the emotional capacity, maturity and knowledge to properly dissect "truth from lies, virtue from vice, propaganda from fact."[78]

"Do you think that little Ivan would be left to read, interpret, and digest these letters by himself?" she wrote. Scarff, along with other US citizens, was sure that letters exchanged between American students and students on the other side of the Iron Curtain would be "censored" and "misconstrued." She saw the project as a way for the Soviets—"our mortal enemies"—to exploit and influence American schoolchildren.[79]

The nature of the project was questioned: Would communist propaganda be avoided? Most of the anti-pen pal letter writers were concerned that communist propaganda would seep into the minds of US students if the project continued. Porter recognized the possibility of Soviet government intervention in facilitating correspondence with Russian students. However, Porter was certain that, if Russian fourth graders did correspond with Oregon fourth graders, the content would be overseen by Janice's teacher, McFetridge, and other community members. Porter wrote to schoolteacher Scarff that any propagandist activity would be "detected and counteracted without trouble."[80]

✳✳✳

In July of 1959, Porter, along with 16 other congressmen and senators, met and established the *Congress for World Peace Through Rule of Law*.[81] The organization reflected Porter's unfaltering promise to "spend at least a third of my time doing what I could, however little, for the interests of peace."

At the time, President Eisenhower agreed with Porter's peace-through-law notion. In a United World Federalists statement report, titled "One World ... Or None," Eisenhower said, "It is my purpose to intensify efforts ... to the end that the rule of law may replace the rule of force in the affairs of nations."[82] Porter, in his 1959 Policies for Peace speech affirmed, "Peace is surely too important to be left to the State Department—or the politicians. It is everybody's job, yours as well as mine."[83]

A United World Federalists report outlining the organization's mission to "attain world peace through world law."

MEN OF VISION . . . .

The United World Federalists' movement to attain world peace through world law by way of a strengthened United Nations constantly is finding increased support among leaders of world opinion. Reproduced here and on succeeding pages are a few of the current statements on this subject.

"All peoples are sorely tired of the fear, destruction, and the waste of war. As never before, the world knows the human and material costs of war and seeks to replace force with a genuine rule of law among nations.

"It is my purpose to intensify efforts . . . in seeking ways to supplement the procedures of the United Nations and other bodies with similar objectives, to the end that the rule of law may replace the rule of force in the affairs of nations."
— *Dwight D. Eisenhower*

THE CAPITAL BANK
NATIONWIDE INSURANCE CO.

Within the United World Federalists report, Eisenhower conveyed his hopes that "rule of law may replace the rule of force" between nations.

✹✹✹

In an attempt to redirect the Riverside School pen pal project, Assistant Secretary Macomber suggested that Classroom 15 correspond with "non-Communist countries"[84] through People to People International (called, in Janice's day, the People-to-People Program)—a not-for-profit organization intended to facilitate international friendships, originally endorsed by President Eisenhower.[85]

To Eisenhower, ensuring understanding between other countries, cultures and governments meant actively working toward strengthening friendships across borders through government engagement. Governments can assist the people, he said. But it's up to the everyday people—"professors, students, executives, travelers abroad"[86]—to engage and exchange with other countries in order to achieve "peace through understanding."[87]

Eisenhower's granddaughter and now-president and chair emeritus of People to People International, Mary Eisenhower, said about her grandfather: "My granddad realized that world peace had to come from the soul of human nature and that governments could not dictate the human heart, only reflect it."[88] Even Mary Eisenhower's present-day email signature rings the same: "Peace like hostility is a learned behavior. Teach peace."[89]

President Eisenhower criticized the communist way of government for its propaganda program, which meant strict control by state authorities trying to force conformity of the people to government rule. But Eisenhower was also optimistic. "What we must do is widen every possible chink in the Iron Curtain and bring the family of Russia," he said, "or of any other country behind that Iron Curtain, that is laboring to better the lot of their children, to sit down between us to say, 'Now, how do we improve the lot of both of us?' "[90]

The People to People International was launched just four years before Classroom 15 began their pen pal project.[91] In 1987—over 25 years after the start of the project—students under this program traveled to Russia (and met former Soviet leader, Mikhail Gorbachev) after People to People International facilitated trips to both China and Russia.[92]

Classroom 15, of course, didn't intend to travel to Russia. They just wanted to write letters. But while students 20 years past the Red Scare would have that right and more, Janice and her cohort were discouraged from even the most meager effort to reach out. Porter disagreed. His ideologies were close to Eisenhower's regarding intercultural dialogue. They both believed in "peace through understanding."[93] Porter believed that students on both sides of the Iron Curtain would be better off communicating with one another, despite the risks and unpredictability of censorship and propaganda. To Porter, controversy was the "heart of democracy."[94] When we discard controversy, he thought, we give up the opportunity to engage in democracy.[95] He continued to worry "about the growing tendency of men and women in this country to shut themselves away from thoughts, written and spoken, which may not concur with theirs. I can't help but feel that free and open discussion means a strengthening of the democratic process."[96]

✼✼✼

During February 1960, Congressman Porter telephoned the Letter Writing Committee secretary of the People to People International, Carolina Botsford, for more information about the program and protocol for Russian correspondence. Porter never specified his reasoning for requesting information on Russian correspondence from the People to People International, but, given the letters were among all Russian pen pal materials in Porter's RUfiles, and given that the timing of his letters from People to People International correspond with the timing of the pen pal project, it seems logical to presume his extensive research efforts were for or related to Classroom 15.

"We receive very few requests from the Iron Curtain countries," Botsford responded. However, she wrote, the organization would "do its best" to serve his request.[97]

LETTER WRITING COMMITTEE
THE PEOPLE-TO-PEOPLE PROGRAM
45 EAST 65TH STREET   NEW YORK 21, N.Y.

MISS ANNA LORD STRAUSS
CHAIRMAN

FEB 8 1960

February 5, 1960

The Honorable Charles O. Porter
252 House Office Building
Washington 25, D. C.

Dear Congressman Porter:

In accordance with your telephone request for information about
our program we are sending the enclosed leaflet.

The Letter Writing Committee is a center for international exchange of letters between the United States and people in other
lands. We receive very few requests from the Iron Curtain
countries, but if and when we receive them we do our best to
have the correspondents also served.

Sincerely yours,

Carolina R Botsford

Carolina R. Botsford
Secretary
Letter Writing Committee

CRB/ms
Enclosure

A letter from Secretary of the People-to-People Program Letter Writing Committee, Botsford, who followed up about Congressman Porter's inquiry of the Program's protocol for communicating with Iron Curtain countries.

LETTER WRITING COMMITTEE
THE PEOPLE-TO-PEOPLE PROGRAM
45 EAST 65TH STREET   NEW YORK 21, N.Y.

MISS ANNA LORD STRAUSS
CHAIRMAN

FEB 17 1960

February 16, 1960

The Honorable Charles O. Porter
252 House Office Building
Washington 25, D.C.

Dear Congressman Porter:

As a follow up to my letter of February the 5th, I am sending you a copy of the form letter we send to U.S.A. requests for correspondents from Russia when we cannot fill them, and a copy of the slip we send to those that we can serve.

If there is any other information you would like to have please do not hesitate to ask of us.

Sincerely yours,

Carolina R Botsford

(Mrs) Carolina R. Botsford
Secretary Letter Writing Committee

CRB
Enclosures.

A letter from the People-to-People Program Letter Writing Committee Secretary, Botsford to Congressman Porter outlining the Program's form letter protocol.

> You are one of the few carefully chosen Americans to receive a name
> from behind the Iron Curtain. May we suggest, for the protection of
> your new correspondent, that political discussions be avoided? If,
> on the other hand, you receive communist propaganda, we would like
> to know about it. It would also be of great interest to us to know
> the general trend of your correspondent's letters.
>
>   LETTER WRITING COMMITTEE
>   45 East 65th Street
>   New York 21, New York

A copy of the form letter alerting letter writers about propaganda.

In a follow-up letter to Porter 13 days later, Botsford sent to Porter a copy of form letters regarding the organization's protocol for foreign correspondence.[98] It is still unclear why Porter requested these form letters, but it does confirm his active role as a pen pal project proponent. He wanted to know more about the People-to-People program, and more about how US–Russia relations were facilitated by programs like this one.

Addressed hypothetically to a would-be participant in a correspondence with Russia, the form letter read:

"You are one of the few carefully chosen Americans to receive a name from behind the Iron Curtain. May we suggest, for the protection of your new correspondent, that political discussion be avoided? If, on the other hand, you receive communist propaganda, we would like to know about it. It would also be of great interest to know the general trend of your correspondent's letters."[99]

Although this was just a form letter and not directed toward Classroom 15's pen pal request, it showed Porter that, under the hypothetical circumstances that Classroom 15 chose to seek help from the program in connecting with Russian students, People to People International would have sought to have a heavy monitoring role.

In an unaddressed letter found in Porter's files, the chairman of the People-to-People Program, as it was then called, Anna Strauss, wrote that requests from the Soviet Union for American correspondents were rare and that she didn't have any on file. However, if the correspondence was directed toward

LETTER WRITING COMMITTEE
45 East 65th Street
New York 21, N.Y.

Dear

We have received your letter of   and are gratified
that you are interested in participating in the international correspondence
program for which this committee serves as a clearing house.

~~We regret that~~ We seldom receive requests from the Soviet Union for
American correspondents. At present we have none on file. When we do receive
the name of a Russian who seems to answer your requirements, we shall notify you.

In the meantime, if you are interested in carrying on a correspondence
with some one with similar interests in another country, we shall be glad to
try to satisfy your request. We suggest that you give us the names of several
countries in the order of your preference. By so doing you will assure yourself
more prompt establishment of a letter writing exchange than otherwise.

We appreciate your interest in the program. For your general information
we are enclosing a copy of our brochure on the letter writing program of the
People-to-People Program.

Sincerely yours

Anna Lord Strauss
Chairman

An unaddressed letter from Chairman Strauss specifying the circumstances and likelihood of Russian correspondence.

another country, she would gladly satisfy the request and ensure a more "prompt establishment of an exchange than otherwise," insinuating a delayed establishment, if any, of a Russian exchange.[100] Perhaps a free world country, as Macomber suggested, would offer a more efficient relationship.[101]

Whether or not Porter was the recipient of Strauss's letter is inconclusive, though the letter was found in his files. Given that Porter's files were this letter's final resting place, this appears to be another form or example letter from Chairman Strauss. This trio of letters (the original letter from Botsford, the follow-up letter with the form letter attached, and the unaddressed letter from Chairman Strauss) made clear that People to People International did not serve as an entryway for all international correspondence requests as the organization proclaimed.

Instead, People to People International curbed any chance of American-to-Russian correspondence by explicitly redirecting Porter and the unknown letter writer to explore other countries. The People to People International Program was founded on Eisenhower's belief that "the surest way to break cycles of fear and misunderstanding was for people to understand one another."[102] But if world peace could only be established through understanding, the program didn't uphold its fundamental values because the organization didn't give the students of Classroom 15 a chance at understanding their Russian counterparts. Further communication between Porter and the People to People International was not documented in Porter's files.

The program wasn't ill-intentioned in discouraging Russian pen-pal-ship or foreign exchange. In fact, their mission to this day is to "enhance international friendships," not prevent them.[103] But there were other factors at play in 1960. In the thick of the Red Scare, the program felt it had to consider US foreign relations alongside its role as a liaison for international friendships.

✸✸✸

Classroom 15's project was halted, and the news coverage dissipated, but a new class project was emerging simultaneously—also, coincidentally, in Roseburg: a class that wanted to go on a "Friendship Tour to Mexico."[104]

The tour unfolded in a similar nature to Janice's class project. In January 1960, during the same time that Room 15 attempted to make friends with Russian students, the Friendship Tour began with the "out-loud thinking" of Roseburg High School Spanish teacher Berton Bailey.[105] The students raised money for their trip through candy sales, Mexican dinners, and car washes.[106] They also promoted the trip through advertisements, one which asked for donations: *Your Purchase Will Help Us Take The Friendship Tour of Mexico. Muchas Gracias!*[107]

In February 1960, less than one month after Janice's initial contact with Porter, Bailey also sent a letter to Congressman Porter. Bailey asked for Porter's support in funding the campaign. He explained to Porter that the tour was a way to "further friendly relations between Mexico and the United States," which was "indicative of the community spirit of Roseburg."[108] Porter called the tour a "good project" and facilitated funding and press for the Roseburg students.[109]

A Roseburg High advertisement intended to prompt funding for the class's trip to Mexico.

"Volumes of correspondence filled the mails from Mexico to Roseburg," an *Oregonian* staff writer reported on the Friendship Tour in 1960.[110] There was, however, one major difference between the pen pal project and the Friendship Tour: The Friendship Tour saw no intervention from the State Department. There was no evidence to suggest that Porter felt obligated to pass along Bailey's request to the State Department, as he did for Classroom 15's.

Porter even reached out on the high school's behalf to a Mexican delegate in the United States for help facilitating the project. He sent a letter in February 1960 to Vicente Sanchez Gavito, Mexico's ambassador to the United States and the Organization of American States (OAS), who was also "a good friend" to the United States, according to Porter.[111]

The OAS is an organization that dates back to the 1800s with a mission to facilitate democracy, cooperation and peace between the 35 independent states of the Americas.[112] As a representative to the OAS, Gavito was responsible for adhering to the OAS's fundamental principles, among which was the mission to "promote representative democracy, with due respect for the principle of nonintervention,"[113] which concurs with Eisenhower's notion that governments could only "point the way" toward peaceful diplomacy.[114] The rest was in the hands of everyday citizens, and, in the case of the Friendship Tour, in the hands of high school students.

Porter initially reached out to Gavito to help publicize the tour so that the class could raise the necessary money for the Friendship Tour to ensue. He wrote to Gavito that the students were "receiving wonderful cooperation from Mexican authorities."[115] Gavito responded to Porter that he was eager to help. "Both you in the United States and we in Mexico need more of this. In democracies such as ours, international relations sooner or later are bound to reflect prejudices, animosity, sympathy, appreciation, and admiration."[116]

Three months and over $900 in funding later, the students left for Guaymas on the Friendship Tour. Guaymas—a city about 400 miles south of Tijuana and the border, with a population of only 35,000 people in 1960—welcomed 36 high school students, for whom the Guaymas Chamber of Commerce arranged a private home for their lodging, according to the *Oregonian*.[117] Teacher Bailey wrote to Porter that the class was "declared official guests of the City," after both countries' flags were displayed and both national anthems rang aloud.[118] The Roseburg class lost the international basketball game the group had organized, 45-22, as the June 1960 *News-Review* reported.[119]

After the tour, in a follow-up letter to Porter, Bailey conveyed that American and Mexican students had many common interests. "All students signed certificates pledging themselves to the task of cementing good relationships between the countries," *The Oregonian* reported,[120] adding that the students behind the Friendship Tour "were heading for a tomorrow rich in good relations."[121]

✳✳✳

Sixty years later, Peter DeFazio now occupies what was formerly Porter's position as Oregon's 4th congressional district representative.

When DeFazio visited the University of Oregon campus in the fall of 2019, he responded to the hypothetical scenario: What if he had been the one to receive Janice's letter?

"I don't know who would be against something like that. It's a great idea," DeFazio said. But he understood the political tensions of 1960 because he lived them.

> There was this prevailing feeling. This could all end. I remember when I was a kid, I was home and I had math homework. I'm up in my room and I turn on my little transistor radio and it was about a Cuban missile crisis. And I thought "What the heck. Why should I do my math homework if I'm not going to be here tomorrow? We're going to have a nuclear war."

He contemplated what the pen pal project would look like today. "I know for certain North Korea would not let the letters in. And China would be problematic." China, he thought, would let the letters in, but with heavy censoring. "I think the problems would be on the other side of the ocean rather than on our side," DeFazio said. "But under this administration," he added, referring to the Trump presidency, "who the hell knows?"

DeFazio's own political experiences in Washington mimic political polarity even on a domestic level. Republicans and Democrats can't communicate cordially within the United States, let alone with people across oceans and borders, he thought. In the same spirit of Porter and Eisenhower, DeFazio acknowledged that, "Anytime you can get a dialogue going between people, they aren't as polarized as they seem."

Notes

1   Porter, Charles O. "Russian Pen Pals." Received by Mrs. Naomi Scarff. Box 32, Charles Orlando Porter Papers, Ax 088, Special Collections & University Archives, University of Oregon Libraries, Eugene, Oregon.
2   "Russia Off Limits for Pen Pals." *San Francisco Chronicle*, January 28, 1960, pp. 6–6. Box 32, Charles Orlando Porter Papers, Ax 088, Special Collections & University Archives, University of Oregon Libraries, Eugene, Oregon.

3   Porter, Charles O. *Autobiography, Preparation: 1932–1952*. pp. 4–28, *Autobiography, Preparation: 1932–1952*. Box 43, Charles Orlando Porter Papers, Ax 088, Special Collections & University Archives, University of Oregon Libraries, Eugene, Oregon.

4   *Ibid.*

5   *Ibid.*

6   Porter, Charles O. *Chronology*. Charles Orlando Porter Papers, Ax 088, Special Collections & University Archives, University of Oregon Libraries, Eugene, Oregon.

7   Porter, Charles O. *Autobiography, Preparation: 1932–1952*. pp. 4–28, *Autobiography, Preparation: 1932–1952*. Box 43, Charles Orlando Porter Papers, Ax 088, Special Collections & University Archives, University of Oregon Libraries, Eugene, Oregon.

8   *Ibid.*

9   *Ibid.*

10 *Ibid.*

11 *Ibid.*

12 *Ibid.*

13 Burton, Robert E. "CHARLES O PORTER - EMBATTLED LIBERAL." *University of Oregon*, 1964. Word processed from a copy of the original by Sam Porter, December 2007.

14 Porter, Charles O. *Autobiography, Preparation: 1932–1952*. pp. 4–28, *Autobiography, Preparation: 1932–1952*. Box 43, Charles Orlando Porter Papers, Ax 088, Special Collections & University Archives, University of Oregon Libraries, Eugene, Oregon.

15 *Ibid.*

16 "Porter, Charles Orlando - Biographical Information." *Biographical Directory of the United States Congress*, bioguide.congress.gov/scripts/biodisplay.pl?index=P000439.

17 Porter, Charles O. *Autobiography, Preparation: 1932–1952*. pp. 4–28, *Autobiography, Preparation: 1932–1952*. Box 43, Charles Orlando Porter Papers, Ax 088, Special Collections & University Archives, University of Oregon Libraries, Eugene, Oregon.

18 *Ibid.*

19 *Ibid.*

20 *Ibid.*

21 "Porter, Charles Orlando - Biographical Information." *Biographical Directory of the United States Congress*, bioguide.congress.gov/scripts/biodisplay.pl?index=P000439.

22 Burton, Robert E. "CHARLES O PORTER - EMBATTLED LIBERAL." *University of Oregon*, 1964. Word processed from a copy of the original by Sam Porter, December 2007.

23 "Oregon State Bar Bulletin — APRIL 2006, In Memoriam." *Welcome to the Oregon State Bar Online*, www.osbar.org/publications/bulletin/06apr/obits.html.

24 Mapes, Jeff. "Charles O. Porter 1919–2006." *The Oregonian*, January 4, 2006.

25 "'Peace Congressman' Porter Lays Defeat to 4 Factors." *Portland Reporter*, December 22, 1960, pp. 4B–4B. Charles Orlando Porter Papers, Ax 088, Special Collections & University Archives, University of Oregon Libraries, Eugene, Oregon.

26 "Porter, Charles Orlando - Biographical Information." *Biographical Directory of the United States Congress*, bioguide.congress.gov/scripts/biodisplay.pl?index=P000439.

27 Burton, Robert E. "CHARLES O PORTER - EMBATTLED LIBERAL." *University of Oregon*, 1964. Word processed from a copy of the original by Sam Porter, December 2007.

28 Porter, Charles O. "Member of Congress: Four Years Before the Mace, Introduction." pp. 1–3. In file "Autobiography." Charles Orlando Porter Papers, Ax 088, Special Collections & University Archives, University of Oregon Libraries, Eugene, Oregon.

29 Abell, Ron. "Ron Abell on Charles Porter." *Willamette Week*, March 22, 1976, pp. 1–8.

30   Flegel, Al. *Prepared By The Re-Elect Porter to Congress Committee*. Eugene *The Register-Guard*, 0AD, pp. 1–1, *Prepared By The Re-Elect Porter to Congress Committee*. Charles Orlando Porter Papers, Ax 088, Special Collections & University Archives, University of Oregon Libraries, Eugene, Oregon.

31   "Transcript - Porter - Dellenback Debate." *KVAL-TV*, October 20, 1966, pp. 1–11. Charles Orlando Porter Papers, Ax 088, Special Collections & University Archives, University of Oregon Libraries, Eugene, Oregon.

32   *Ibid.*

33   "The Register-Guard." *The Register-Guard*, January 31, 2006, pp. D1–D4.

34   Mapes, Jeff. "Charles O. Porter 1919–2006." *The Oregonian*, January 4, 2006.

35   Abell, Ron. "Ron Abell on Charles Porter." *Willamette Week*, March 22, 1976, pp. 1–8.

36   Porter, Charles O. "Russian Pen Pals." Received by Mr. Samuel Bowles, February 26, 1960. Box 32, Charles Orlando Porter Papers, Ax 088, Special Collections & University Archives, University of Oregon Libraries, Eugene, Oregon.

37   "The U.S. In Soviet Bloc Propaganda—U.S. Pen-Pal Exchange Decision Derided." *U.S. Information Agency, Office of Research and Analysis*, February 3, 1960.

38   Porter, Charles O. Received by Unknown, October 10, 1960. Charles Orlando Porter Papers, Ax 088, Special Collections & University Archives, University of Oregon Libraries, Eugene, Oregon.

39   Porter, Charles O. Received by the Editor, Eugene *The Register-Guard*, October 18, 1960. Charles Orlando Porter Papers, Ax 088, Special Collections & University Archives, University of Oregon Libraries, Eugene, Oregon.

40   Porter, Charles O. *Our Policies for Peace: An Evaluation*. Yale Forum, 1959, pp. 1–8, *Our Policies for Peace: An Evaluation*. Charles Orlando Porter Papers, Ax 088, Special Collections & University Archives, University of Oregon Libraries, Eugene, Oregon.

41   "UPI-84 (Passports)." 1959. Charles Orlando Porter Papers, Ax 088, Special Collections & University Archives, University of Oregon Libraries, Eugene, Oregon.

42   Porter, Charles O. Received by Honorable Christian A. Herter, August 19, 1959. Charles Orlando Porter Papers, Ax 088, Special Collections & University Archives, University of Oregon Libraries, Eugene, Oregon.

43   "Despite Supreme Court Setback Porter to Continue China Case." *The Register-Guard*, December 8, 1959, pp. 3A–3A. Charles Orlando Porter Papers, Ax 088, Special Collections & University Archives, University of Oregon Libraries, Eugene, Oregon.

44   "UPI-84 (Passports)." 1959. Charles Orlando Porter Papers, Ax 088, Special Collections & University Archives, University of Oregon Libraries, Eugene, Oregon.

45   Olive, Ralph. "Professor Who Took Issue With Porter Not Eager for Clamor." *The Register-Guard*, December 13, 1959, pp. 9A–9A. Charles Orlando Porter Papers, Ax 088, Special Collections & University Archives, University of Oregon Libraries, Eugene, Oregon.

46   Baker, Richard. "Professor Blasts Porter's Stand On Relations With Red China." *The Register-Guard*, November 12, 1959. Section B. Charles Orlando Porter Papers, Ax 088, Special Collections & University Archives, University of Oregon Libraries, Eugene, Oregon.

47   Abell, Ron. "Ron Abell on Charles Porter." *Willamette Week*, March 22, 1976, pp. 1–8.

48   Porter, Charles O. "Member of Congress: Four Years Before the Mace, Introduction." pp. 1–3. In file "Autobiography." Charles Orlando Porter Papers, Ax 088, Special Collections & University Archives, University of Oregon Libraries, Eugene, Oregon.

49   Porter, Charles O. *Our Policies for Peace: An Evaluation*. Yale Forum, 1959, pp. 1–8, *Our Policies for Peace: An Evaluation*. Charles Orlando Porter Papers, Ax 088, Special Collections & University Archives, University of Oregon Libraries, Eugene, Oregon.

50   Ciliberto, José Angel. "Charles O. Porter." *El Nacional*. Translation (Spanish), Trip—Venezuela. Charles Orlando Porter Papers, Ax 088, Special Collections & University Archives, University of Oregon Libraries, Eugene, Oregon.

51   "Porter's Six Points, A Man Behind An Ideal." *Visión*, 1958, pp. 15–15. Translated (Spanish), Rep. Charles O. Porter being interviewed by newsmen at Caracas.

52   Porter, Charles O. *Our Policies for Peace: An Evaluation*. Yale Forum, 1959, pp. 1–8, *Our Policies for Peace: An Evaluation*. Charles Orlando Porter Papers, Ax 088, Special Collections & University Archives, University of Oregon Libraries, Eugene, Oregon.

53   Porter, Charles O., and Robert J. Alexander. *The Struggle for Democracy in Latin America*. New York: The Macmillan Company, 1961.

54   Porter, Charles O. *Our Policies for Peace: An Evaluation*. Yale Forum, 1959, pp. 1–8, *Our Policies for Peace: An Evaluation*. Charles Orlando Porter Papers, Ax 088, Special Collections & University Archives, University of Oregon Libraries, Eugene, Oregon.

55   Porter, Charles O. "An Interview With Fidel Castro." *Northwest Review*, January 1, 1963.

56   Porter, Charles O. Received by Mr. Erik Wensberg, September 13, 1965. Page 2. Charles Orlando Porter Papers, Ax 088, Special Collections & University Archives, University of Oregon Libraries, Eugene, Oregon.

57   *Central Intelligence Agency*, Central Intelligence Agency, www.cia.gov/library/readingroom/document/cia-rdp75-00149r000600370005-4.

58   Porter, Charles O. Received by the Honorable Veroslav Vagner, Cuban Affairs Officer, February 16, 1965. Charles Orlando Porter Papers, Ax 088, Special Collections & University Archives, University of Oregon Libraries, Eugene, Oregon.

59   Porter, Charles O. Received by the Honorable Wayne Morse, October 7, 1964. Charles Orlando Porter Papers, Ax 088, Special Collections & University Archives, University of Oregon Libraries, Eugene, Oregon.

60   "Transcript - Porter - Dellenback Debate." *KVAL-TV*, October 20, 1966, pp. 1–11. Charles Orlando Porter Papers, Ax 088, Special Collections & University Archives, University of Oregon Libraries, Eugene, Oregon.

61   Porter, Charles O. Received by the Honorable Wayne Morse, October 7, 1964. Charles Orlando Porter Papers, Ax 088, Special Collections & University Archives, University of Oregon Libraries, Eugene, Oregon.

62   Porter, Charles O. Received by Hessel E. Yntema, Jr., Special Assistant, Bureau of Security and Consular Affairs, April 11, 1964. Charles Orlando Porter Papers, Ax 088, Special Collections & University Archives, University of Oregon Libraries, Eugene, Oregon.

63   "Charles O. Porter - Resume CV."

64   United States, Congress, "An Interview With Fidel Castro." *An Interview With Fidel Castro*, 1963, pp. 1–22. General CIA records. https://www.cia.gov/library/readingroom/document/cia-rdp75-00149r000600370005-4

65   *Northwest Coyote by David Schneider*, www.bigbridge.org/PW-DS2.HTM.

66   *Ibid*.

67   United States, Congress, "An Interview With Fidel Castro." *An Interview With Fidel Castro*, 1963, pp. 1–22. General CIA records. https://www.cia.gov/library/readingroom/document/cia-rdp75-00149r000600370005-4

68   *Northwest Coyote by David Schneider*, www.bigbridge.org/PW-DS2.HTM.

69 "Northwest Review." *University of Oregon*, nwr.uoregon.edu/.

70 Porter, Charles O. "Russian Pen Pals." Received by Mrs. Naomi Scarff. Box 32, Charles Orlando Porter Papers, Ax 088, Special Collections & University Archives, University of Oregon Libraries, Eugene, Oregon.

71 Porter, Charles O. "Russian Pen Pals." Received by Miss Judy Hamilton Church, March 1, 1960. Charles Orlando Porter Papers, Ax 088, Special Collections & University Archives, University of Oregon Libraries, Eugene, Oregon.

72 *Ibid.*

73 Wood, Morton S. "Russian Pen Pal." Received by Mr. Porter, February 23, 1960. Charles Orlando Porter Papers, Ax 088, Special Collections & University Archives, University of Oregon Libraries, Eugene, Oregon.

74 Stephens, Eugene B. Received by Mr. William B. Macomber, Jr., January 29, 1960. Charles Orlando Porter Papers, Ax 088, Special Collections & University Archives, University of Oregon Libraries, Eugene, Oregon.

75 Bowles, Samuel. Received by Hon. Charles Porter, January 29, 1960, Essex, Connecticut. Box 32, Charles Orlando Porter Papers, Ax 088, Special Collections & University Archives, University of Oregon Libraries, Eugene, Oregon.

76 Thomas, Frances. Received by Mr. Macomber, February 5, 1960. Box 32, Charles Orlando Porter Papers, Ax 088, Special Collections & University Archives, University of Oregon Libraries, Eugene, Oregon.

77 Church, Judy Hamilton. Received by Charles O. Porter, February 6, 1960. Box 32, Charles Orlando Porter Papers, Ax 088, Special Collections & University Archives, University of Oregon Libraries, Eugene, Oregon.

78 Scarff, Naomi. Received by Charles O. Porter, 1960. Box 32, Charles Orlando Porter Papers, Ax 088, Special Collections & University Archives, University of Oregon Libraries, Eugene, Oregon.

79 *Ibid.*

80 Porter, Charles O. "Russian Pen Pals." Received by Mrs. Naomi Scarff. Box 32, Charles Orlando Porter Papers, Ax 088, Special Collections & University Archives, University of Oregon Libraries, Eugene, Oregon.

81 "M Of C for W.D." From the Office of Joseph S. Clark, 1959. Charles Orlando Porter Papers, Ax 088, Special Collections & University Archives, University of Oregon Libraries, Eugene, Oregon.

82 United World Federalists. *One World ... Or None*. The Capital Bank Nationwide Insurance Co., pp. 24–24, *One World ... Or None*. Charles Orlando Porter Papers, Ax 088, Special Collections & University Archives, University of Oregon Libraries, Eugene, Oregon.

83 Porter, Charles O. *Our Policies for Peace: An Evaluation*. Yale Forum, 1959, pp. 1–8, *Our Policies for Peace: An Evaluation*. Charles Orlando Porter Papers, Ax 088, Special Collections & University Archives, University of Oregon Libraries, Eugene, Oregon.

84 "Russia Off Limits for Pen Pals." *San Francisco Chronicle*, January 28, 1960, pp. 6–6. Box 32, Charles Orlando Porter Papers, Ax 088, Special Collections & University Archives, University of Oregon Libraries, Eugene, Oregon.

85 NC State University Libraries. "People-To-People Partnership: The White House Conference." *People-To-People Partnership: The White House Conference - AV2_FM_296-people2people - NC State University Libraries' Rare and Unique Digital Collections | NC State University Libraries' Rare and Unique Digital Collections*, November 9, 1956.

86   *Ibid*
87   "The History of People to People International." *PTPI*, ptpi.org/about/the-history-of-people-to-people-international/.
88   "History." *People to People International Europe - PTPI.eu*, www.ptpi.eu/history/.
89   Eisenhower, Mary Jean. "Letter Writing." *Letter Writing*, August 26, 2019.
90   NC State University Libraries. "People-To-People Partnership: The White House Conference." *People-To-People Partnership: The White House Conference - AV2_FM_296-people2people - NC State University Libraries' Rare and Unique Digital Collections | NC State University Libraries' Rare and Unique Digital Collections*, November 9, 1956.
91   "The History of People to People International." *PTPI*, ptpi.org/about/the-history-of-people-to-people-international/.
92   "History." *People to People International Europe - PTPI.eu*, www.ptpi.eu/history/.
93   "The History of People to People International." *PTPI*, ptpi.org/about/the-history-of-people-to-people-international/.
94   Porter, Charles O. Received by Unknown, March 10, 1958. Box 32, Charles Orlando Porter Papers, Ax 088, Special Collections & University Archives, University of Oregon Libraries, Eugene, Oregon.
95   *Ibid.*
96   *Ibid.*
97   Botsford, Carolina R. "Letter Writing Committee The People-to-People Program." Received by The Honorable Charles O. Porter, February 5, 1960. Box 32, Charles Orlando Porter Papers, Ax 088, Special Collections & University Archives, University of Oregon Libraries, Eugene, Oregon.
98   Botsford, Carolina R. "Letter Writing Committee The People-to-People Program." Received by The Honorable Charles O. Porter, February 16, 1960. Box 32, Charles Orlando Porter Papers, Ax 088, Special Collections & University Archives, University of Oregon Libraries, Eugene, Oregon.
99   Letter Writing Committee. Received by Unknown, 45 East 65th Street, New York 21, New York. Box 32, Charles Orlando Porter Papers, Ax 088, Special Collections & University Archives, University of Oregon Libraries, Eugene, Oregon.
100 Strauss, Anna Lord. Received by Unknown, Letter Writing Committee, New York, New York. Box 32, Charles Orlando Porter Papers, Ax 088, Special Collections & University Archives, University of Oregon Libraries, Eugene, Oregon.
101 "Russia Off Limits for Pen Pals." *San Francisco Chronicle*, January 28, 1960, pp. 6–6. Box 32, Charles Orlando Porter Papers, Ax 088, Special Collections & University Archives, University of Oregon Libraries, Eugene, Oregon.
102 "Student Travel Programs: About People to People International Travel Programs." *People to People*, www.peopletopeople.com/about/.
103 "People To People International." *PTPI*, ptpi.org/.
104 *The Oregonian*. "Roseburg Spanish Students Pay Own Way On Visit to Old Mexico." Charles Orlando Porter Papers, Ax 088, Special Collections & University Archives, University of Oregon Libraries, Eugene, Oregon.
105 *The Oregonian*. "Roseburg Spanish Students Pay Own Way On Visit to Old Mexico." Charles Orlando Porter Papers, Ax 088, Special Collections & University Archives, University of Oregon Libraries, Eugene, Oregon.
106 *Ibid.*
107 "Your Purchase Will Help Us Take The Friendship Tour of Mexico." 1960. Charles Orlando Porter Papers, Ax 088, Special Collections & University Archives, University of Oregon Libraries, Eugene, Oregon.

108 Bailey, Berton M. "Roseburg Spanish." Received by The Honorable Charles O. Porter, August 29, 1960. Charles Orlando Porter Papers, Ax 088, Special Collections & University Archives, University of Oregon Libraries, Eugene, Oregon.

109 Porter, Charles O. "Roseburg Spanish Class." Received by Vicente Sanchez Gavito. Charles Orlando Porter Papers, Ax 088, Special Collections & University Archives, University of Oregon Libraries, Eugene, Oregon.

110 *The Oregonian.* "Roseburg Spanish Students Pay Own Way On Visit to Old Mexico." Charles Orlando Porter Papers, Ax 088, Special Collections & University Archives, University of Oregon Libraries, Eugene, Oregon.

111 Crain, Larry. "Students Plan Display of the Trip's Mementos." *The News-Review,* June 16, 1960. Charles Orlando Porter Papers, Ax 088, Special Collections & University Archives, University of Oregon Libraries, Eugene, Oregon.

112 OAS. "Organization of American States: Democracy for Peace, Security, and Development." *OAS,* 1 Aug. 2009, www.oas.org/en/about/who_we_are.asp.

113 *Ibid.*

114 "People-To-People Partnership: The White House Conference." *People-To-People Partnership: The White House Conference - AV2_FM_296-people2people - NC State University Libraries' Rare and Unique Digital Collections | NC State University Libraries' Rare and Unique Digital Collections,* November 9, 1956.

115 Porter, Charles O. "Roseburg Spanish Class." Received by Vicente Sanchez Gavito. Charles Orlando Porter Papers, Ax 088, Special Collections & University Archives, University of Oregon Libraries, Eugene, Oregon.

116 Gavito, Vicente Sanchez. Received by Mr. Charles O. Porter, March 2, 1960. Charles Orlando Porter Papers, Ax 088, Special Collections & University Archives, University of Oregon Libraries, Eugene, Oregon.

117 *The Oregonian.* "Roseburg Spanish Students Pay Own Way On Visit to Old Mexico." Charles Orlando Porter Papers, Ax 088, Special Collections & University Archives, University of Oregon Libraries, Eugene, Oregon.

118 Bailey, Berton M. "Roseburg Spanish." Received by The Honorable Charles O. Porter, August 29, 1960. Charles Orlando Porter Papers, Ax 088, Special Collections & University Archives, University of Oregon Libraries, Eugene, Oregon.

119 Crain, Larry. "Students Plan Display of the Trip's Mementos." *The News-Review,* June 16, 1960. Charles Orlando Porter Papers, Ax 088, Special Collections & University Archives, University of Oregon Libraries, Eugene, Oregon.

120 *The Oregonian.* "Roseburg Spanish Students Pay Own Way On Visit to Old Mexico." Charles Orlando Porter Papers, Ax 088, Special Collections & University Archives, University of Oregon Libraries, Eugene, Oregon.

121 *Ibid.*

Chapter Eight

THE DECADES-OLD DOSSIER

by Zack Demars

In which student journalist Zack Demars closes a 58-year loop and presents Janice with her FBI "dossier."

***

"When I was 9 years old, I was about as deep as a wading pool."

–Janice Boyle, June 2019

***

On a warm Sunday afternoon in Eugene, Oregon, Janice Boyle walked into a conference room in the University of Oregon's Allen Hall. Around the table were journalists of various walks: the editor of the local alt-weekly, the former director of the paper of record's editorial page, a former foreign correspondent who spent years reporting for CBS News in—yes—Russia. Aside from her younger sister and "chauffeur" Jodi (who came complete with a long Mercedes to drive Janice to and from various locations during her visit back to Oregon), Janice was the only person in the room who wasn't a professional journalist (or on track to be one, in the case of the students in the room). Journalism was the topic of the discussion, which had drawn participants from halfway around the globe. From her seat at the head of the table, Janice looked on quietly as the discussion's participants connected, via Skype, with other journalists in Italy. The journalists on screen were discussing a forthcoming documentary on the topic of "slow news," an academic and practical movement to combat the acceleration of the 24-hour news cycle. Around the table in Eugene, the group listened as the Italian journalists described their film, the methodology behind their reporting and their upcoming trip to the United States. Listening to what they had to say, Janice was "making friends" and learning "their ways," 58 years after she'd sought to do the same with Russian students abroad.

But this was much different than her 1960 experiences. The school's dean didn't come down the stairs to confiscate the computer from which the Italians spoke, nor did the university's president drive to the whitewashed Federal Building on 7th and Pearl in downtown Eugene to alert the FBI of a group's attempt at international communication. The event did not make national headlines for the Bureau's censorship of curious young people. No, this attempt was far more successful, as the Italians spoke and the Americans listened. What's more, this attempt at communicating globally was far simpler: There wasn't a months-long string of correspondence required with Congress, Assistant Secretaries of State and American communists from New York. There was simply a Skype call. The young journalists listened along with Janice and surprised her with copies of the files she had long sought.

The journalists and newspaper editors around the room nodded with interest as Janice told them of the attention her class had garnered in 1960, and the attention she now continued to generate all these years later from a new generation of enterprising students who continued to prod her about her experiences. "If our project had been now, with the internet and stuff, it would never have been an issue," Janice said to the group, reflecting on the challenges her class faced with the pen pal project. "It's very telling of the times."

Janice recounted her experience in an almost flippant manner, telling the group how little the letters, memos and investigations actually mattered to the students of 1960. "It meant absolutely nothing to me," she said. "When I was nine years old, I was about as deep as a wading pool." Janice went on to say that, after the three or so weeks of media coverage, the entire escapade was quickly forgotten about as the students returned to the important parts of life—what was on TV, and what was for dinner. "It wasn't like every year in January we'd have a little Russian party and celebrate—we didn't do that. It was done."

The events, though, were clearly not the same for district administrators and the FBI, as Janice received her mail from Charles Pemberton. That June 2019 day in the university conference room was the first time that Janice read the mail intended for her back in 1960. She had discussed the letters with the team of reporters because she had to sign a document before the National Archives would release her files but had yet to see what the federal government had written about her.

"Can I have my dossier?" she asked, as the fat stack of FBI documents sat on the table in front of her.

One of the documents was read aloud. "It is of course true that the Soviet Government is a dictatorship and that censorship would be likely, however this is the kind of world we live in, and I think the sooner that boys and girls like yourself understand that these controls exist, the better for you personally and for the kind of nation we will have when it is in your charge." Fifty-eight years later, Janice remembered that letter. It was from Congressman Porter. It was the class's first and last taste of help from the federal government.

Janice gazed at another photocopied document — this time, the letter from Charles Pemberton, the avid American letter writer.

"I never saw it," Janice said, gazing at a Pemberton's typewritten message. "I never knew this letter existed."

"Just 60 years too late," commented one of the conference participants as Janice held the letter in her hand, quietly scanning his typewritten message, reprinted with an archivist's "best possible image" certification across the top and a string of serial numbers across the bottom. The whole file had been "screened by NARA" in 2013, as if there was some potential for the release of some sensitive information about the Hoover FBI's anti-elementary-school-propaganda campaign.

After reading in less than a minute the message she'd waited over half a century to see, Janice came to her conclusion about the censorship she faced at the time. "No one told me about it. I can see why, and I understand why, at nine years old if I had read this I'd have gone, 'What? I don't know what he wants,'" she said, Pemberton's pages of communist literature sitting untouched on the table in front of her.

"So it probably would not have been a bad thing for me to read it, because I wouldn't know what he was talking about," she continued. "Now that I read it, I think, 'holy crap.'"

✳✳✳

"This is a childrens world, many of them are deep thinkers. Us adults should encourage them at all times."

– F. A. Nowey, a social activist who sent a letter of support to Janice's family.

✳✳✳

At that June meeting in Eugene, Janice was in the midst of her own historical project – to catalog her personal genealogy. She found as many newspaper stories she could which mentioned her name in relation to the pen pal project.

The independently researched historical record supported Janice's later accounts of how she felt about the project at the time. Then, the papers show, the intent was simple, unassuming and nothing near what nearly any of the bureaucrats—not Superintendent Deller, not Assistant Secretary Macomber, not Special Agent App—had assumed. "You see, we want to learn their way of life. Maybe they would like to learn our way of life. And we would like to make friends," Janice said in her original letter to Congressman Porter, according to an account in the *Oregonian*.

Similar to what Charles Pemberton had displayed with his letter to Janice, the idea of a young student seeking to be "friends" with Soviets is an attractive prospect for encouragement—not only from innocent civilians in the name of "international connectedness," but also for domestic activists. LeRoy Wolins, a Chicago native, was clearly supportive of the idea of friendship, having served as the secretary of the National Council of American-Soviet Friendship, according to an FBI file on the man who would later help establish the Chicago chapter of "Veterans for Peace in Vietnam" and "Vietnam Veterans Against the War." His 2005 obituary in the *Chicago Sun-Times* described him as an "anti-war, anti-greed, pro-environment crusader" who was "noticeably different from other kids" during his childhood because of his preference for listening to political speeches on the radio over playing outside with other children. That difference carried over into the Korean War veteran's political views in adulthood, as he was, according to his file, eventually identified by Hoover's FBI as a member of the Communist Party in the United States. As did some notable communists at the time, Wolins testified before the House Un-American Activities Committee, the arm of the US Congress which acted as the legal instrument to investigate and harass those it found "subversive."

As a prolific "communist" letter writer of the period, Wolins sent letters to children, encouraging them to learn more about the ideology. Janice, the now-nationwide target of propaganda that she was, was sent one such letter. Wolins described to Janice, in his sharp and slanted cursive penmanship, his recent visit to Stalingrad. He told her about a family that he'd met, and that they had a young daughter about Janice's age, who, he thought, might be interested in corresponding with Janice and her classmates. Education, like Charles Pemberton's letter to Janice, was a central theme of Wolins's as he extolled the virtues of the Russian school, in which students were taught entirely in English after the fifth grade. It is here, however, after eight short lines of neat text, that the historical record fails: The letter is cut off after "might like to correspond with you and your" in the FBI file. For one bureaucratic reason or another, only a portion of the letter was kept by the National Archives and released in response to Freedom of Information Act requests about the young Janice, leaving the rest of Wolins's likely words lost to the spiraling winds of history—or at least some government-issue wastebasket.

While other letters might have been sent but not included in the federal government's records, Janice's dossier included one final letter outside of those from Congressman Porter, Assistant Secretary Macomber and communist sympathizers Pemberton and Wolins. Just the day after the story of the pen pal project's demise was published in *The New York Times*, someone by the name of F. A. Nowey penned a letter different in a number of ways from those by Wolins and Pemberton. Nowey chose to address the letter to Edward Boyle, Janice's father. In nearly unintelligible cursive and sporadically connected sentences, Nowey described an effort to promote pen pal relationships for children worldwide. It's unclear whether Nowey was offering Boyle a business deal or simply encouraging Boyle to encourage Janice to continue in her efforts.

That her father had been the recipient of a letter about the incident surprised Janice. Her father, she said, typically refrained from engaging in business that he considered the government's. "In his eyes," Janice's sister Jodi recalled, "It would've been, 'It's the government's business, it's none of my business.'" According to Janice's memory, her father and mother both were interviewed by the FBI, but the Bureau has no records of such meetings.

The most notable difference, other than the addressee, of Nowey's letter compared to Pemberton's and Wolins's was Nowey's intention. It's clear from what was written that Nowey had no interest in propaganda or communism generally, as Nowey didn't comment once on the actual content of what a pen pal relationship might entail. Instead, Nowey simply praised the virtues of the idea of pen pals. Nowey's letter is the closest of the bunch in the files to supporting what teacher McFetridge and young Janice sought to do with their efforts—to make friends.

"The idea which Janis has brought to the public's attention merits consideration with active exploration," Nowey wrote. The letter continued by admonishing Mr. Boyle in favor of supporting his daughter's efforts, whether those efforts had purely educational or even seditious tendencies. "This is a childrens [sic] world, many of them are deep thinkers. Us adults should encourage them at all times."

✸✸✸

"Portland is conducting no investigation and this matter is being considered Referred Upon Completion by this office."

– Memo from Portland Field Office, Federal Bureau of Investigation, March 1960

✸✸✸

In the prologue of the Portland FBI's memo recounting the Roseburg hubbub, with letters and Chinese propaganda attached, the regional office requested that the Bureau's offices in Chicago, New Haven and New York research other actors in the case and report back any findings. In a final procedural shoulder-shrug at the end of its addition to the government's growing file of Charles Pemberton's suspicious activities, the Portland office

announced—like William Macomber had announced in his letter months earlier to the group of enterprising students about their inspired project—that its bureaucratic reach into the activities of Ray McFetridge's Classroom 15 was closed.

Outside the National Archives building is a statue upon which is inscribed a quote from Shakespeare's *The Tempest*, reminding visitors to the archives that history is always repeated: "What's past is prologue."

Chapter Nine

PROGRESS AND THE PRESS

by Julia Mueller

In which student journalist Julia Mueller takes off her editor's green eyeshade to analyze lessons journalists and the rest of the public can learn from Classroom 15.

"What you're putting together," says Janice Hall, née Boyle, of the book being written about that anomalous 1960 winter of her youth, "again, not many people will probably even care about it." She refers to the book project by its early-draft nickname, Janice 101. Janice signs her emails that way now—Janice, with a parenthetical 101—triumphant to know that there's a manuscript-in-progress with her name on it. Nine-year-old Janice could never have known how her adult life would unfold: motherhood, the workforce, retirement and then a journalistic inquiry. Even adult Janice has her doubts.

"It didn't mean that much to me," she shrugs. Her youth detached her from full understanding: The pen pal project existed to her in a world without political repercussions, without media influence, without cultural consequence. The news cycle moved on quickly, and so did she. She grew up and away from the Riverside School's Classroom 15. She left behind Ray McFetridge, and the classroom's spinning globe and the fourth-grade geography lesson on "How People Work Together." Neither her parents nor her teachers sat her down to explain what had happened and why. Reminiscing, Janice calls the project "little"—the same word she uses to describe herself in retrospect.

Eager as she may be to be interviewed, or to show off yearbook pictures, or to sign her name with "101" on emails, Janice seems acutely aware that the insignificance she once ascribed to the pen pal project may be similarly noticed even by readers of the *in media res* manuscript. A little project. A little impact. "But," says Janice, "it does have an important point."

For the last 60 years, Janice has lived a life wrapped up like a double helix with the media. She rocketed to local notoriety at nine years old, her picture splashed across the front page of the *The News-Review* after trying to reach beyond the Iron Curtain. She reveled in a teenage stint as her high school paper's entertainment editor, running up and down the Vegas strip to interview Dean Martin and Liza Minnelli. She reached toward a life in journalism herself—then settled into a career as a media liaison in a Nevada courthouse, brushing past lawbreakers and lawmakers alike in the hallway.

She grew up as America passed through more than one landmark era. The nascence of McCarthyism. The hydrogen bomb and the Cold War. Color television. The Civil Rights Movement and Second-Wave Feminism. The Cuban Revolution. She lived through the construction and destruction of the Berlin wall; she watched Neil Armstrong take one giant leap for mankind. The Pentagon Papers and the first personal computer. War, war, war: on Korea, on the Persian Gulf, on drugs. Medicaid, climate change, and the attack on the World Trade Center in New York. About 40 years after her high school was desegregated, Janice saw the country elect its first Black American president.

The world has changed around her—sometimes, she thinks, for the better. It's having lived to trace connecting lines through US history that leads Janice to conclude that the pen pal project and the book being written about it are of value beyond the original Classroom 15.

"It does have an importance in what's going on now," Janice says confidently of Janice 101. "It does have something to do with what could happen in the future."

❋❋❋

"I think he probably knew that this was going to happen," says Janice. She's talking about her fourth-grade teacher, the late Ray McFetridge, who, unlike his eight- and nine-year-old students, would have been dialed in to what she calls "the mentality of the times." A young Janice might not have made the connection between a pen pal program with the USSR and the mid-twentieth century tension with communism, but McFetridge likely would have. His family thinks the same.

Throughout the pen pal project's attempted launch, its brief stint as a lightning rod for local attention and the subsequent government intervention into the mailbox of Roseburg's Riverside School, Janice remembers a ready, steady McFetridge, dogged in his attempts to get the project off the ground but silently resigned when the project was abruptly dropped. To her, these actions—and lack of action—are indicative of a man who knew exactly what line he was toeing, eager to push the boundaries but understanding when they would not budge.

"I don't think he was surprised by it, because he was very emphatic. Russia this, that. 'Write this letter. Do that.' I think he probably sat there and thought it all out and said, 'Now, let me see what kind of reaction we get.'"

But even if McFetridge had been working to shepherd his class toward controversy, his students likely didn't know much—if anything—about where they were being led. Even in her fifth year of public school, Janice was still struggling to grasp the concept of a world as disparate from her Roseburg life as the USSR. She'd heard the word "communism" but didn't know the definition.

It wasn't only school that had kept her, at least to that point, insulated. At home, her family shared a terse relationship with news consumption and political discourse.

"We did not discuss politics," says Janice. "We just didn't." Her parents were Republicans, but they kept their viewpoints to themselves—or else they tried to imply rather than emphasize them. "It didn't matter to us what was going on."

When they lived in Roseburg, two daily newspapers were delivered to the Boyle family: the *Oregonian* in the morning and *The News-Review* in the afternoon. They listened to anchorman Walter Cronkite deliver the CBS Evening News. To Janice, the news felt more like family-home furniture than an important fixture in her life.

"We would watch the news. The local news and then the national news. Every night," says Janice. "It was on. I did not sit down and watch it. It was just there; it was there." She heard only voices telling monotone stories, rarely piquing her interest. "For the most part it was just right before dinner. When it was done, dinner was ready. We sat down and ate dinner. And we did not discuss politics at dinner."

As she reminisces, Janice sits with her hands clasped in front of her on a wide, white desk in an empty classroom at the University of Oregon's School of Journalism and Communication. Her younger sister, Jodi, is at a chair further back in the room, watching her sister tell the story of their childhoods, waiting for pauses to fill with her additions to the narrative they share. "We were just coming out of the Second World War," says Janice. "The Russians were just taking over all of Europe."

"And then the Korean War," Jodi supplies.

Her sister nods and continues as if uninterrupted. "So, we were just coming out of that. And I think they were thinking—if you're not an American, if you're not an American born, then you're no good." Janice explains the American ethos as she came to understand it in adulthood—the idea that America was the international breadwinner, the heavy-lifter—but she's quick to shake her head and refute the assumption. "We didn't win the war by ourselves. But I think that's what we were taught."

Jodi speaks again from the back of the room. "The era of McCarthyism. They were pinko commies. If you're red, you're dead."

Their classrooms kept the girls' world feeling small and estranged, and the austere fireside-chat-esque news at home did little to inform them any further.

Looking around at the flatscreen-lined college atrium and the wired-up podium at the front of the classroom in which they now speak, the Boyle sisters remark at how different their schooling has been from the hyper-connected twenty-first century. Their classrooms had no radio, no television, no internet.

Janice is quick to correct when Jodi talks about the lack of electronic media in the classroom. She describes a semicircle of schoolchildren in her fifth-grade classroom huddled around her teacher's personal television, which had been lugged to the school from her home so her class could watch the swearing-in of President Kennedy in 1961. "But again, it didn't mean that much to me," says Janice coolly. "It meant I didn't have to do any school work that day."

Janice grew up riding bikes down rainy Oregon neighborhood roads, playing for long hours outside with her sisters, but she was also living under the incessant stress of the Cold War. Nine-year-old Janice may have barely understood the myriad ways the war impacted her, but, as she grew up, she became painfully aware of the pressure on her family, her town, her nation—and her own childhood. The threat of mutually assured destruction loomed. Talk of bomb shelters. Anti-war protests.

"They don't know what it's like," says Janice of children growing up in the modern climate. She's been talking to her grandchildren, the oldest of whom is already in his twenties. "They don't have a clue at all what it was like to be in the Cold War with the Russians. They've heard about it because they've heard about it in school but they don't know what it was like."

The tensions of the Cold War, a particular blend of propagandized drama and an intangible conflict with an all-but-invisible antagonist, stoked what is arguably a too-common characteristic: *fear of the other.*

Such a fear was nothing new: The country was already highly polarized on racial issues as the Civil Rights Movement strengthened. Race riots, internment camps and the uneasy brewing of yet another war for the twentieth century meant Americans lived on a livewire of hostility and violence, both domestically and internationally.

The Boyle sisters are quick to disclaim that, though their father was wont to let slip ideology every now and then, they were raised in a politically ambiguous home. They're proud to have been raised in such a way that they "were never taught racism" in their Roseburg home.

"But I must say," Janice says, "until we moved to Las Vegas, I had never, ever interacted with a black person." She explains the grim history of the Oregon Constitution that her great-great grandfather aided in writing—early laws banned Black Americans settlers from the state, the vestiges of which

were not fully removed from the state's constitution until 2002[1]—and the collective moral revolt of Roseburg residents at the thought of Black Americans
moving into the town. "If they came into town, they ran them out on a rail. It
was the way it was."

"Jim Crow laws were in force, let's put it that way," adds Jodi.

"I must say, though," Jodi continues to interrupt her sister, "our dad was a
bit of a racist." She recalls wanting to ask a Latino boy to a girls' reverse dance
in high school. "My dad threw a fit."

"You learn as you get older," says Janice simply.

Whatever that learning is that happens in between naïveté and wisdom,
it seems America was teaching itself throughout the 1960s. Looking back on
the pen pal project of Classroom 15, Janice sees that it was likely political
tensions, international wariness and that *fear of the other* that contributed to the
censorship-esque cessation of the project-in-motion.

She speculates that it came from a lack of access to information. She's
aware of how little she understood about her fourth-grade teacher's exploits,
and wonders how much he knew, too. Lacking as Classroom 15 was in the
ability to internet search, Janice sees their pen pal initiative as a reaching-out
toward an understanding of the other.

"When we were looking at this at the beginning," Janice explains, "they
were children who happened to be living in Russia. That's how we looked at
it. We never looked at it as: These people are going to be horrible, wait 'til we
write to them and they're gonna tell us all these horrible things. No, they were
little kids, like us, who lived in Russia. And that was our whole goal, to see if
we could connect with them."

That the Soviet children "were little kids, like us," was what Ray McFetridge
seems to have been attempting to teach his students in his 1960 lesson on
"How People Work Together." McFetridge instructed his fourth graders to
write down stories about their own lives alongside questions about others'—
strangers from an unfamiliar, far-flung place. But if Ray McFetridge was, in
fact, calculating his class assignment to encourage communication through
the Iron Curtain, it begs the question: Did he know what would happen?

"Is this what you wanted to teach us? Is this the point you wanted to make?"
asks Janice decades after the pen pal project attempt. "What is that supposed
to teach us? What was your point?"

In rapid back-and-forth, Janice and Jodi discuss the pen pal project's con-
ception, demise and aftereffects. Maybe McFetridge wanted to teach the class
that there weren't any differences between American and Soviet children, or
maybe he just wanted to stir the pot. Maybe he just wanted reactions from his
students—maybe from the national news. Did he want to highlight prejudicial
labels, or was he trying to enforce them?

"He was not a stupid man," says Janice. "He was an adult. He watched the news. He knew what was going on."

As Janice now knows well, the project was stalled at the State Department and the students' handwritten letters were never delivered to Russian students. The story spent a brief moment under the limelight of local news—with a jaunt at the national level, too—but McFetridge chose not to capitalize on that attention.

Janice remembers the short-lived thrill of seeing herself in a black-and-white photograph in *The News-Review,* standing next to two classmates and McFetridge, holding her classroom's spinning globe. "I called my mother and I said, 'Ma, I'm on the front page of the newspapers!' I was beside myself." She's quick to concede that the project lost its luster unceremoniously: Her childhood concerns were more focused on schoolyard play than on international relations she could not yet understand. Even the gravity of her above-the-fold photograph didn't last much longer than the morning-of, and the procedural drama of the project getting pushed from desk to desk within the State Department didn't come into further discussion in Classroom 15.

"It was done," says Janice. "And after that we never talked about it again. He never discussed it in class. Never finished off the project. It was just dead."

Perhaps the project's abrupt end signals that McFetridge had no idea what he'd gotten his class into—or perhaps it signals that he knew the implications exactly.

Of course, McFetridge did, ultimately, receive Russian children's letters intended for his fourth-grade class that winter—the national profile of the Roseburg story was enough to help postcards find the Riverside School address—it's just that he took them home to his cedar chest instead of to show-and-tell. But what brings Classroom 15 to light as an example of '60s censorship is not how effective the censorship was, but rather the fact that censorship was attempted—albeit from just one side of the letter-writing, as the State Department curtailed the Oregonians' efforts to find Russian contacts and as McFetridge kept the Russian postcards private. And albeit without much follow-up, as the FBI, for example, only seized the propagandizing Pemberton letters after they had arrived, addressed to the young Janice, in Roseburg.

With the benefit of 60 years' retrospect, the Boyle sisters have both realized the futility of that *fear of the other* that they now believe was the whetstone for what happened in and around Classroom 15.

"Categorizing people should stop," says Jodi. "So they're black. So they're white. So they're green. So they're purple. Who cares?"

"You can't just say that because you are a Muslim, oh, you're bad, you can't be around me," says Janice. "What if they came in and said, well, you're a Methodist, I can't be around you?"

This all begs the question: Would Janice's grandchildren, with the world inside the smartphones in their pockets, be as ignorant of global politics as she was at their age? Would a group of fourth graders today be more engaged in a pen pal initiative with a foreign country? How would a hardcopy-letter exchange play out, if at all? And in the modern political landscape, would it be successful?

"I think nine-year-olds now or then are still nine-year-olds," says Janice, but she feels that she and her sister were disadvantaged by the "more sheltered life" that McCarthy-era fourth graders lived relative to her grandchildren's hyper-connected modernity. "I mean, there was just so much that we knew nothing about."

✸✸✸

At far right, Janice in her self-proclaimed "Go-Go Girl stint" during her sophomore year of high school.

The Boyle girls' elementary-school ignorance started to erode after the family's 1963 move to Las Vegas, Nevada, and the brave new world of high school. Suddenly, Janice—once inclined to ignore the static murmur of Walter Cronkite's newsreel—was required to read sections of the newspaper as a daily class assignment. This practice morphed quickly from homework into a hobby, though Janice remembers it happening much to her father's dismay. She took to reading her father's paper before he did—he'd come home from work and bellow for whoever had messed up the creases.

Janice started at Valley High School for the 1965–66 school year, a member of the inaugural student body: the Valley Vikings. In her first year, she and the rest of the journalism class in which she was enrolled published the school's first yearbook—called *Valhalla* after the warriors' heaven of Norse mythology—and established the school paper, *Thor's Hammer*.

Pictures of the Las Vegas Valley High School in the students' inaugural 1966 yearbook.

Valhalla '66 had a special dedication—to one Mr. Ron Schiessl, who "contributed graciously of his time and efforts to the Student Body by seeking to establish a Valley tradition of ethical journalism."

Schiessl provided Janice with her first formal foray into the world of journalism. He gave his students the Batman Test: Watch the show's weekly broadcast and pay attention. Each Friday, he quizzed the class on minutiae. "He would pick out the most obscure little things—what color Robin's glove was or whatever. So that you would have to watch and pay attention," says Janice. "And really I thought, this is so much fun."

SPECIAL DEDICATION

Left: **Janice's credit on the first page of the *Valhalla 66* yearbook. *Right:* The yearbook's special dedication to Ron Schiessl, with a nod to the journalism teacher's "Batman Test."**

Janice was the entertainment editor of *Thor's Hammer,* and her older sister, the late Pam Boyle, worked as feature editor. High-school-age Pam and Janice would get home from school to scarf down their dinners, ask littlest-sister Jodi to do the dishes, and run back to the school's mimeograph machine. Working with Schiessl's aid and encouragement, the two sisters hand-created every column for the paper.

"I liked the talking, I liked the looking, I liked the putting stuff together," says Janice of the girls' process.

Thor's Hammer came out every Friday, after a long Thursday night with mimeograph fluid and stencils.

"I was so proud of that," says Janice. "I loved and I loved and I loved everything about it."

The school's proximity to downtown Las Vegas gave the journalism class a unique opportunity to fill their small paper's pages with the glitz and glam of Sin City. Janice would make at-random calls to Vegas hotels, asking after celebrities who might be staying there—and whether or not a representative of Valley High School Journalism could make a press visit. She'd dial and be directed to hotel clerks or, at best, the star's manager.

One afternoon after school, Janice was excited to have gotten ahold of the manager for actor-singer Dean Martin—or so she thought. "I talked to Dean Martin on the phone!" Janice is giddy at the memory. "I thought I was talking to his representative, but he said, 'Oh, darling.' As soon as he said that, I knew."

If a successful call opened the door to an in-person meeting, young Janice would rush into the city and run up and down the Vegas strip, darting in and out of hotel lobbies. She met with pop stars like Neil Sedaka and Petula Clark, bands like The Turtles and The Righteous Brothers, comedians like Corbet Monica and Johnny Carson. If a celebrity stopped through Las Vegas, Janice—the proud *Thor's Hammer* entertainment editor—would call.

"My favorite, favorite interview: Liza Minnelli," says Janice. "And she was only 20 or 21. She was either married to or just-dating Peter Allen at the time, but when we were there at her hotel, we interviewed her before the show." The interview was interrupted by a phone call from Minnelli's mother, checking in on her daughter's visit to Vegas. "I thought, I'm so cool!"

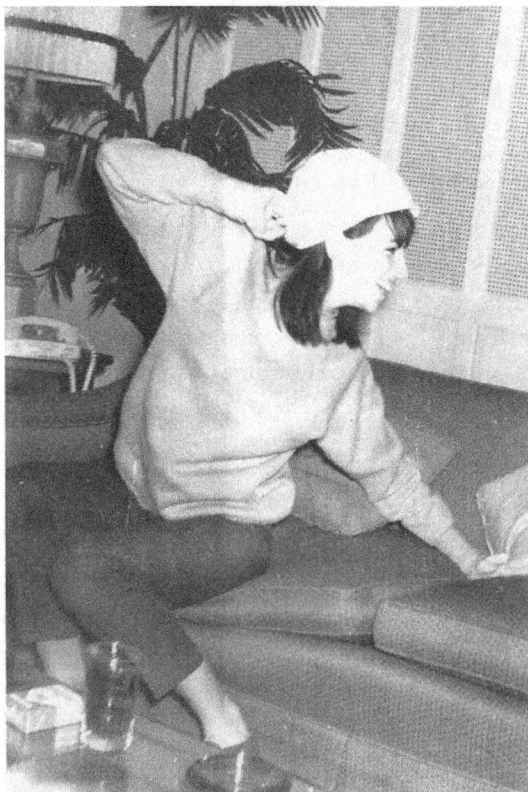

Janice's photograph of Liza Minnelli, taken during their 1966 interview.

The hardcopies of Janice's Liza Minnelli interview—and the many others she published in *Thor's Hammer* throughout her time in high school—have been lost to time, but Janice remembers the thrill of taking the story back to class and getting feedback from Schiessl. She waited on Schiessl's approval as if he was an ambassador for the journalism industry, eager for affirmation from the field she was falling in love with.

"It was exciting for me because it was an outlet. I was able to get my thoughts out and down on paper."

1st semester editorial staff: standing—bob ruff, carol wilson, sid goldstein, rich opperman, jan boyle, bruce rugar, mike onstott, mike lloyd. seated—pam boyle, robert lloyd, mary rose, rod rose.

Janice stands at center frame in a 1966 yearbook photo of the *Thor's Hammer* staff at the Las Vegas Valley High School. Her older sister, Pam Boyle, is seated at a typewriter to her left.

The 1960 pen pal project was not Janice's only experience with a student effort curtailed by administrative censorship.

In her senior year at Valley High School, Janice stepped back from *Thor's Hammer* to work as editor for the school's first literary journal—if memory serves her, the title was *Abstractions Unlimited*, though the school has no record of its early student publications. The journal promised to be a showcase of student creativity: short stories, poems, drawings and photographs.

Janice and her peers were, as she remembers them, an expressive lot—the Vikings stormed another school during class time to intimidate their rivals before the state basketball championship—and the late 1960s stoked the students' expressive fervor. The editors and writers of the literary journal leaned into the friction and controversy of the political moment.

"Please remember," says Janice, "this was 1968, a time of great conflict between students and teachers." The school, which opened in 1966, was "on the cusp of integration and in the heart of the Civil Rights Movement." She remembers the Vikings experiencing, in her freshman year of high school, "not one but two race riots in the lunch room." Black Americans were being brought by bus into the all-white neighborhood around the school, and the desegregation process caused conflict. During one such riot, "tables, chairs, food, books" and lit cherry bombs were hurled across the room. "Unfortunately, I was the lucky one sitting in the chair under which one chose to detonate. I was unharmed, but it scared the bejeesus out of me." Socioeconomic cliques also formed, further delineating the differences between students and fostering a sense of bitterness toward the administration.

All this channeled into the literary journal, culminating in a final work that, in addition to sharing artistic expressions of the student experience at Valley High School, touched on race, drugs and war.

To protect their work as they began this flagship project, Janice recalls that the students entered into an agreement with the school administration: no interference from the adults.

"I had hoped," says Janice, "this would allow the many skeptical students to submit their work without the fear of retribution or backlash from the staff."

But the students' first journalism teacher—beloved mentor and advocate of ethical, honest journalism Mr. Schiessl—had left after Janice's sophomore year. Schiessl was replaced by Walter Lukas, Janice's English teacher, a man "with no journalism background" and with whom she often "butted heads." After one in-class disagreement, Janice was thrown out of Lukas's English course and forced to "sweet-talk" herself into another, or else come up shy of the requirements to graduate.

When he saw the penultimate draft, Lukas disregarded the agreement allowing students to curate and publish the journal without administrative interference.

"Participants were stunned to see their work badly edited or whole sections cut out," says Janice of the final product that was published. "He removed everything he found to be offensive, which was the bulk of our work."

Lukas's slashing edits to the journal removed editorial criticisms of the Vietnam War, drawings that "included or alluded to" marijuana and art that displayed female breasts—the latter was deemed "pornographic."

"As the editor, I should have taken the blame for the final published product," says Janice in retrospect. "But I was so angry that I made it very clear I was in no way responsible for the rag presented to the student body." She wrote a simultaneously searing and clarifying editorial "setting the record straight" and slated it for publication in *Thor's Hammer* following the journal's release—but the editorial never appeared in print.

***

In 1966, Janice received Valley High School's first-ever Most Valuable Staffer award, presented to her by the *Las Vegas Review-Journal* for outstanding contributions during the school year. She remembers with pride that winners were selected with help from recommendations from journalism teachers like Schiessl.

Though she retains a meager paper record from her time at *Thor's Hammer*, the fading plaque remains one of her prize possessions, a reminder of her Sin City escapades as a teenage journalist. A reminder of Thursday nights at the mimeograph machine beside her sister. A reminder of the passion and purpose she found—but also a reminder of that passion curtailed.

"As I got older, I found out, or I realized, I wasn't going to be able to do that," Janice says of journalism. "We didn't have the money for me to go to college." She talks about her high school career with nostalgia, solemn when she shares that she never worked as a writer again.

"If circumstances were different in 1968 when I graduated, I might have attended your school and continued in a career of writing," she says in the University of Oregon classroom. "But it did not turn out that way.

"If you didn't go to college and get a degree, which women at that time were not expected to do, you got married," says Janice frankly. She finished up her time at *Thor's Hammer*, punctuated her senior year with *Abstractions Unlimited*, graduated with the Valley High School class of 1968 and married in 1969.

"I got married just a couple months after I turned 19. What did I know?" She married a man she'd only just met and got pregnant soon after. She lost her first child just after his birth in August 1970 and gave birth to her second in October 1971. Before her daughter, Kristen, was a year old, Janice and her husband had separated. She suddenly found herself as a homebound young mother and wife turned divorcee. "I got married because I didn't know what to do." After her early separation from her husband, Janice would be a single mother for nearly three decades after the separation, until her remarriage in July 2000.

"Jodi was in high school, and I was living at home again because I had no place to go. I was working at the bank at the time. And it was just not what I wanted. It was *not* what I wanted. But it was what it was."

Janice's Most Valuable Staffer Award, presented by the *Las Vegas Review-Journal*.

What Janice *wanted* was to go to school for journalism—to rocket to stardom as a writer and keep interviewing, editing and publishing with the passion she'd had in high school. But the circumstances were against her, both societal and familial. Not only was it out-of-the-ordinary, says Janice, for a young woman to choose college over wife- and motherhood, but the Boyles' father didn't agree with his girls continuing their education post-high school.

This position goaded another member of the Boyle family tree: the girls' aunt Ianthe.

Ianthe was the granddaughter of Delazon Smith, a politician who started papers in both New York and Ohio before moving out West to serve in the Territorial House of Representatives, participate in the drafting of the Oregon Constitution and found the *Albany Democrat* newspaper in 1859. The Boyle sisters remember their aunt working at the newspaper—Albany's first, for which Smith was editor. She started out in the newsroom, quickly entangled herself in the local gossip and was promoted to the society editor, a position she held for more than 40 years.

Ianthe Smith

ALBANY - Ianthe Smith, 78, of 1023 West Sixth St., died Friday in a local nursing home.
  Born in Tangent, she was a life-long resident of the Albany area. She was a veteran Oregon newspaperwoman. She was the editor of the society section of the Albany Democrat-Herald for more than 40 years before her retirement in 1966. She was the recipient of numerous journalism awards and was named Linn County Woman of the Year in 1966.
  She helped found the local chapter of the Betta Sigma Phi Sorority which was named after her. She attended the University of Oregon and majored in journalism.
  She was the granddaughter of Albany's first newspaper editor, Delazon Smith, who established the Albany Democrat in 1859.
  Survivors include sister, Mary Boyle, Salem.
  Services will be at 2 p.m. Tuesday at AAsum mortuary and interment in Masonic Cemetery.
  The family suggests contributions to the United Methodist Church.

Left: **Ianthe Smith at the grave of her grandfather, Delazon Smith.** *Right:* **Ianthe Smith's obituary.**

"She was a hoot and a half, I have to tell ya," says Janice of her aunt. "She was quite the character."

"She was the only one in the family, I'm sure, that was a smoker," Jodi adds. "And she drank."

"She drank like a sailor."

"You either loved her to pieces or you couldn't stand her," says Janice. "She had a razor tongue. She could cut you in half."

Janice spent a high school summer with her aunt Ianthe in Salem, Oregon, and the pair bonded over mutual admiration for the media. Janice ran through stories of her *Thor's Hammer* exploits and Ianthe shared glimpses of her life in the newsroom. Ianthe was excited to see another woman in the family interested in reporting and eager to both stoke and reward Janice's enthusiasm: Just before Janice's junior year at Valley High School, Ianthe offered to pay in full for Janice's attendance at the University of Oregon, for a degree in journalism.

But Janice wouldn't learn about this offer until she'd reached middle age. *Your mother never told you?* her aunt asked one afternoon. The realization hit Janice with retrospective regret and she felt a wash of resentment toward her father for keeping the offer a secret. "I thought, 'I'm gonna kill you!' 'Cause I really, really wanted to do it."

Thus Janice, having met with obstacles to what she felt were her two main options—her marriage annulled and her university dreams quashed—sought work.

She started out as a file clerk at the Clark County Clerk's office, but the thrift and grit she'd honed as a high school journalist served her well. She was quickly promoted to work in the research department, indexing.

"I loved it," says Janice. "I would spend hours. I found records that they had been looking for for years because I just wouldn't give up. And I would be so proud of myself." After indexing and a stint xeroxing filling copy orders, she was reassigned to the computer division as assistant to the division's head.

Left: **Janice with a Clark County Clerk's office coworker.** *Right:* **Janice with her husband Tom and their dog.**

In her 20 years with the computer division, Janice worked with and trained attorneys, police officers and Nevada State Supreme Court personnel alike in case-tracking software. In that same capacity, she also served as a media liaison between the Clark County Clerk's office and both national and local news outlets.

It was at the Clark County Clerk's office, through her role as liaison for the Eighth Judicial District Court, that Janice met her now-husband Tom Hall.

Tom was part of a newly initiated news department, in charge of the assignment desk at a local Fox affiliate. His job was to oversee story pitches, dole out reporting assignments and begin amassing backstories for the brand-new Channel 5. The pair met in 1998, when Tom began calling the office several times each day for the latest information on a court case. They married two years later.

Janice and Tom at their wedding in 2000.

But what was a mutual ardor for reporting and a determination to carve out space to share the news changed over the years as Janice and Tom began to see the industry around them change itself from the inside out.

"He didn't like that it became about the ratings," Janice explains. "About how much better can we be than the guy across the street." She and Tom both find fault with the 24-hour news cycle. "They will take a story and they will run it into the ground for days on end with nothing new to report, nothing that they have changed. It's the same story over and over and over again."

Janice explains that she and her husband, both with long careers and unique angles on the journalism industry, are disappointed in what they see today from the profession. Gone are the days Janice would rush to beat her family to the afternoon paper. "I don't read the newspapers at all. I rarely will find a magazine that I can stand to read." She blames this newfound apathy for what she once loved on "the tilt" that, in her eyes, now pervades the journalism industry.

"I don't want their point of view. I just want the information." She's critical of the fast-paced, quick-turnover news cycle and the rush to entertain for the ratings. "I think a lot of stuff that they report on is inconsequential, is not important or has nothing to do with what's going on right now."

The Boyle-Hall family is nostalgic for the days of Walter Cronkite-style news, frankly told and quickly disseminated, without pomp and circumstance.

"He just said this is what happened, have a nice night. Goodbye. And that's the way it should be. That's the way I think it should be. And then we have these other people who come in and say this is what happened and this is why you should be sad about it, and these are the people that you should hate."

"Well, it's the editorial news," adds Jodi.

Janice agrees. "It's all, again, pointed at making you fear. It's your fear that feeds their ratings. They create the fear because it gets them their ratings."

Jodi nods. "It's the sensationalism of it that keeps you wanting to read more."

Janice and Tom learned that a paper they once read religiously had been bought by a billionaire intent on throwing money at the publication until, as they perceived it, every article bent in his favor. The Halls canceled their subscription. Nowadays, Janice won't pick up a magazine from the racks.

"And I don't miss it," she says.

Should the evening news accidentally come on when Janice gets home, she retreats to her office while Tom gets his limited fix—or, as in her teenage years, she'll head to the kitchen and start dinner.

"And now he drives a limo," says Janice of Tom. "And he's very happy."

So what is *good journalism*, as defined by someone like Janice, who has dealt with it on both personal and professional levels? It's well-researched, objective storytelling. It shares the facts and admits when there's a lack of them. It doesn't rush to be the first to break a story if that rush could compromise the story's accuracy. It doesn't lean into stereotypes or overgeneralizations. It doesn't stoke fear—that *fear of the other*—but instead promotes understanding, sharing information from both sides of an issue and facilitating readers to make their own conclusions.

"I don't want anyone to tell me how to think."

Throughout her 27 years at the Clerk's office, Janice committed herself to technical writing and personnel training, finding an outlet for her creativity in her professional work. Retired now, she compiles her family tree.

All the same, the lost opportunity to pursue an academic career in journalistic writing is not easily forgotten.

"I just wanted to do it because I loved it," Janice says. "I love writing. I still love writing."

Janice has been digging into her family history, pouring through records like she used to at the Clerk's office. She's found traces of her family stretching back down the Oregon Trail, to the pilgrims' journey to America, all the way back to, she proudly insists, the year 709.

"Looking for these things, I tell myself, I am doing kind of a journalism thing. I'm doing the research I love to do. And I will spend hours doing it. People say, I don't know how you can sit there and do that. Well, I love it."

In conversation with the journalism students telling the story of Classroom 15, Janice indulges herself in imagining the life she might have had—if her father hadn't so flatly declined her aunt Ianthe's tuition offer. If she hadn't gotten married to a man she'd just met. If she hadn't let her journalistic writing settle into lost archives after her *Thor's Hammer* glory days. She wonders what her life might have ended up looking like if society itself were different. If women had more options and fewer expectations.

"I'm up to 246 pages," Janice brags of her working draft on her family's genealogy. "I tell ya, I can't shut up."

✳✳✳

The narrow focus of this book—of the Janice 101 research—is on the life of just one young girl from one small classroom in one small town in the 1960s, and yet, this book reaches into the annals of history and expands the life of an ordinary person into a quasi-historical figure, highlighting the dramatic up- and downswings of her life, attaching her to political movements and using her story as an example of the American experience during McCarthyism and the Cold War.

That's because Janice, when we've zoomed out on her story to see the steps and switchbacks and successes, does serve as a prime case in point. Although the specificities of her professional life path, from Ron Schiessl to Aunt Ianthe to the Clark County Clerk's office, are idiosyncratic, her history is rife with large-scale thematic throughlines: childhood learning, student activism, cross-border communication, political censorship and the pursuit of *pure* journalism.

These themes aren't unique to Janice's life. Journalism permeates the stories of many of the pen pal project's main characters: Ray McFetridge's son Scott is a news editor for the Associated Press in Nebraska-Iowa. Charles O. Porter worked as a reporter for *The New York Times*. What this story makes clear is that, whether or not someone has a direct connection to the professional journalist's world, every American life has been impacted, on some level, by some form of journalism. Reporting is the gatekeeper of fact and the foil to governmental censorship. It was, after all, the Roseburg *News-Review* that initially brought Classroom 15 into the spotlight—so effectively, in fact, that letters came from the Soviet Union to the Riverside School (even if those letters were never seen by the schoolchildren there). And it was, after all, *The New York Times* that first exposed our cohort of University of Oregon journalism students to rediscover the Classroom 15 story and delve into its complexities.

Janice has been wracked by a love-hate relationship with the country's growing culture of constant communication. She's watched the United States graduate from handwritten letters to sticky-key typewriters, and then to a rabid 24-hour news cycle that she and her husband change the channel to avoid when the television flicks on. But she still believes in the beauty of communication and journalism's potential to be a force of good in the wrought modern world.

Now, the student writers behind this book have set another pen pal project in motion. It's a modernized version of the 1960 initiative: Small-town Oregon schoolchildren will write anew to schoolchildren in Russia. They no longer have the Iron Curtain to worry about, but a host of contemporary barriers to mutual understanding are still stacked up before them. This time, though, the letters will be hand-delivered, carried to Russia by one of our cohort's journalism students to ensure their receipt. To ensure that—this time—the pen pal project (2.0) comes full-circle.

What does Janice think of this twenty-first-century re-do of her fourth-grade class project? "I think that's amazing. I think that's such a cool thing," she says. "And my advice to them is: Make your own decisions. Make up your own mind. Don't let an adult change your view—if you're excited about it, don't let someone come in and say, 'Oh no, these are terrible children, you should not be doing that.' No, no. You don't know that. The only way you're gonna find out is to interact with them. If you interact and you find out you don't like them, that's one thing. If you interact and find out you are just crazy about 'em, then that's something else. You can make up your own mind. Even at nine years old, you can still use your mind."

And so the original lesson continues: learning how people work together.

JAN —
thank you for the card and the
love that prompted it —
thank you for being the weird,
wild love of my "Life Among the
Teenagers" I forgive you for the
times you hurt me with your sharpness
— forgive me for the times I hurt
you with my coldness — I couldn't
stand being cold + official - that's
why I had to get out.
I will miss you kids and you more
than most because you were my thick.

Please be the fine, perceptive
women (with a touch of sharpness)
that I know you have it in you
to be.
    You are very important to me, and
what you do with your life, whether
I know about it or not matters greatly.
Be a little easier on people - for me.
I will miss you deeply, Jan my thorn;
I shall never have another like you.
                                    R.S.

**A letter from Schiessl to Janice upon taking leave of Valley High School.
Note: Images courtesy of Janice Hall.**

Note

1   Associated Press. "Many voters opt to keep racist language in Constitution." *The Daily News*. November 7, 2002. https://tdn.com/news/state-and-regional/many-voters-opt-to-keep-racist-language-in-constitution/article_d1bea75e-4398-55bb-8f0b-eea4e9df5ad9.html

Chapter Ten

CLASSROOM 15 TODAY

by Vaughn Kness

In which student journalist Vaughn Kness visits a contemporary Douglas County, Oregon, fourth-grade class to learn that teacher Ray McFetridge's ethos lives on in another Oregon classroom. Intriguing footnote—and one who helped Kness gain access to the school: His little sister is a Yoncalla Elementary fourth grader.

I

The year is 2019. Five circular tables dot the room, each surrounded by chairs low enough to the ground for the third- and fourth-graders' feet to touch the floor. A mix of bald pencils and papers lined with writing that looks more Picasso than Hancock lie atop them. The walls are adorned with crayon artwork. A map adorns one wall, too. It's a map of the United States, where this classroom's children can visualize their tiny home of Yoncalla, Oregon, in comparison to the overwhelming visual might of the whole country.

The other map is spherical—a globe—concentrated today on areas west of this small Oregon town. Russia is centered, facing the classroom, not only because it is the Earth's largest country, but for its significance to the class.

This class has been given the opportunity to write pen pal letters to children in Russia, a modern-day equivalent to the project that tried and failed in nearby Roseburg in 1960. Back then, one of Roseburg's Riverside School fourth-grade teachers, Ray McFetridge, proposed a similar plan to his students, though under a somewhat different political context: Write letters to students in the USSR.

Nearly six decades later, under a veil of animosity and surreptitious dealings, the two countries are once again linked. Years past the Cold War of finger-pointing and "size" measuring the United States and Soviet Union once partook in, the current-day hotbed of activity between the two countries has continued to simmer in recent years. Russian meddling in the United

States' 2016 and 2020 presidential elections still rages as both debate and firestorm in the States. Tensions between the two countries have ebbed and flowed since President Trump's election, with air and artillery strikes in Syria, the poisoning of a former Russian military officer in the United Kingdom and a renewed arms race among the points of contention between the two countries in the last few years.

All of this parallels the political intrigue of nearly 60 years ago to an eerie degree.

Fears of Russian intervention in United States society? Check. The use of espionage and counter-intelligence? Check. Raised awareness and a growing anxiety of the threats these two countries propose to each other? Check.

All that is needed now is a group of grade schoolers to write peaceful letters to one another, and the cycle might be completed.

II

A globe centered on current-day Russia provided the first image of a new world for the children of teacher Diana Fast's third/fourth-grade class. In a class still learning proper grammar and multiplication tables, the idea of a country so large and so far away as Russia seemed unknowable. Unattainable.

"I pulled up a picture on the map and pulled out the globe and showed them where it was," said Ms. Fast. "Because Yoncalla is very, very small, it's quite a concept to them to see how big things actually are."

Yoncalla, Oregon, may be the epitome of the phrase "middle of nowhere." The two largest towns nearby are Roseburg and Cottage Grove, both nearly a 30-minute drive away. A single road stretches through the small town. On one side are the buildings and homes of those who live here, on the other are the woods and overgrown grasses that separate the town from the I-5 freeway that cuts from California up into Oregon and Washington. In a way, Yoncalla appears like a town of old photographs, perfectly simplistic and idealized for its small-town feel. Yoncalla itself is the home of two schools, a post office, a mini mart, a coffee shop and, as of 2017, 1,066 people. In a population so small and insulated, Yoncalla prides itself as a town of "who's-who" and a community so tight-knit that many live their entire lives among people they've known since grade school.

Yoncalla might not be known for much besides the stories those who live here know well. The town was named by settler Jesse Applegate after a local Native American tribe that spoke a language called "Yoncalla." Applegate himself was influential in early Oregon government and helped to find an alternative route to the Oregon Trail: the Applegate Trail. Applegate's home still stands today, one of the oldest known residences in Oregon, one that offers a bit of tourism and pride for those in the town.

The small life in a small town is almost a rite of passage, a ceremony of unceremonious birthrights. Parents give birth to the next generation of Yoncalla neighbors, who repeat the process. Many never stray too far from the familiar roots of Yoncalla, staying within the welcoming hands of Douglas County, which houses Roseburg and Yoncalla both. While this homebound lifestyle is certainly an issue of poverty—Douglas ranks as Oregon's thirtieth-best county for median income out of 36 counties, according to a 2010 US Census Bureau study—the reason is more familial than that. Sons and daughters often emulate their parents, as if theirs is a chosen path of destiny meets fate: Mill workers become mill workers, loggers become loggers (in Douglas County timber reigns supreme, despite its decreased production due to conservation efforts and safety concerns).

These facts served a great purpose to Ms. Fast in attempting to make the world accessible for her students. Ms. Fast has expressed that desire to her students, who believe the bigger cities of Roseburg and Eugene are their doorways to the world, though she's wanted them to know there's much more out there.

"There are other people in the world and it's bigger than Yoncalla," Ms. Fast said. "And that was my biggest motivation to get them to write, was that you might go to Eugene or Roseburg, but that's small compared to the world. I want them to know that there's a huge world to explore and that it's fine to want to explore it and not feel like 'Well this is Yoncalla, my parents didn't go anywhere, and I'm not going to go anywhere.' I tell them not going to college is fine, but not to settle on just working at the mill because my dad does and everyone says that's where I'll end up. If you want to try something, go out there and do it."

To Ms. Fast's surprise, then enjoyment, several kids expressed their interest in writing to children across the world in Russia. She showed them the map of the country that includes 11 time zones and could fit the landmass of the United States twice over. She detailed, briefly, a Sparknotes-esque catalog of facts from Russia's history, glazing over the more macabre aspects. To the still-developing mind of a fourth grader, the lesson must have appeared as land in an explorer's telescope; here was something new, undiscovered, a whole new world and people most of these children hadn't previously known about.

"Because Yoncalla is very, very small, it's quite a concept to them to see how big things actually are," Ms. Fast said. "I had a student last year; we were in Roseburg and passed the river over there, and she goes 'Oh look it's the ocean.' So, when we actually went to the ocean for a field trip I said, 'This is the ocean.' And they were fascinated."

III

For the day of the interview, Diana Fast wore a red shirt. Nothing special, not a shirt decorated with ornate designs or logos, but a shirt with consequence. For the past few months, Ms. Fast has worn red every Wednesday, a symbolic showing of solidarity for the "Red for Ed" teachers strike that swept the nation as teaching conditions and wages worsened in our education system.

Ms. Fast is like many other teachers: she loves her job and her "children," as she calls them. When she goes out to buy supplies or gifts for her class, she will make a point of telling the cashier she is shopping for all 13 of her children.

"These are my kids, and I have some parents that say Ms. Fast is your at-school mom. And I've been called mom so many times. I would do anything for these guys." That "anything" extends beyond the normal realms of instructing the children in reading, writing and mathematics, to the grimmer tasks that have come along with the job in recent years.

"We talk about, with our emergency procedures, I will do anything to keep you safe," Ms. Fast said. She speaks of lockdown drills where children must hide in cupboards and under desks, forced to practice procedures for the all-too-real chance their school might be the location of the next mass shooting. It is a harrowing reminder of the current times, just as the "duck-and-cover" drills students participated in during the Cold War were a reminder of the threat of nuclear annihilation.

Ms. Fast continued, saying, "If it's shoving you in a cupboard to make you hidden, I will find a way. They giggle and don't take me seriously, but I will. Some of them understand that I will do everything in my power to protect them."

From a young age, Ms. Fast applied herself to a future in teaching. She took daycare and teaching classes in high school, then began a stay at Western Oregon University, working toward a Master's degree for eight years.

Her career at Yoncalla began as a second-grade teacher for the 2017–18 school year. The following year, she followed her class to the third grade and inherited the school's entire fourth-grade class, as well. The sudden split in grades and the constantly shifting dynamic of students has proved difficult.

"This has been a very hard class," Ms. Fast said. "Very small class. I've lost a lot this year, gained a couple. Academically I have a wide range of kids. Ones that are to the Oregon standard of grade level and some above and some below. So it's a big, wide range."

Over the course of the year, Ms. Fast's class began with 21 students, but, due to dwindling opportunities in Yoncalla and children moving between different caregivers, her class has dropped to only 13. The teaching challenges have forced her to change curricula and approach to each student with a style that she describes as "firm but fair."

But through every challenge this year, Ms. Fast has endeavored to hold fast to what led her to teaching to begin with. As with many teachers, Ms. Fast's connection to her students comes from a selfless want to contribute to the next generation.

"My big thing is I love when I'm teaching them something and they get that 'OH!' moment and it's like yes, I did my job. I love it. I love interacting with kids and I'm very much a goofy, kind of out-there person. I get nervous talking to adults, but with these guys I dance around and sing and try to embarrass them as much as possible."

And in small-town Yoncalla, Oregon, there come the extra-curricular aspects of teaching. In a place as isolated and off-the-grid as Yoncalla, teachers like Ms. Fast are tasked with the unenviable prospect of widening their students' scope, when all they've known thus far is rooted in family lineage and the streets they were raised on.

IV

The acceptance of the *Classroom 15* reporters' request to renew a decades-old Russian pen pal program was not the first attempt by Ms. Fast to provide a larger scope of the world into her class. Previously, she had reached for the lofty aspiration of sending and receiving letters from a student in each of the 50 states, an operation dubbed The Great Mail Race. In this "race," students wrote letters to children of a similar grade in other states, sharing their personal experiences, enjoyments and information about their community. A pen pal program closer to home, without the vast chasm of difference perceived between separate countries.

Part of the fascination for the project came from Ms. Fast's own experience with pen pals. In fifth grade, she was paired with a student from another state. Though she cannot remember the specifics of who she was paired with or where they lived, fixing only on some vague details, like the stranger she communicated with through letters being a boy.

"I remember being really excited about getting matched up with another student," Ms. Fast said. "I don't remember the end, but I do remember that I was always so excited about getting a message and then being able to respond." Hoping to recreate that excitement for her students, Ms. Fast attempted The Great Mail Race and then used the momentum of that project to attempt communication with Russia.

That want to connect to a wider range of people intersected perfectly with the idea of recreating Roseburg's pen pal plan of 1960. Ms. Fast requested members of her class fill out a letter, and of her 13 students, four returned with letters. Those four, named Ivee, Brinleigh, Tori and Kara, wrote to children they may never see. They inserted their personality into the letters. Some wrote of their state, describing Oregon as a grade school mind would interpret it: best known for trees, Nike, and former University of Oregon quarterback Marcus Mariota. Some detailed their class schedules and favorite colors, but all offered a peek into the life of a rural student through their writing—linked only by age and grade, separated by distances and differences of land and sea, politics and culture.

Ms. Fast hopes simply to receive a response from a Russian student, which would allow her to show her students physical proof of an abstract concept and broaden their perspective on the world. And though Ms. Fast doesn't stay too informed on the current-day political climate of US–Russian relations, finding most of the news too depressing to digest, she is eager, like Ray McFetridge before her, for her students to reach out to parts and people unknown.

"The ones that first volunteered did it because they were excited to do another letter to a school. Once I told them where it was going, I had a couple more volunteer. They didn't quite understand about it being a different country until I showed them a map of the world and where they would be writing to compared to where we live."

Brinleigh Lewis, one of the fourth graders to write a letter to Russia, described the class as excited and confused about the prospect of talking to students in another country. "When the teacher said, 'Who wants to write to Russia?' everyone said, 'Me, Me!' so I think they were excited by it," Lewis said. "I don't think they know anything about it. Like me, I know they have vodka there."

Lewis shared her sentiments on what the class wanted most to know about their Russian counterparts: what they do for fun, what they eat. And though many of the students ended up writing about their lives, the hope that a student they may never meet in person could reply to their hand-written notes jolted the class with a palpable sense of excitement and wonder.

And for Lewis, at least, writing letters proved easier than communicating face-to-face. "Because it might be fun to learn about different people without, like, having to talk to them in person."

V

A pen pal program is, in many ways, more than a correspondence between two cultures, but an interaction between two cultures. Perhaps, in the days of Ray McFetridge, Janice Boyle and Genee Parr, the paranoia of the day—itself a side effect of the Red Scare and the rise of McCarthyism—played a part in small-town Roseburg's high-profile involvement in the Cold War. The mere idea of any Americans, whether government officials or naïve fourth graders, interacting with the enemy of the times, would've proved as contentious as any actual collaboration.

As Ms. Fast heard the story of Ray McFetridge's class-project-turned-political-thriller, she appeared aghast. All she said was: "Oh, wow."

"For the most part, teachers are good people," said Ms. Fast, composed seconds later. "Teachers want to be here for the kids and do everything in their power to protect and guide and teach. And I am very much a goody two-shoes. If that happened to me, I'd be freaking out and calling my mom up like, 'Mom what do I do?' And I'd be asking myself, 'What did I do, what did I say, what brought this on?' I would be very much confused and panicked. I'm sure that's how he felt back then."

Someone like Ms. Fast is qualified to speculate as to the mood of that fourth-grade class so long ago. The plan of recreating that pen pal program today would most likely not end in an FBI intervention, though those tensions and anxieties felt by Mr. McFetridge long ago can be appreciated by teachers whenever and wherever they teach fourth graders.

So too can the temperature of that 1960s class be measured by looking at the classroom today. What would students like Genee Parr and Janice Boyle have felt? Some students, such as Mark Wilborn, are determined, all these decades later, to desert that incident in the past. The emotions of students may depend on their own involvement and investment in the project.

Ms. Fast can make guesses as to how her students would react if a group of FBI agents intervened in their classroom and school.

"I think they would be more curious than scared or nervous and be like, 'What's happening?' Confused. What are they doing? Kids are fairly innocent, and they wouldn't know the gravity of that situation."

Brinleigh, who is only 10 years old, said she would feel "scared and wouldn't know what to do." Beyond that, empathy is hard to find for the fourth grader, as the situation placed on the likes of Janice Boyle and Genee Parr is too bizarre to truly understand. And certainly, if a modern fourth grader can barely comprehend the mere thought of such a peculiar position, then the actual event, as it was lived in nearly 60 years ago, must have felt like fiction come to life for all those involved.

VI

So, little has changed between Classroom 15 and Ms. Fast's classroom, at least when comparing a current fourth grader's knowledge of history and politics to that of a child 60 years ago. Ms. Fast herself believes students should be aware of a broad issues, but not gritty details.

"My students, I believe, are old enough to learn some aspects about what happened, but can wait until they get older to know the specifics. They know too much mature content right now as it is that some things should wait 'til they have the maturity to process it." And while Ms. Fast doesn't believe that should exclude the students from many social issues, such as those concerning race, sexuality, religion and gender, those more macabre aspects of society, like war and human conflict, should wait until later in life.

But that cannot always be the case, as is demonstrated by Janice Boyle's class 60 years ago, and the string of contemporary violence in schools that is of concern for every student and parent of today. One must wonder, then: At what point children should be taught the ways of the world, especially as it concerns their place and understanding of it?

Are students of today better equipped to handle the hardships of that world that often qualify as barometers for adulthood? Can they know that today's political climate is eerily similar to that written in textbooks concerning times 60 years before? And, if so, are they able to comprehend their place in it?

The answers might come from the way America educates its children. English, math, science and history remain the four pillars of a proper education, just as they were in the previous century. With the advancement of technology through the internet and social media, as well as the advancement toward greater globalization, one may believe children today are more connected to the pulse of the world than ever before. And though that may be true, life today acts as a funhouse mirror reflection of history.

"The youth now differs, in my opinion, from the youth in the '60s with ways they communicate. Back then they had a lot more face-to-face contact and were better equipped to work in large groups and had the patience to solve a problem. A lot of kids nowadays get frustrated more easily if something doesn't come as quickly to them and they have a harder time communicating face-to-face with people because usually they use video games or social media to do that."

Communication. The way students are given information and how they process it, as well. What divides a student of 60 years ago from a student today is the methods of their communication, which back then were relegated to teachers, books, radio and three-channel televisions. Today, communication is global and ever-expanding, as is its accessibility to children. In the age of the internet, a child may grasp at whatever threads pique their curiosity. Whatever wormholes or dead-ends they reach depends only on how far their mind wishes to travel. All of which is to say that, wanted or not, vital information of the world, information that might've illuminated the confusion Janice and her classmates were shadowed by in 1960, is within the grasp of fourth graders today.

Ms. Fast herself spoke highly of a student who, when the Russia pen pal program was first introduced, brightened at the thought of writing. This fourth grader, unnamed by Ms. Fast as he didn't ultimately finish his own pen pal letter, had a deep-seated interest and knowledge of World War II and the Cold War that followed it: things many fourth graders wouldn't and, according to some, shouldn't know.

Even Ms. Fast believes that world readiness comes from the person—their heritage, their parents, their outlook on life. "When you are a kid, being confident in yourself and being able to know the difference between right and wrong helps you make good choices as you grow up," Ms. Fast said.

She continued, saying, "My parents were not strict, and they trusted me. That allowed me to have more freedom than all my other friends. My mom always told me that I need to do my best in school, but she didn't expect me to get straight A's. She expected me to do my best and she was not a parent that was on my back all the time. She was there when I needed her, but also gave me the space to grow and make my own decisions and mistakes."

And that might be most important of all when considering if a child is at an optimal age to be taught about the world they live in. When taught with maturity and confidence, a child might look at the troublesome world we all inhabit and meet it head-on, unafraid. But when they are taught by more fearsome methods—a school lockdown or an FBI intervention in their school life, for examples— then so becomes the world.

As society progresses, so too does our ability to judge past generations. We may look back and realize what faults needed fixing. From there, we develop new ways to process the world. After all, what isn't constantly evolving is made obsolete by time. So, we can look back at a fourth-grade class long ago, one consumed by a frenzy of media and Cold War fear, and wonder how to better the narrative for future generations, if ever they are wrapped up in dealings they have yet to be taught. And we can hope to improve, though that offers its own equal challenges, too. We can judge past generations as society progresses, but can never properly judge the current ones.

VII

The globe sits near the classroom's front door, a model of a world grown old. The Soviet Union no longer stretches beyond the borders of Russia to include 14 other republics. So much has changed in the 60 years since a fourth-grade class in Roseburg attempted to communicate with a group of children located somewhere in the Soviet Union, for years the United States' formidable enemy. Maps have been remodeled, even, and new globes have been placed in US classrooms that put a stamp of difference on those changing times.

Many children today, in towns smaller than what Roseburg once was, like little Yoncalla, have yet to learn of those times. They marvel at the grandiose nature of a country the size of two United States. They revel in the opportunity to speak with children of different cultures, different mindsets than their own. And they wonder at just what responses they might receive, if ever replies are sent.

Yet they are mostly unaware of what brought about this moment. Fourth graders years before, now climbing age's ladder to its uppermost steps, who were fitted with the same chance as these students today: a chance to discover not only what students of another country ate or did in their free time, but to open their worlds to something so drastically different that it can only be visualized on a map.

The globe in Diana Fast's Yoncalla classroom.

And open it they did. Janice Boyle and her peers gained wisdom few fourth graders are ever gifted—or cursed—with. In a time of paranoia bred from fear of the unknown, they were stopped

Impossible is the task of understanding what might have been different had the fourth graders back then chosen a different country, or had the government left alone those innocent children.

It is both a harrowing and uplifting message, then, that life hasn't much changed since the days of Classroom 15. The countries' borders may have shifted, the players substituted for more modern alternatives, but what remains is what came before: students willing to reach out to others to understand a life they may never interact with outside of hand-written grade-school postcards and letters. Teachers willing to protect and enrich their children through any means possible. And countries that still hide their hostilities behind paranoia and fear.

One can look at a globe and begin to understand how history has molded it. All one needs to do is listen to the stories it inspires in those who look on it for the first time and discover that the world isn't the walls of their small hometown. One need only look at these to understand what has been achieved, and what is still being worked toward.

Chapter Eleven

NASTYA HAS A CAT NAMED CHRIS

by Zack Demars

In which student journalist Zack Demars concludes the attempt at igniting a pen pal relationship between students in Oregon and Russia, gathers a Russian perspective on the 1960s project and closes the questions he opened at the outset.

Teaching aids and informational signs adorn classroom walls in Gimnazium 14.

Ms. Fast's classroom is, of course, not the only one in the world with a map hanging on the wall. In another, the map was also centered on a large country, which allowed the students to spot their city in the vastness of their state. This one, however, was covered in Cyrillic script—the alphabet of the Russian language—and centered on the school's home continents: technically Europe, though some definitions argue that Asia lies across the Don River, just a stone's throw from Gimnazium 14.

Aside from the map on the wall, the school and its city bear resemblance to Yoncalla, the students of which could soon become new friends. While Rostov-on-Don, the city designated by President Vladimir Putin as one of "Military Glory" for its efforts in defending the fatherland,[1] is home to about a million people, it, like Yoncalla, is far smaller than its local (and in the world's largest country, a 16-hour train ride might as well be "local") metro comparator: Moscow, a city with about three times as many residents as the whole of Oregon.[2] Rostov-on-Don's industrial and agricultural economy compares, too, though Oregon timber is traded for port traffic, helicopter manufacturing and sunflower production.[3] What's more, the city is just 400 kilometers away from the Otradnenskoye District—the home of the school that sent letters to Riverside students after hearing of their plight in 1960.

While Gimnazium 14's cafeteria offerings are better than one could ever expect in any American public school—with homemade (yes, as in, made-from-scratch) borscht, pierogi, chicken and pork cutlets and pickled green tomatoes, among other local selections—the feeling of community within the schoolhouse walls mirrors that in Yoncalla. Many of the teachers—22 of them, said Principal Tatyana Kornilova—in the Russian school had graduated from there years before.

A student bags the pastries he has selected for lunch.

The most obvious parallel between the two worlds-apart schools was the center of it all: the key to a successful international friendship, classrooms full of enthusiastic students. Throughout the wood-floored halls of Gimnazium 14, the excitement was palpable, perhaps even greater than that of the Oregonian friends who'd written letters to them. What differed, though, was their familiarity with American culture. In one of the classrooms, a poster detailed the basic parts of American government. Would a visitor find something similar for Russian government in an American primary or secondary school? While the Yoncalla letter-writers were curious to tell about American and Oregonian culture, the Russian students were curious to ask. Fourth graders wondered about American musicians, while 11th graders were curious about American films.

Despite differences in previous cultural knowledge, what remained between the two schools was genuine excitement. Upon seeing the letters from their unknown American friends presented to them, an entire auditorium of fourth graders smiled and squirmed with anticipation. And they had been waiting— before the letters had even arrived, the students had preemptively written to their future pen pals.

Letters to new friends await their long journey to Oregon.

In a gift bag, adorned with the white, blue and red of the Russian flag and emblazoned with the coat of arms of the Russian Federation, 45 letters sat, awaiting their journey to the hands of their recipients. "To my friend," reads the sealed envelope of one—and another, and another, and most of the pieces of correspondence. The line, as simple as it is, puts on display exactly the emotion a child might feel when penning such a letter—the hope that the letter will arrive *to* someone, the fact that person is yet unknown to the child and the goal above all that the recipient will become *my friend*. From the variety of letters, it is obvious the students' teachers had assigned the letter writing as a class project—likely an assignment for practicing English skills. The letters vary in every way: Most are taller but less wide than a standard American envelope, some are white and others are blue or printed with floral designs, others are covered in stickers of school buildings, dolls, pencils, cats, stars or rabbits, still more are adorned with pictures of statues or drawings done by the young students.

A series of details from the envelopes and letters penned by Russian students.

Unsurprisingly, these young students were curious about pretty much the same things as the ones in Yoncalla—and, we can assume, the ones in Roseburg some time ago.

"I am fond of chess," wrote Samuel. "I like swimming."

"I often go to the cinema with my dad," Taya wrote to her new, unknown friends. "We have a beautiful park near my house and I often go there when the weather is good."

The only inkling of "adult" conversations were about family—a popular topic among the students' letters. Something that hadn't appeared in any of the American students' letters, but was present in many of the Russian notes: a list of their family members. "I have got a mother a father and a sister," Lida wrote. "We are four in my family," said Bogdan. Other popular topics of discussion are best friends and pets: Kirill's best friend is Bogdan, and Lida's is Sasha. Ksenia has "many pets: goldfish, snails and a hamster." And Nastya has a cat named Chris.

What the letters lacked—to no one's surprise—was any hint of the political. There was plenty that teachers or government functionaries could have instructed students to cover in their letters: election interference, proxy wars over the globe, the spreading of misinformation. *Friend, I like to swim, but my government did not manipulate the election of your president. What is your favorite class? Mine is "Good Democracy" and "Respecting the Lives of Former Russian Agents."* But no, none of that—just English class, *are you good at maths?*, sport and computer games.

✳✳✳

Principal Kornilova likes to decorate her school. The walls and floors are relatively mundane on their own, beige and various shades of brown abound. The outside of the school is a sponge-like yellow-tan brick with plain white windows arranged neatly across the front. To enter, one must walk through, first, a clear glass door and, second, a brown slab of hinged metal which serves as a barrier from the cold December days. Beyond that, a visitor must walk up gray concrete steps, around a wall and through a baseball stadium-like turnstile. From that anteroom, they pass through a nondescript brown wood door, only to be greeted by a security guard and metal detector (a common facet of shopping malls, train stations and most any other public buildings in Russian cities like Rostov-on-Don and Moscow). Once the visitor gains the blessing of the security guard, they are free to move about the school, creaking its well-loved wooden floors and getting lost in its passages and alleys next to the French and German classrooms.

But the macabre-sounding building is far from mundane. The tan bricks are adorned with a mosaic image of trumpets and books on a rainbow background. Inside the first anteroom, stairs leading to the metal door are covered with admonitions to entering students: *be hopeful, be loving, be unique, be kind-hearted, be sociable.* During the holiday season, too, New Year's decorations like ornament-adorned fir trees and tinsel-wrapped wreaths (things you might expect of an American Christmas celebration, though people in Russia hold

larger celebrations for New Year's than Christmas, which comes later in the
Orthodox calendar) bring life to the brown and gray school entrance.

**Gimnazium 14 from the outside on December 11, 2019. New Year's trees,
lights and wrapped packages sit inside the school's windowed entrance.**

The school's common areas are similarly styled—and given cultural themes
to evoke the countries about which students learn in their classes. What was
once a blue and white cafeteria turned, at the hands of Principal Kornilova,
into a "French" café, with purple teapots and flowers sitting on color-washed
white-wood shelving installations. Kornilova had plans to decorate an upstairs
floor in an "American" style, which is to say with *Marvel* superheroes. On the
ground floor, what was once a dark corridor frequented by students taking a
break turned to a slice of UK life—more precisely, a spitting image of *Harry
Potter*. Books of spells sat in stacks on shelves, a stuffed owl portrayed the novel's
Hedwig and a sign on the wall warned of the "forbidden forest." On one wall,
what was once nothing more than white paint became a gallery of British
notables: William Shakespeare, Winston Churchill, the Beatles.

On the opposite wall, what was once a statue of Soviet dictator Vladimir
Lenin in the Gimnazium 14 of the past had become a London-esque red
phone booth. The school staff, Kornilova remembers, was ordered to remove
the statue of Lenin from the school grounds over the course of one night
after the death of one of the Soviet Union's leaders. After graduating from

Gimnazium 14 in 1977, she worked there between 1988 and 1999 before spending a few years as the principal of another nearby school and eventually returning to her alma mater as its new principal when the job opened up.

A decorative telephone booth sits where a statue of Vladimir Lenin used to be in Gimnazium 14.

"We are patriots—not of the USSR, but of our native schools. It was home," said Kornilova of the move, and of the fact that many of the school's teachers today were also once students wandering the halls under the watchful eyes of Vladimir Lenin.

Kornilova couldn't recall the exact year the statue had to come down, but the image there today is evocative enough. What was once a representation of one of Communist Russia's most brutal dictators—and the author of many of its central beliefs—was literally westernized, democratized and "capitalized" by placing on its former post a symbol of Western Europe, a symbol of one of the world's foremost capitalist countries and a symbol of communication. And beyond the poetic irony that the Lenin-turned-phone booth provides a western observer of today, it also symbolizes a logical challenge to the assertion that a pen pal project of 2019 is politically equivalent to one of 1960—that teachers and administrators would act the same now as they would have then, that the height of national political tensions would have the same impact on schoolhouse projects now as it would have had in the time when Ray McFetridge had his students pick the farthest-away country they could imagine. Today, a phone booth is almost technologically obsolete, with the need for one replaced by cellphones and digital technology.

Fortunately, beyond providing a venue for the reignition of a pen pal project, Gimnazium 14 also presents—with its "glorious history," as a guide in its museum called it—a wealth of institutional knowledge about how a school would have reacted to such a project in the midst of the Cold War.

Even the architecture gives clues about what the school might have been like during the Cold War. There's a stained-glass window in Principal Kornilova's office suite, in the wall above a few couches that form a sitting area. It's made up of two panels in bright colors: blue, yellow, red and orange. Light passes through from an unknown background to portray Communist imagery which is now, according to another Gimnazium 14 graduate Zhenya Belyakov, just part of history. On the left, the glass portrays two nondescript people, standing. One of them, a woman in a yellow dress with hair to match, stands with her arm raised, symbolizing the Soviet desire for excellence in the space race, according to Belyakov. On the other side, a man stands triumphantly inside the swirls of color, wearing a patchwork suit of orange and blue. Around his neck, a red tie billows in an implied breeze—a "Pioneer tie," said Belyakov. The Pioneers (more formally the Young Pioneers' Organization) made up the youth arm of the USSR's Communist Party between 1917 and 1991,[4] until the fall of the Soviet Union. With activities much like those in Scout groups across the western world, the Pioneers pledged upon entry to the organization to devote themselves to homeland, party and Communism.[5] As part of their school uniforms, said Belyakov, Young Pioneers would wear their Octoberist-red kerchiefs to school—and then remove them upon leaving the schoolhouse gates.

"When the school day was over, we were going out of school and we took off our Pioneer ties—everybody had to wear the red tie. So we took it off," Belyakov said. "Why, why care? No, we just did not want to belong. Everybody understood the fake nature of Communism at that time."

Belyakov and Kornilova spent a few minutes, sitting under the stained glass window, talking in Russian about teachers they had who really believed in the Communist idea—but for most others, Kornilova remembered, communism was "just an obligation."

Stained glass in the head teacher's office offers a window into Gimnazium 14's Soviet-era history.

What was not just an obligation, however, was the want for international communication—international friendships. Kornilova remembers having pen pals in the United States and Great Britain during her years as a student at the school, and Belyakov recalled being part of a "Club of International Friendship," which met after classes to find friends abroad and write letters to them. They were encouraged, primarily, to find friends within other socialist or communist countries, but farther-fetched aspirations were permitted by teachers and administrators as well.

After writing and before sending, Belyakov remembers, letters would be checked by teachers to ensure they were "politically correct." But students were never explicitly told what to write, as far as Belyakov could remember. Instead, he said, "all the children knew what to write to be politically correct." Students would mention that they were "very happy to be a Soviet Pioneer," and sometimes there were campaigns, like in opposition to the Vietnam War. Belyakov especially remembered movements in support of American political activist Angela Davis, a self-proclaimed communist who was on trial for aiding[6] an attack on a California courthouse—as if reporting that "the 7-year-olds supported Angela Davis" would help much, he quipped. (Regardless the impact of 7-year-olds' support, some accounts estimate that at least 5 percent of Soviet Russia's propaganda efforts in 1971 were dedicated specifically to the Davis case.) Students weren't required to write about the "campaign" at hand—but it was generally understood that letters without that content wouldn't be sent.

Stained glass in the head teacher's office offers a window into Gimnazium 14's Soviet-era history. Zhenya Belyakov remembers removing the red tie pictured—representative of the "Soviet Pioneer"—at the end of each day, in an attempt to recognize the "fake nature" of Communism at the time.

Students wouldn't write about the negatives of communism, those things which made their lives harder or less enjoyable—but, in fairness, who would? Certainly, it couldn't be reasonable to expect pen pal friends to begin their friendships by writing about life's hardships, so it seems far-fetched to argue that the failure to include this could be called "communist propaganda."

Put more simply: The US State Department of 1960, the one which rejected an Oregon class's request to make friends abroad because they assumed it would result in propagandizing, was only partially correct. Students, at least in this anecdotal case, wouldn't be directly instructed what to write, but their writing would naturally include remnants of what they were taught to believe. As Belyakov remembers, "The brainwashing was good—but not 100 percent effective." Surely, American letters would include something similar, like images of baseball, freedom or free-trade super-market apple pies. The resistance to allowing these kinds of letters—even if they have inklings of political feelings which percolate from a school's daily "political information" sessions (which Belyakov and Kornilova remember, for that matter, to be more about practicing English than teaching political ideology)—seems overbearing.

"You cannot praise capitalism; you cannot blame Communism. At least you have just to be neutral. You write about your stuff. We play football, we enjoy life, grass is green, sun is bright."

✸✸✸

At the time, in Kornilova's view, propaganda was coming the other way—from the United States to Russia, and from the US government and media to its own people. Beginning in 1945, the US State Department was deeply engaged in an international communication project of its own, in the form of *Amerika* magazine. In the words of a 1951 journal article lauding[7] the work of the magazine, "*Amerika* is a handsome, slick paper, Russian-language magazine written and printed in New York by our Department of State. It is the same size as *Life*, has 76 pages, 12 of which are in color, and is filled with articles on every phase of life in the United States including art and culture as well as business and industrial features." The magazine, which ran until 1994, focused mostly on describing the best aspects of American life—prosperous facts and figures as the result of capitalism, the ease of construction and agricultural production, the (allegedly) high quality of life of the "American negro[sic]." But, later in its life, *Amerika* became more active in its depictions, providing, for example, patterns for making western clothing or basketball coaching manuals.[8] The magazine was tolerated by Soviet officials under an agreement[9] to exchange them with copies of a similar magazine about Soviet life to be sent to America for distribution— but not without dissent and counter-propaganda to counteract the rosy picture of America that *Amerika* painted.

A 1947 US State Department summary[10] of a critical article published by the Communist Party, for example, recalls "[the Soviet criticism] article asserts illustrations and articles in [the] magazine *Amerika* do not depict actual American life or show real living people who actually create wealth: It's the story of a disunited country with wealth concentrated, workers oppressed, Okies wandering homeless, Indians discriminated against and Negroes lynched, and the article says *Amerika's* editors fear drawing back the curtain on these matters and instead give something like embellished operetta scenes."

The State Department, however, continued on, rejoicing in this scathing review of its publishing: "Embassy considers mere appearance … article in this authoritative journal encouraging sign that *Amerika* penetrating consciousness … Soviet intelligentsia too deeply for comfort of party leaders. … writer cannot find more specific points in *Amerika* magazine itself vulnerable to attack, but rather deals in generalities, is indication our method of presentation has been very successful."

For Belyakov, that couldn't be truer—at least in regards to *Amerika's* presentation of American cars. The few times he could get an issue, in spite of low circulation (prescribed by the government) and long lines at newsstands when new issues were available, Belyakov remembers seeing images of new American cars and thinking that—while life in his country wasn't so bad and the quality of life was hard in America with no jobs and no equality, according to his government—they have nice things in capitalist ones. Culture, he and Kornilova felt, was one of the biggest forms of persuasion there was.

"Rock and roll did a lot to bury down the Communism here. Rock and roll, American jeans, records. It was not just consumption involved," Belyakov said, after remembering listening to rock concerts on western European radio signals. "I'm talking about culture. Culture brings values. There were lots of values incorporated into what we wished for. We were looking for a free, joyful life. 'Capitalism' provided that.' At least the concept of it."

For Kornilova, though, the propaganda must have been inside the United States, too. "Propaganda in the United States," she said, "was also propaganda against the Soviet Union." She experienced that firsthand in 1985, when her husband was invited to work as a professor of journalism at Silesia University in Poland and his family moved with him. For three years, the family lived in an international hotel, with the families of other professors from all around the world. France, Germany, New Zealand and Yugoslavia all found representation in the university's faculty, and all found families and children living in that international hotel.

Kornilova had a special role in the hotel—being part of the family with the hotel's largest room, it meant that she often played host to children and friends who needed a place to play and make friends from around the world.

"My daughter was 3 years old, [an American professor's] daughter, Raylin, was 10 years old, one more child from France was 6 years old and two Polish children," Kornilova remembered. "They played together and, after two weeks, they started speaking all the languages."

But, while the young children at the time played indiscriminately with one another—just excited, one can assume, to be able to travel, and that Kornilova was always prepared to feed the children when they played in her room— there was another game being played, one that Belyakov aptly called a "game of adults."

The father of Raylin, one of the American children who played in Kornilova's room, was also working at the university at the time, with Kornilova's husband. She recalled one of their first times meeting: "We moved by bus. It was the first or the second meeting with him. He, very carefully …" she grabbed the corner of a shirt and rolled the material between her fingers, pretending to investigate the material's threads as the American professor had "… did such, to my dress. I asked him, what are you doing?"

"And he said, 'Really I'm amazed. It's normal, it's an ordinary dress you wear,'" she said quietly, almost whispering as if the professor had been completely shocked by the normalcy of her dress's material. "He was surprised that I can cook well, that my daughter spoke three languages at that time. It was very strange to them. Some foreigners mistook us as some strange people who wear fur or I don't know what else. He was really surprised by my English at the time."

Of course, it's impossible to say why an American professor did what he did in 1985, but the broader issue for Kornilova is the misconception that the professor—obviously someone educated well enough for the role, and with the international mindset to be selected for international work—held, and what it indicated about Americans' perceptions of Soviets. They thought, she said, "maybe that we were—people here in the Soviet Union—were ancient people. He was surprised at the time. A normal, ordinary woman!"

That perception wasn't just outside the United States, either. When Kornilova visited Mobile, Ala., among other states on an exchange program the school ran in the '90s, she faced similar misconceptions on the ground.

"When we came to Mobile, we met people in the United States who—it was the first time they saw Russian people." She told a story about how she'd gone to purchase comfortable clothes and shoes and, at breakfast the next morning, "Americans were surprised by my appearance. They said that I ... look very much like American women, and it was surprise."

The reason for this, Kornilova thought, was easily explained—easy enough to be the justification for so much more than just misconceptions and misunderstandings. It was the same reason that the distribution of *Amerika* was heavily restricted in the Soviet Union, the same reason anti-communists in the United States feared infiltration into the moviemaking industry, the same reason an assistant secretary in a federal government office denied a congressman's request for the names and addresses of peer schools.

"If you mean propaganda, propaganda was also abroad," Kornilova said.

✳✳✳

Perhaps, on further review, a discussion of propaganda might be the wrong conversation to have. Perhaps the conversation should instead accept that propaganda might occur, but there's more to the game than that. It comes down to framing—perhaps, before one can even look at propaganda, we have to ask why it occurs, and if it would still occur if two sides had a better understanding of the other. An 11th-grade class at Gimnazium 14 had this, tacitly, on the top of their minds when they began a series of presentations and discussions with what they thought most important for an outsider to know about their *motherland*: the truth about certain "Russian myths and rumors."

The myth of "Russian drunkenness?" Nothing, compared to other European countries like Italy or France, the presenter said.

The myth of the worst roads in the world? "Yes, roads are our misfortune, but not only ours," said the presenter, who went on to telling about other states which "inherited" poor roads from the Soviet Union.

The myth that every Russian man wears earflaps? Sure, some Russian men wear them—but so do units of the Canadian military or German police.

The myth that bears roam the street in Russia? Yes, parts of Russia have bears—but they "proudly march around the world," too.

The most important stereotype, though, that the students wanted to share: "Russia is most famous for its people. Whoever comes to Russia always finds wonderful people who live in different cities, settlements and villages. They are alive, openhearted and ready to help their friends. They sing, dance and do it all with soul, with heart."

She ended the presentation with a quote from Alexander Suvorov, a Russian Empire military leader during the eighteenth century:[11] "He who loves his country sets the best example of love for humanity." There was hardly any talk of politics at all—just the stereotypes you see in movies and TV shows that make it easier to identify someone who's supposed to be of a certain background. But, as the two students showed in just a few minutes of their presentation, many of those film stereotypes are easily debunked with a little learning about what's being stereotyped.

Comparisons were easy, too, as students offered their stereotypes about Americans: that Americans eat a lot of fast food, that American universities are easier than foreign ones, that Americans tend to smile even when that facial expression isn't an accurate characterization of how they feel. Many of these misconceptions, the students said—similar to the misconceptions about Russians—come from the American films that students watch. But global politics are not immune from blame, either.

"Because of the politics, I think that many Russians think that Americans hate them, and of course many Americans think Russians hate them," one student, Sasha, said. "It's not the truth."

The 11th graders at Gimnazium 14 had similar questions to the fourth graders, and similar questions to what Belyakov remembers being curious about with his pen pals of the past: American schools, movies (most were appalled by the price of a standard American movie ticket), music (no one knew Tame Impala or Rex Orange County, but the students promised to listen once their names were written on a whiteboard, alongside their visitor's Instagram handle). But, for the 11th graders, international politics were impossible to ignore when considering how citizens of the two countries think about one another.

"I think that Americans and Russians are supposed to be out of the politics and be friends instead of all the quarrels between us," said Mikhail Plotnikov, one of the students who'd also given a school building tour. "I think that we shouldn't concentrate on the politics. The relationships between simple people should be more important than political and economic interests."

It is important, however, to consider who was in the room—American President Donald Trump was not in that room, Russian President Vladimir Putin was not in that room and neither Angela Davis nor Joseph McCarthy nor any of their successors were not in that room. It was nothing more than a group of young people—and a few adults—trying to connect with one another. In thinking about the ability to communicate, some acknowledged the barriers created by the Cold War—and that those barriers are melting away with the rise of the internet and the loss of those who remember the reasons for Cold War tensions in the first place.

"The younger generations really want to communicate with people from America and from other countries," said one student.

"It's very important for us to use the internet nowadays because using the internet at even playing video games we can find different people and friends for us, such as pen pals," said another named Misha. "For example, me and my friends were playing video games and we found a man—an American—who helped my friend write an essay about one of our things for our homework."

❊❊❊

In reality, the discussion need not even be as profound as crossing oceans to find new pen pals. Perhaps it need not be profound at all.

After the discussion ended, the students went about their days— to their next class, back to their homes or to the cinemas to watch new movies. The next day, they were planning a cultural performance, wherein students would learn about another country or culture and present about it to their peers, pageant style. With that, they'd build just a little bit more understanding and empathy for a different group of people, just by learning a bit about them—the things that make them *them*, the human things, like art, culture and dress.

"Everyone writes, 'Write me back as soon as you can!'" Kornilova reported about the fourth-grade students' letters to their new friends. There was a sense of urgency in her voice, like the same hurried and excited energy with which those same students had raised their hands to ask questions and tell about themselves. But there was only so much that could be done about the urgency—that is, nowadays, one of the key features of a physical, letter-based pen pal friendship is the slowness it requires, the patience necessary as you wait to hear from your friend as letters traverse oceans and cities.

By any guess, the children would largely forget about the letters they'd written in a few days. As Belyakov put it, "Children can pretend, and get fun from everything." In a few weeks or months, perhaps they'd be excited when they got a response, stamp, envelope, and all—perhaps that same excited energy would return to the tall hallways of Gimnazium 14. But for now, the students' new friendships were just blips in their school days, seeds sown with small piles of dirt rising above the ground—but no sprouts yet. On a number of occasions, former class secretary Janice from Roseburg lamented about how minor her class's failed attempt at making pen pal friends was in her life.

Perhaps, though, by watering the seeds planted in Yoncalla and Rostov-on-Don, these letters *To My Friend* can be more than blips and can become what Ray McFetridge had hoped in 1960: a lesson on "How People Work Together."

Gimnazium 14's fourth graders didn't consider the future political implications of the letters they scrawled, but one of their 11th-grade schoolmates tacitly had:

"I think talking about friendship, especially now, is very important because old wars, old conflicts are going away—they are becoming past. It's very important to become friends right now. Because nobody knows what would be—perhaps something bad."

Letters to new friends await their long journey to Oregon.

Notes

1   "Putin Named Five New 'Cities of Military Glory,'" vz.ru, May 6, 2008, https://vz.ru/news/2008/5/6/165649.html. *(Translated from Russian via Google Translate.)*

2   "U.S. Census Bureau QuickFacts: Oregon," Census Bureau QuickFacts, 2019, https://www.census.gov/quickfacts/OR. *Compare 2010 figures to:* "The population of Russia, federal districts, constituent entities of the Russian Federation, districts, urban settlements, rural settlements—regional centers and rural settlements with a population of 3 thousand people or more," Federal State Statistics Service, 2010, https://rosstat.gov.ru/free_doc/new_site/perepis2010/croc/perepis_itogi1612.htm. *(Translated from Russian via Google Translate).*

3   "Rostov-on-Don: land of sunflowers and hi-tech hub," RT, June 2009, https://web.archive.org/web/20130203093653/http:/rt.com/programs/russia-close-up/rostov-on-don-land-of-sunflowers-and-hi-tech-hub/.

4   "Soviet Young Pioneers," Historical Boys' Uniforms, April 18, 2009, https://www.histclo.com/youth/youth/org/pio/pioneer-ussr.htm. *See also:* Kaminskaya, Masha, and Stolyarova, Galina, "Schools Hit Books for New Methods," The *St. Petersburg Times*, January 19, 2001, https://web.archive.org/web/20041030082731/http:/www.sptimesrussia.com/archive/times/637/top/t_1644.htm.

5   "Pioneer Memories," Anna & Vladimir Popravko, 2004, http://www.just-so-site.com/archive/pioneer/pion_songs.htm. *(Translated from Russian via Google Translate.)*

6   "Search Broadens for Angela Davis," The Eugene *The Register-Guard* (Associated Press, April 17, 1970), https://news.google.com/newspapers?id=4BkRAAAAIBAJ&sjid=NuEDAAAAIBAJ&pg=6482%2C3554926.

7   Peet, Creighton. "Russian 'Amerika,' a Magazine about U. S. for Soviet Citizens." *College Art Journal* 11, no. 1 (1951): 17–20. Accessed August 22, 2020. doi:10.2307/772791.

8   Mike O'Mahony, "Juvenile Delinquency and Art in Amerika," Art on the Line, 2004.

9   "Draft of Letter to Party Organizations concerning the Dissemination of the Magazine America in the USSR," Central Committee of the Communist Party of the Soviet Union, July 30, 1956, http://www.bukovsky-archives.net/pdfs/usa/1200_us56-6-Eng-Olynyk.pdf. *(Translated from Russian by Marta D. Olynyk, December 2010)*

10 Walter Bedell Smith, "The Ambassador in the Soviet Union (Smith) to the Secretary of State," U.S. Department of State (U.S. Department of State, August 13, 1947), https://history.state.gov/historicaldocuments/frus1947v04/d403.

11 Philip Longworth, "Aleksandr Vasilyevich Suvorov, Count Rimniksky," Encyclopedia Britannica (Encyclopedia Britannica, Inc., May 15, 2020), https://www.britannica.com/biography/Aleksandr-Vasilyevich-Suvorov-Graf-Rimniksky.

EPILOGUE

THE PROCESS

by Hayley Hendrickson and Zack Demars
with notes from Madie Eidam,
Isabel Burton, Carol Kress and Robert Kessler

The behind-the-scenes story of how a University of Oregon class turned a 30-minute exercise into a two-year project, with a retelling of each step along the way and dispatches from the reporters in the field.

Reporting II Class Syllabus, Winter 2019

In this era of seeming transparency, consequential reporting is more important and valuable than ever. Sources are "media trained," corporate headquarters hide on websites with no street addresses, so-called citizen journalists pose opinion as fact. Overloaded news reporters too often find themselves reduced to stenographers rewriting press releases. Hoards of reporters descend on the Big Story, leaving fascinating and critical news left unreported. Critics of journalists call us "enemies" peddling "fake news."

Conjuring a story from what may appear to be nothing but a mundane street scene or what seems an inconsequential exchange between passersby is a thrill. Finding nascent story elements and reporting them into a tale worth telling that an audience wants to consume is our stock in trade as journalists. Creating narrative nonfiction journalism is both great fun and can be an art form. But as important as aspirations to journalistic art may be, the essential tools of journalism remain a deep knowledge of and practical experience in basic news reporting techniques.

This class is designed to develop, improve and professionalize students' reporting, story development and storytelling skills—from the discovery of subject matter and characters to the creation of a well-told news story.

A University Classroom Stumbles Across Classroom 15

"Find that girl!" was the call of the day. It was not a typical call in the corridors and computer labs of Allen Hall, the headquarters of the University of Oregon's School of Journalism and Communication. Outside, the college town of Eugene was in the height of a cold winter. The January 2019 day was overcast, soggy, definitionally "dreary." The inside of Allen Hall was stuffy and humid from students who'd left their dorms for class too late, gotten too wet on the walk over and sweat too much on the three-story climb to the top of the building. The 14 students in room 306 were typical, too—sitting in silent anticipation, waiting for their esteemed and eccentric professor to arrive just on time, as he always would.

And, as was typical, he did. He sauntered in with a copy of *The New York Times*, which was not unusual. The *Times* was required reading in class. But this day, as was every day in Reporting II, was different.

He demanded to know who'd read the Tuesday paper's "On This Day in History" column on the inside of the front page, January 29, 2019. No one had, of course—the course syllabus was clear, reading *The New York Times* was only required reading on the days we had class, not on weekends! Instead, the class sat in silence, as it so often did in response to a question from Professor Peter Laufer. As was typical, his question ended in him explaining what led him to ask it.

Atypically, though, his question also ended, some two years later, with the volume you now hold.

❋❋❋

On This Day in History
A MEMORABLE HEADLINE FROM THE NEW YORK TIMES

U.S. BARS A GIRL'S PLEA FOR RUSSIAN PEN PALS

January 29, 1960. The Times reported on some disappointing news delivered to Janis Boyle, a fourth-grader in Roseburg, Ore., who was informed that "the State Department opposed allowing her and her friends to write letters to Russian children." The request had gone (almost) all the way to the top: After she requested some names of children to write to, "her Congressman, Representative Charles O. Porter, a Democrat, advised her that Assistant Secretary of State William B. Macomber Jr. had refused, fearing Soviet censorship and propaganda."

❋❋❋

When Professor Laufer began to read us an article that was published in that day's *The New York Times* about a fourth-grade girl named Janis Boyle who was censored by the US State Department, we had no idea that her story would eventually consume our entire curriculum. But as soon as we started the investigation, we couldn't stop.

When Laufer first read it out loud, we sat in quiet confusion. We were intrigued by the story—it was about a relatively local town (since *The New York Times* doesn't get out to our west-coast state all too often) and had the intrigue of Cold War bureaucracy and political interference—but we weren't quite sure what relevance it had to us today or, more frighteningly at the time, what Laufer wanted us to do with it. We had read stories in class from *The New York Times* before and discussed aspects of them like their relevance in the current news climate, how the story was structured or what possible local stories might be spun off from the *The New York Times* national one. But this time, unbeknownst to us students, Laufer had something unconventional in mind. More than just a discussion today, he was planning a brief, 30-minute reporting exercise in class before we moved on to our next topic.

He posed the question to the class: "If I were a reporter trying to find out information about this character Janis Boyle, how would I go about getting it?" One of us raised an uncertain hand and mentioned that we could go to the county courthouse to search for details on the case. Other journalistic techniques were proposed—from simple Google searches to a road trip down I-5 to Roseburg. In response, he immediately started doling out tasks for each one of us to complete in order to obtain more background on the girl and the controversy.

Day One: Finding Janis

Laufer had only given us a 30-minute window to find as much information as we could. At first, we were flustered and tense. However, once everyone had jumped head-first into their assigned tasks, the classroom started to function as a newsroom with Laufer acting as assignment editor. Someone was looking at *The New York Times'* archives to find the original story the recent column was memorializing. Another was looking for the Roseburg *News-Review*—if it was in *NYT*, it must've been in the local paper, right? Someone was looking at obituaries somewhere—no, New Jersey! Look to New Jersey, can someone call this county's clerk and ask about wedding records for Janis Boyle? That's J-A-N-I-S!

When the half hour was up, Laufer told us to stop our work, assess our results, and close up shop. None of us did. We were too close to give up. We'd found at least half a dozen Janises and Janices Boyle who just might have been *that girl.* We just needed to get one of them on the phone and have her tell us she'd lived in Roseburg around 1960, and we'd be back to the class session listed on the course syllabus.

It was agreed, then, we'd search for 10 more minutes before moving on. We were hooked on the journalistic search, and Laufer was hooked on seeing us get a rush of adrenaline from the work he'd practiced, perfected and taught for decades.

By this time, we had attempted to call a few sources who were a part of the story such as Janice herself and her classmates, but we were still moving at a snail's pace in journalistic terms. As compelling as the story was, the truth of the matter was that we barely got started. Some students had successful conversations with people tangentially involved with the story while others hit a dead end. Most of us, being relatively inexperienced journalists, had no idea how to overcome obstacles that got in our way and were still unsure of just how far to push potential sources. We all had our various tasks—newspaper archives, libraries, county clerks, personal information directory websites— but each came with a paywall, a wrong subject, an unanswered call.

As a class, we continuously tried and failed to find the "real Janis Boyle." One of us would research and find a "Janis Boyle" who matched the age and location we were seeking, only to discover that this was not the Janis Boyle we were looking for.

We consistently hit the same stumbling block: There were many Janices out there who might be our young class secretary, but not too many Janises. We were running in circles and an added layer of difficulty in our search was the misspelling of Boyle's name in *The New York Times* article. It took us precious time to deduce which spelling was correct—"Janis" or "Janice"— as it was hard for us to believe that *The New York Times* would be so careless as to misspell the main subject's name. We wouldn't know, we decided, if the *Times* (and the AP reporter they reprinted their wire copy from) had spelled our subject's name correctly until we spoke to her.

At this early point in the process, Janis/ce Boyle could be anywhere. We were not positive she was even alive. The confidence in the classroom waned with every misidentified Janis/ce Boyle.

"I think I found her," someone would call out. The class would perk up and ask for the details about the Janis/ce that had been found, and the reporter would read out what details they could find—until the reporter would read out the fatal detail. She'd lived in another state her whole life, or she was too old, or she simply couldn't have been alive at the time.

And then the right Janice Boyle picked up the phone.

Maddie Moore had found her—this one lived outside of Las Vegas, Moore said. Laufer's next direction was obvious: Get her on the phone. Moore didn't have success immediately. She called Janice the very first day of the project and heard the beep tone of an answering machine. She called her again, at Laufer's pushing, twice more through the course of the class session. Almost a week later, Moore called again and again hit an answering machine. But after our class session had ended that day during the first week, Laufer encouraged her to try again. Begrudgingly, Moore agreed. She expected to leave another voicemail but was surprised when a woman's voice traveled through the phone with a welcoming, "Hello!"

We'd found our Janice.

As we learned, a well-formed journalistic story doesn't arise without an abundance of research, determination, and as it turns out, a little bit of luck. Or a lot of luck. Janice Boyle lives in Henderson, Nevada, a suburb just outside of Las Vegas—and Moore was scheduled for a sorority trip over spring break at the end of March. To Las Vegas.

"It really is serendipitous," Laufer mused.

Janice agreed to meet Moore for an interview. She was extremely coopera-tive and excited at the prospect of talking about a memory from decades ago. She referred to the events that transpired in 1960 as her "15 minutes of fame," and looked forward to telling her story again, a couple of generations after that fame. By the end of the first week, we had an interview scheduled with the main subject of the story.

Suddenly, this innocuous class exercise had turned into real reporting.

"Reporting II" Turns into "Janice 101"

This week, along with continuing our normal Reporting II class curriculum, we started to dive further into Janice Boyle research. We had two specific sources that we wanted to contact amidst the preliminary stages of our work. The first source was possibly the most intriguing research aspect of Janice's story: the FBI.

At this stage, after several of Moore's phone conversations with Janice, our collective understanding was that the FBI had raided the Boyle family home in order to obtain the fourth-grade letters that were to be sent along to Russia. Therefore, we assumed that the FBI had these files hidden away somewhere having not seen the light of day since 1960. This is the perfect tool for a reporter, the first-hand documents filed away in some government archive. We made two incorrect assumptions: first that the FBI had these documents in their possession, and second, that they would merely hand them over to us.

But, where to find them, and how to get them? If the government had touched them, Laufer reminded us, they must have kept a record of them. And, many records kept by the government are public and therefore (theoretically)

accessible. Sure, we had class assignments to look forward to, but Laufer was lenient as he was as intrigued as we were by the Janice story. In the name of "experiential learning," a buzzword so often sought by professional schools like ours, it began to overtake whatever readings and assignments were listed on the printed syllabus as Laufer found "teachable moments" like a short lecture on the Freedom of Information Act.

At this point, our main goal was to find out as much as we possibly could about Janice Boyle and it seemed that one effective avenue to accomplish this was through filing a FOIA request to obtain the documents the FBI had taken from Janice. One of our reporters, Zack Demars, had the most experience filing FOIA requests and took up the task that second week by filing one for any Janice file the Bureau may have had. He'd go on to file several more about Janice and her compatriots under various names and spellings, often to receive only denials from the agency or responses that they had no such records.

One agenda item was to get in contact with a school in Roseburg that could serve as an almost mirror image to Janice's elementary school in 1960. We wanted to implement an experiment by finding a willing participant to go through the same process Janice's fourth-grade class went through. Vaughn Kness, another of our reporters, had a sister in the fourth grade at Yoncalla Elementary School, only a half hour up the road from Roseburg and also in Douglas County. Vaughn spoke with the teacher of the fourth-grade class, Diana Fast, who said she was more than willing to participate in the project. She planned to have the students who were interested write their own pen pal letters to potential Russian friends. With another excited and committed participant, we continued to charge forward.

✹✹✹

Week three of research brought about a major mischaracterization of the story we had formed thus far. Moore had been speaking to Janice frequently to confirm details we unearthed and improve our understanding of the story we sought to recount. After talking with Janice over the phone again, Moore discovered that the FBI had not "raided" the Boyle home as we thought they had. Janice said the agents had actually "raided" the school for the letters. This painted a different picture in our minds of the role the FBI had played in the story. Raiding an elementary school and involving principals and administrators only would have increased the imprint the FBI left on the town of Roseburg—but would not have been as dramatic as we'd imagined the agents breaking down the door to young Janice's home.

This discovery led to our desire to gather more information on the school and its employees, specifically teacher Ray McFetridge. Demars filed another

FOIA request in hopes of obtaining the file we presumed the FBI had on him. At the same time, Demars received a letter from the FBI which claimed that they were not allowed to hand over the information on Janice as she was still alive—because, apparently, the federal government cares for "personal privacy" only when it comes to releasing information to journalists. In order to obtain any file they had in their possession, Janice would have to file an FOIA request herself or sign a form giving us permission to do so. While disappointing that they didn't hand over any files with their response, simply seeing a letter in response to our query with the FBI insignia at the top was exciting.

U.S. Department of Justice

Federal Bureau of Investigation
Washington, D.C. 20535

February 6, 2019

MR. ZACHARY DEMARS

EUGENE, OR 97403

FOIPA Request No.: 1428112-000
Subject: BOYLE, JANICE

Dear Mr. Demars:

This acknowledges receipt of your Freedom of Information Act (FOIA) request to the FBI.   The FOIPA Request Number listed above has been assigned to your request.   Below you will find informational paragraphs relevant to your request.   Please read each item carefully.

You submitted your request via the FBI's eFOIPA system.

☐   We have reviewed your request. Consistent with the FBI eFOIPA terms of service, future correspondence about your FOIA request will be provided in an email link.

☑   We have reviewed your request. Consistent with the FBI eFOIPA terms of service, future correspondence about your FOIPA request will be sent through standard mail.

You have requested records on one or more third party individuals.   Please be advised the FBI will neither confirm nor deny the existence of such records pursuant to FOIA exemptions (b)(6) and (b)(7)(C), 5 U.S.C. §§ 522 (b)(6) and (b)(7)(C).   The mere acknowledgement of the existence of FBI records on third party individuals could reasonably be expected to constitute an unwarranted invasion of personal privacy.   This is our standard response to such requests and should not be taken to mean that records do, or do not, exist.   As a result, your request has been closed.   Please visit www.fbi.gov, select "Services," "Information Management," and "Freedom of Information/Privacy Act" for more information about making requests for records on third party individuals (living or deceased).

Please be advised per standard FBI practice and pursuant to FOIA exemption (b)(7)(E) [Title 5 U.S.C. § 552 (b)(7)(E)], this response neither confirms nor denies the existence of an individual's name on any watch lists. This is a standard response and should not be taken to mean that any individual's name appears, or does not appear, on any watch list.

Even though we were not yet able to obtain information from the FBI on Janice or her family, we realized that perhaps we could get it straight from them. Janice Boyle's family included a mother, father and two sisters. With the help of the class, reporter Hayley Hendrickson managed to track down Janice's sisters along with their contact information. She called Janice's older sister, the late Pam Nord, and youngest sister Jodi Alsbaugh, who were both willing to be interviewed for the story. Both sisters were surprised that a story from 1960 about their sister was garnering so much attention from an entire class of journalism students. They were also unsure of how much their memories would be of use to us as they were not the focal point of the story. But they were happy to provide everything they remembered.

In talking with Nord and Alsbaugh, Hendrickson gleaned two pieces of knowledge that proved to be integral to the story. According to Janice's sisters, the fourth-grade class had received a box of letters from a Russian class. Riverside School then hired a Russian interpreter to translate and read out loud the letters from Russia to the students in Janice's fourth-grade classroom. This new development was perplexing to us as we couldn't yet figure out how or why a Russian class would be inclined to write letters to Janice's class when the Roseburg class's letters had never been sent to Russia. The portrait was slowly being painted for us, but we couldn't see the full picture yet. The next order of business was to find the Russian translator who had made the trip down to Roseburg in 1960.

Before looking into the logistics of the newly discovered Russian letters, we wanted to get a better perspective of the event from students in Janice's class. Carol Kress and Madie Eidam decided to do some deep internet digging to find some of her classmates. Eidam and Kress tracked down two Riverside School alumni and asked them about their memories of the infamous event. Kress located Genee Parr, one of Janice's classmates who laughed and laughed when the story was mentioned to her. She mused that "she had not thought about it for a very long time." She did make an interesting claim that McFetridge chose Russia for the pen pal project because it was the height of the Cold War. She didn't remember anything about an FBI "raid" but she agreed to be interviewed for the story and provided us with another classmate's name— Mark Wilborn. After Eidam called Wilborn, she reported to the class that he was helpful but did not have very much to report.

"I'm so sorry to tell you my memory is not very clear in regard to this project. I was nine years old and was more interested in sports," said Wilborn.

In addition to McFetridge and Boyle's family, another subject we wanted to dig deeper into was Charles O. Porter, the congressional representative who forwarded Janice's letter seeking help finding Russian students to the State

Department. We wondered if there was even a minute possibility he had kept the letter Janice had sent to him. It became apparent that most of his old files, however, were already right in our lap—across campus in the university's Knight Library. In the immediate aftermath of this fortunate discovery, Laufer enthusiastically ordered Isabel Burton to take on the task of sorting through Porter's extensive files. At the time, it seemed like yet another wild goose chase. Porter's files were voluminous and the likelihood of finding anything of value was low. But as we came to learn throughout the process of writing this story, good things come to those who look down every possible route.

It was at this point where the future of this project seemed to solidify for us. Laufer asked for a vote: Should we throw out the rest of our scheduled class curriculum in favor of putting all our resources into continuing to work on the story? The answer was immediate and unanimous, so the next assignment due, he assured us, wouldn't be what was listed on the syllabus and would instead be Janice-related. We began research into various publications that would be interested in a long-form story such as this one. We were confident in the compelling consequential nature of the events within the story, but we were not quite sure that we had managed to put all the pieces together to make it a compelling feature article for a magazine.

There was no doubt that the events that transpired in 1960 were news-worthy events. But we worried that as a class we had gotten caught up in our enthusiasm. After weeks of research, gathering data, and interviewing sources, we suddenly reflected: Does this story even matter in 2019?

We gave countless practice elevator pitches to each other in our Allen Hall classroom. Laufer brought in two former CBS and NBC foreign correspondents, stationed in Moscow, as guest speakers, and we began solidi-fying our story. By this point, we'd found an old whiteboard in Allen Hall and scribbled away each corner of the project—one section dedicated to FOIA requests, one dedicated to people to call, one section dedicated to classmates, another section dedicated to who would do what. Every few class sessions, Laufer would invite another professor or a former colleague of his into class. We still didn't know what the story *really* was, but each time one of us would attempt to explain it in a compelling way to impress whichever guest had given us their time and insight before we, with much fanfare, turned the whiteboard around to show the guest all the ideas we had for the reporting.

Some asked if the story was fact or fiction. Some wondered how the story had not garnered more attention in 1960. In every pitch, the excitement generated in our newsroom was visible on our eager faces and palpable in the tones of our voices. Now, it was simply a matter of narrowing our scope, setting a goal for publication, and actually writing the story.

With each guest, Laufer or a student would ask if this, to the guests' trained ears, sounded like a viable story or a complete waste of time. And each guest told us that, with the right work, this could be something.

❋❋❋

Jan–March 2019 Reporting Log for Individual Research (Excerpt)

Zack Demars

~30 January
~12:00 PM — The Boyle Project begins as an in-class exercise run long.

4 February
4:08 PM — FBI FOIPA request submitted for records of Janice/ Janis Boyle/Hall. Fee waiver requested.

6 February
2:45 PM — FBI FOIPA request submitted for records of Ray McFetridge, Patricia Boyle, Edward Boyle. Fee waiver requested.
3:16 PM — FOIA request submitted to State Department for records for the events in which State was involved.

13 February
5:00 PM — Letter from FBI received. Informs that they cannot send records for Janice, if they exist, due to privacy exceptions to FOIPA.

15 February
5:00 PM — Letter from FBI received. Informs that they cannot send records for Edward et al., if they exist, due to privacy exceptions to FOIPA.

20 February
4:00 PM — Letter mailed to Janice for her to forward to FBI to provide consent for the release of records related to her name.

25 February
5:47 PM — Email comes from Janice, informing that the request letter she was asked to forward isn't quite accurate. Her home wasn't visited by the FBI—only the school was.

26 February
4:00 PM — Revised letter sent to Janice.

4 March
1:51 PM — Janice forwards letter to FBI records.
9:00 PM — Time spent searching for obituaries or death records of McFetridge, Edward, and Patricia.
11:57 PM — Documents sent to FOIPA; questions email address, as instructed by FOIPA PIO.

```
6 March
   3:31 PM        Attempt to find verification of death of McFetridge.
                  Seeking Oregon Death Index in Knight Library.
                  Research desk provides call number and refers
                  me to microform library. In place of microfilm
                  box is "see microform desk" card. Technology
                  desk person claims not to know what that means,
                  refers to circulation desk. Circulation desk
                  refers to microform desk on the left, which does
                  not exist.
   8:42 PM        Contract UNLV libraries for Patricia's obituary.
11 March
   9:12 AM        Obituary obtained from UNLV.
12 March
   7:16 AM        New request submitted for Patricia's records.
   3:42 PM        Oregon Death Index listing Raymond H. McFetridge
                  located in Knight Library on microfiche.
13 March
  10:53 AM        New request submitted for McFetridge's records.
```

***

In the last week of the term, progress had significantly slowed down. We were awaiting the much-needed interview with Janice that would come in one more week. Moore was set to interview Janice in her home in Nevada. We were patiently waiting for a response from the FBI about FOIA requests regarding Patricia Boyle, Janice Boyle's mother and Ray McFetridge. Well, maybe not so patiently. So far, the FBI had been fickle about the amount of information they had or were willing to divulge, and we had reaped nothing from the many FOIA requests filed.

It was finals week of the university's winter term. According to the Reporting II syllabus, we were, by the end of the week, supposed to be turning in a final draft of a 1,000-word story on some topic of interest to us and our college town. But, Laufer instead told us that our final would be to write 1,000 words on our piece of the pen pal project.

There was one point of contact that did pique our interest in the dwindling hours of the class we had coined "Janice 101." Reporter Amelia Salzman had successfully contacted McFetridge's son, now an Associated Press reporter headquartered in Iowa. He provided the contact information for his older sister, who immediately asked if we were inquiring about the Russian letters. We hoped that McFetridge's family would lead us to more information regarding the letters, as McFetridge had passed away in his forties and did not leave any explanation behind for why he had started the pen pal project.

***

Dispatch: Isabel Burton, Congressman Charles O. Porter, Reporter and Library Researcher

I was tasked with looking through the political and congressional files of Charles O. Porter, representative for Oregon's
4th congressional district in 1960 and with searching for
evidence of Porter's involvement in the Riverside class's pen
pal request.

The congressman's files were located within the Special
Archives unit at the University of Oregon library. During
my exploration, I came across frail newspaper clippings,
Polaroid and black-and-white photos, books and speech drafts
and lengthy political reports. The process of looking for
Riverside materials was grueling and tedious. There was a
possibility I would find nothing about the innocent Riverside
pen pal attempt. I dug through more than 15 boxes—some which
held more than 20 files per box—without seeing any mention of
Russian penpalship, Janice Boyle, or the Riverside School.
I dug through boxes titled Education, *Register-Guard* [Eugene's
newspaper], Censorship, and State Department, naïvely thinking
that the project would uncover itself.

One seemingly average morning at Special Archives, as the
number of boxes to look through—and my patience—dwindled,
I was finally rewarded for the many days I spent cooped up in
the depths of the UO library.

I opened up my last box—Box 32. It was an alphabetical box
that held all of the "R" files, including Radiation, Railroads
and Roosevelt. I came across a file labeled "Roseburg Disaster"
and immediately associated it with the Riverside class
project—although I learned later that the Roseburg Disaster
was a massive explosion that occurred in Roseburg in 1959.
In my mind, the Riverside pen pal project was the biggest
disaster to have occurred in 1960 Roseburg. Disappointingly,
I found nothing in this file about the project.

But right behind this file was another—labeled RU. And all
of a sudden it clicked. RU meant Russia and Russia meant the
Riverside pen pal project. It was this file where I found
letters and newspaper clippings surrounding Porter's involvement in the project.

I never found the letter that Janice sent to Porter though,
which was heavily covered in the news. The thought about where
it could be (and that it's not in our hands) drives me crazy.

❋❋❋

In the two weeks we had been gone, much had occurred. Moore interviewed
Janice in Vegas and brought back pictures along with both poignant and funny
stories. Janice was extremely gracious and more than willing to dedicate time

to the project. Having her enthusiastically on board meant the world to us and the story would never have gotten as far without her willing participation.

After what felt like weeks without a word from the FBI, there was an onslaught of updates about our FOIA requests. The FBI informed us that they had no files on Ray McFetridge and that the file on Patricia Boyle had been destroyed. This struck us as odd, but we simply didn't have time to delve too deeply into conspiracy theories.

The FBI did inform us that Janice Boyle's files had been forwarded to the National Archives and Records Administration. Demars got in contact with a Records Specialist from the National Archive who told him that Janice's file was lumped together with that of a man named Charles Pemberton. Our immediate reaction was confusion and alarm. Janice had never mentioned a man named Charles Pemberton being involved with the case. The helpful NARA staff person said that he would send the Janice Boyle portion of the Pemberton file to us right away—he could mail us a CD or send the files via email. We chose the latter.

Ben Lonergan created a website where we could start organizing the information we possessed. At this point, it was still up in the air about how we wanted to format the story and where we wanted the story published. We decided to keep researching and writing with the hope an appropriate place to publish would become obvious to us as we developed the story—a story that had become increasingly intriguing and complex.

✳✳✳

Dispatch: Carol Kress, Roseburg Reporter

The drive to Roseburg is one of the most beautiful drives I've ever experienced. When I visited, some trees had started to spring new leaves, while others remained bare in the cold of winter. We were surrounded by rolling mountains and every shade of green imaginable. The drive allowed me to ponder the pure excitement I felt at the prospect of going to a new town to interview a woman with direct knowledge of the event that occurred 60 years ago in a small town in southern Oregon.

I learned that Roseburg was known as "Timber Town." As a native to Southern California, where our local fauna was palm trees, I couldn't imagine what exactly "Timber Town" would look like. But as I got closer to Roseburg, I passed truck after truck carrying logs, and then one timber mill after another.

The Coon family lived on a side street that was difficult to find. The sign had been blown over in the snowstorm two months

before and had not yet been fixed. But once I pulled up to the
house, it was exactly as I'd imagined—the All-American house,
complete with flowers under the window, a blue trim on the
house and Old Glory waving at us as we pulled in.

As a newer journalism student, doing interviews had not
yet become second nature to me. Despite all the planning,
preparation and my notebook full of questions and recorders
with fresh batteries, I still felt the pressure of the interview. But Genee Coon, one of Janice Boyle's classmates during
Ray McFetridge's "How People Work Together" lesson, was a
delight. After only a few minutes, it felt like talking to an
old friend. Learning about other people's lives and listening
to their stories is what I love most about journalism.

Half of my time in Roseburg was spent with the Coons and the
other half was allocated to driving through downtown, looking
at the locations we had heard so much about in the previous
months, such as Janice Boyles' old house and the buildings
formerly known as Riverside School.

I also went to the newly-reopened library and looked through
the old newspapers on microfilm. It was a nice break from the
copious amounts of online research and a journey back to our
roots: libraries, microfilms, and ancient machines that took
me way too long to figure out how to operate.

The trip was short, only a few hours in total, but for a
student just beginning to dip my toes into journalism, this
trip only made me want to dive in entirely.

✸✸✸

In the second week of spring term, Salzman, the reporter in charge of
obtaining information on fourth-grade teacher Mr. McFetridge, brought extra-
ordinary news—she had located the Russian letters. The letters sat in an old
box in the house of one of McFetridge's daughters in Sisters, Oregon. Laufer
ordered a round of applause from the whole group. We had tangible evidence
for what had been a mystery for months. To us, locating the Russian letters
was a symbol of our hard work and dedication to this project. We could have
stopped at any point, declared victory and said that any further work would
be fruitless or unnecessary. We never did though, and it finally felt like we were
being rewarded for the countless hours all of us had invested in this story.

It still wasn't clear what the end game for the story was—did we just want
to find the letters? Did we want a feature story in a campus publication, or a
state-wide newspaper, or a special section in *The New York Times*?

"We are *not* writing a book!" Laufer insisted, knowing full well what could
come ahead for the project.

Riding on the back of the Russian letter excitement, Demars had an
update about Charles Pemberton. He told us that apparently Pemberton was

a dedicated communist and prolific letter writer. He wrote to Janice in 1960 encouraging her to research communism and included much communist propaganda in the package he sent to her.

"We couldn't write fiction better than this," Laufer noted in response. Throughout the research process we were continuously amazed at the depth of this story—but this was the icing on the cake. It felt as if a present had been dropped into our lap. The entire term we had been looking for alternate perspectives for the story besides Janice's. We had found many, but none were blatantly communist.

As another heartwarming surprise, Kness brought present-day pen pal letters from the fourth-grade class at Yoncalla Elementary School. We read them aloud during the meeting, enjoying the students' innocence and the lighthearted tone of the letters. It was another piece of the story that helped put things into perspective for us, and it led to us wondering again about where this story could be published. In a further burst of enthusiasm for the project, Laufer suggested, "This could be a book." And in doing so, he planted a seed in all of our minds that maybe, just maybe, our hard work could turn into a published book.

***

Dispatch: Madie Eidam, Russia–United States Relations Reporter

My role in Janice's story began with newspaper clippings and the discovery of Mark Wilborn, who is pictured with Janice and Genee Parr in one of Roseburg's feature stories when word of the pen pal project hit headlines in 1960. I began collecting any and all newspaper clippings I could find in Oregon and across the country about our mysterious pen pals. I soon found Janice's account on Newspapers.com, and her folders of familial research and genealogy tracking records acted as a great help to my own compilations. As I read through articles that were born out of Roseburg and spread through Salem and Portland, and then all the way to the East Coast, my understanding and excitement about the momentum and impact that this story had in the 1960s grew intensely. Janice and her class's efforts were covered in local newspapers in the South, inspired editorial pieces about government interference in New Jersey, and even made their way to newspapers in Russia. The absolute opposite of what the United States government wanted, the Eisenhower administration's actions led to an amplified focus on Janice's attempted pen pal efforts, and ultimately helped the Roseburg fourth-grade class make contact with Russian children. Coverage in newspapers in Europe brought this story of desired connection on to the radar of Russian educators, which led to the writing of letters to Mr. McFetridge's class. As the scale of this story grew before our eyes, we celebrated the power of the press and the ability of news to spread.

I began my efforts to get in touch with Mark. I had found a phone number and nervously dialed it, hoping it was the correct Mark Wilborn who was now 68 and living in Wilsonville, Oregon. That Friday, I left a message explaining who I was and why I was calling. That felt easy enough. *Now, I wait,* I thought. The weekend passed with no word from Mark, and when I returned to class on Monday and gave Laufer the update, he told me, "Well, call him back." So, I called him a few times over the course of the week. The following Monday, I returned to our class still empty-handed. We went around the room, as we did every class after we had effectively blown up our syllabus, sharing our updates on how our piece of the story was developing. Today I was seeking some guidance from my peers and professor. I had left multiple voicemails with Mark and Carol Wilborn and had absolutely nothing after two weeks. This, to me, meant that Mark didn't want to share his side of the story with us. I did not have an email for him, but I did have an address and, at this point in the term, I had begun to embrace Laufer's assertion of persistence. "Can I write a gentle letter to Mark? Maybe if I can explain in more words what we're doing, he'll want to talk with us." With some affirmation and advice from my peers, I wrote a letter to send to Mark. Laufer gave me postage and an envelope, University of Oregon embellished, and I sent out my last hope with a stamp and felt accomplished. After less than a week, I received an email from a Mark and Carol Wilborn! To hear from this mystery man who I had been hoping to speak to for almost a month felt amazing. Mark's memory of the time period was limited to bits and pieces, such as seeing the article in *The News-Review*, and he mused that as a child he must have been relatively protected from the politics of the time. His sentiment about youthful innocence gave the class a chuckle when the letter was read aloud. He wrote, "I'm afraid at that age I was more interested in sports and other activities than school projects."

While Mark may have felt like he had little to say, his recollections were still a beautiful and valuable glimpse into his experience of this strange occurrence in Roseburg. He brought to light something essential to our understanding of this story: Many of Janice's classmates, including Janice to a degree, were fairly oblivious and uninterested in political

agendas and likely processed the termination of this project
with a shrug of the shoulders and then asked to be excused
for recess.

❋❋❋

Though our articles were only in-progress, our research was proving substan-
tive, with promise for much more. Laufer wanted to officially gauge our reaction to writing a book. He briefed the class with a forewarning that it would
be extremely difficult to not only write a book, but to find an appropriate publisher. We would have to put in an increased amount of effort into the project
beyond the classroom, with the understanding that we could end up writing a
book without it ever getting published. Laufer put it to a vote: to write a book
or to not write a book. With little hesitation, the entire class raised hands in
favor of expanding the project into a book. With the green light, we started a
book proposal.

For four hours that night, we brainstormed and, with students taking turns
manning the laptop to type, we sketched out what a book might look like. In
every aspect, we were all on the same wavelength.

Laufer's cry to dull our hopes and expectations changed: "We are not
publishing a book!"

❋❋❋

The book project had been set in motion, but we wanted to remain grounded.
The proposal we'd written up could easily be rejected, and we would have had
to go back to the drawing board. We wanted to remain hopeful but never stray
into the territory of being overly-confident. The plan was to work until all of
our goals were met, fully developing the content and story while finding an
appropriate and interested publisher.

And as the spring term ended, this is exactly what we did.

Spring and Summer 2019

In an effort to keep ourselves on track, and because none of us wanted to
stop the reporting process just because our required Reporting II course was
completed, Laufer set up no-credit meeting times for the spring term so we
could meet once a week as a class and update each other on the progress
we were making. "Janice 101," originally a tentative title for our class, had
now been fully embraced. Heading into spring break, we felt confident and
galvanized to get the job finished—to tell the complete story. We had a story
on our hands, and most of us decided that we cared enough about it to commit

to it for another term. The picture we had been painting the entire term had started to take shape. It was up to us to keep on pushing.

Summer arrived with little fanfare and an abundance of uncertainty. As a cohort, we had just ridden the incredible high of meeting Janice at the Slow News Conference. Seeing the subject of our book, and frankly, the starting point of our entire journey read the files we had uncovered over long, strenuous months of investigation was a surreal sight. We took Janice out to dinner after the conference and the same sentiment was uttered a multitude of times at the table—"I can't believe we're here."

But quickly, the stars faded from our eyes and the precariousness of our current situation set in. Soon we would all be heading off in our own directions with our own unique obligations as the class ended and graduation approached. Laufer worried about the student cohort putting the book on the backburner.

To alleviate some of the concerns that swirled around the book project, Laufer enlisted the aid of a managing editor who would take on the extremely difficult task of getting this rag-tag group of students in order and put our disjointed pieces together into a cohesive piece of literature. Julia Mueller, a student at the UO School of Journalism and Communication, worked at the school's writing center, held more than one student leadership position, and was a published writer—and Laufer introduced her by those credentials to the student cohort at one of our last meetings of the spring term. We deduced that she could write well, edit well, and, most importantly, lead a team. Her reputation preceded her, and we found she was more than qualified to take on the (unpaid) job. Within the first week of her involvement with the project, she met with each writer individually to brainstorm their chapters, research new leads, and plan the expansion of our short class assignments into the narrative arc of a journalistic book manuscript.

✳✳✳

Dispatch: Robert Kessler, Original Cohort Member Researching Russian Pen Pal Correspondence

My first experience corresponding with Russia took place in the middle of the Phoenix Inn and Suites Eugene ballroom at 10:30 pm.

I was accompanied by our colleague Terry Phillips, a former CBS News correspondent based in Russia, who would help make the call and translate if needed. Terry and I met in the hotel lobby, quickly discussing our plan for contacting the Russian school. It was late in the United States, but Russia was just starting its day. With the hope of catching someone at the school before their day became too busy, we quickly grabbed some old foldable chairs and dragged a plastic table to the center of the ballroom.

Terry opened his laptop and dialed the 11-digit phone number into Skype. As the phone rang, I felt my stomach begin to tighten. So many questions started racing through my head. "Would anyone answer?" "Would they speak English?" "Would they even be interested in having pen pals in the U.S.?" The phone rang several times before a woman picked up the phone answering in Russian. I looked at Terry because this was now out of my domain. Terry spoke with the woman for a minute or so in Russian before switching over to English. We spoke for several minutes, and the woman acknowledged that she had received our previous emails and would talk to faculty and the administration before moving forward.

Once we finished the call Terry and I discussed the call. The woman on the phone seemed reluctant and that was worrisome. We were afraid that her reluctance and lack of correspondence to begin with would leave us empty handed. Terry and I parted ways and so began the waiting game. Luckily, it was a short wait. Less than a week later my colleague Allison Barr received an email from a fourth-fifth-grade teacher at the school. We finally had an in. For months we continued correspondence on our end, but the Russian side had gone quiet.

After months of silence, we finally cut ties with the teacher and the school. With our colleague Zack Demars set to travel to Russia and a different school found for us by Terry Phillips, those working on the Russian school contact happily handed our research over. Despite our first attempt falling through this was an experience I will never forget. It was something that finally made me realize "Hey! I'm a journalist!"

***

Fall 2019

Mueller and Laufer called a meeting as soon as the new school year started in October, 2019. Mueller had been hard at work all summer, coordinating dozens of drafts of each individual chapter, and frantically trying to contact writers who had gone radio silent during the break. When the cohort arrived at the meeting, we quickly noticed that the core group had dwindled down even more: As cohort members graduated, studied abroad, or got new jobs, there were few of us in Eugene—and fewer still with the time and energy to devote to the project.

After Mueller had debriefed us on the state of the manuscript and the state of our cohort, Laufer announced that one of the four cohort members present needed to embark on a journey to Russia over the winter break.

Go to Russia? Who would go? When would that writer go? How would we come up with the funds for travel?

Laufer went on to explain that the project as-is was interesting—but that a trip to Russia would solidify the project. Mueller agreed that it would allow the story taking shape within the manuscript to come full circle by having a writer hand-deliver the letters we had received from the Yoncalla fourth graders to an elementary school in Russia. Laufer's final point convinced us: We'd already done everything we could for this book from Eugene. This was the next step. This was all that we had left to do.

We came to the quick consensus that it would be in our best interest to send Zack Demars. Demars had been an integral part of our team, filed countless FOIA requests, secured the compelling Pemberton files, and obtained many of the documents that we utilized to put the pieces of this story together. He was a reporter for the school newspaper, the *Daily Emerald*, and had studied abroad in Eastern Europe, in the former Yugoslavia, the summer before. And he could write quickly—the trip would take place in December, and we would need his finished chapters by the end of the year.

"VISA STUFF?" Demars scribbled on a notepad during the meeting.

Laufer and Demars pursued funding from the journalism school and various departments on campus and a plane ticket was procured. With the help of Terry Phillips, arrangements for translation, housing abroad, and a 16-hour train ride to Rostov-on-Don were settled.

Meanwhile, the cohort was hard at work writing and re-writing, editing and re-editing. We knew the process would be painstaking, but we were not all quite prepared to take on the previous workload of those who had left the project. Mueller and Demars took on rewriting and reorganizing many of the chapters whose authors could not work on their chapter at the time, and Hendrickson helped chapter authors with research—changes needed to be made quickly, and contacting cohort members proved increasingly difficult as the school year continued.

In the middle of fall term, we discussed scrapping the project. As full-time students themselves, Mueller and Demars found that the work of fact-checking, copyediting, rewriting and strengthening 11 chapters—each with a unique author, unique sources, and a unique storyline—was almost too much. But a pep talk from Laufer proved enough to keep the Eugene-based cohort pushing.

This doubling down of our efforts led us to new discoveries. We learned that Congressman Peter DeFazio was coming to campus for an event at the law school in early November, and saw this as an opportunity to get an alternate perspective from a present-day Oregon congressman—Burton and Demars caught DeFazio in a walk-and-talk interview across campus.

At Mueller's direction, the cohort also refocused its efforts on research that may have been overlooked or put to the side in the months prior. Burton and Hendrickson made frequent trips to the UO Special Collections and pored over countless documents from Charles O. Porter's legacy. This additional research aided us in the characterization of Porter and the political campaigns he was involved with.

But despite our steadfast commitment to the book project, Laufer did not want us to lose sight of what we had already worked so hard to accomplish. Through Slack—our primary form of communication— Laufer sent messages meant to simultaneously encourage and galvanize us to keep pushing. In his correspondence, he asserted, "This is our make-it-or-break-it moment."

Laufer repeatedly reminded us that there are "coffee drinkers in every Starbucks with an open laptop who think they want to write a book." Only a small percentage of them push hard enough to get their work finished, and fewer still get published. "Starbucks slackers," Laufer would call us in jest, reminding us to keep working.

✹✹✹

Dispatch: Zack Demars, FOIA Reporter and Russia Correspondent

When you're starting a pen pal project, it's a really good idea to have letters to share. We had them—don't get me wrong—but it's pretty important to know where they are before you get on a plane. In the spring, we'd gotten the initial set of pen pal letters from the Yoncalla, Oregon, class. That first meeting, Vaughn Kness brought them into our team meeting one Wednesday afternoon to an immediate round of applause. We excitedly passed around the loose-leaf correspondence and drawings the youngsters had scrawled in pencil, reveling in how ideal their comments were for fostering such a friendship.

They were to be scanned, it was agreed. After that meeting, the Yoncalla letters went home with someone and, for the most part, were forgotten about for months.

Fast forward to October. At the fall 2019 first meeting, we addressed the elephant in the room: the next logical step in reporting about fourth graders—sending someone to Russia. By some mysterious series of steps, it was concluded that I, of all people, would be the one to go, and I went home that night with a notebook page reading, "Visa Stuff? RUSSIA?"

But there was something I'd failed to write on that page— "letters?" I spent the next two months preparing all sorts of things: answering detailed questions about myself and my family to apply for a visa, researching how to dress without standing out too much, making arrangements with the Rostov school and scouring thrift store racks for low-cost and high-heat outerwear.

In the lead-up too, of course, I ran through all sorts of reportage considerations: Who would I talk to? What about? How would I talk to them? How would I record what they said?

But until about a week before I left, I still hadn't considered that key piece of the project. The damn letters. The Monday before my Saturday departure, I realized my error. I texted Julia Mueller, "You have the letters, right? Will need to get those from you before I go!"

Then, panic. She did not have them. Perhaps Laufer had them in his office? No. Perhaps Vaughn had held onto them? No. Perhaps they really were hidden in a drawer of Laufer's vast desk? Still no. Luckily, though, after calls or texts to every member of the project's team, we located the scans that had been taken of the letters in the spring. With just hours to go before my flight, I got an email with those letters attached—to the joyful reception of new friends in Rostov.

Winter 2020

The plan was to hold our final Janice 101 meeting almost a year to the day after Laufer first introduced us to *The New York Times* article that would set us on our pen pal journey. Demars had spent part of the winter break in Rostov-on-Don, and Mueller had edited the two chapters he turned quickly around as he traveled home. Now, we had some facts to iron out, some last-minute edits to make, and some publication plans to develop. We sat around a table on the second floor of a restaurant in Eugene until it closed, our laptops next to our dinner plates as Mueller read aloud questions and facts to check from the manuscript. We answered the questions and checked the facts then-and-there. The next day, our work would be sent away to publishers and Janice 101 would officially close up shop—until, that is, the next necessary round of edits. At the end of the meeting, Mueller suggested our title: *Classroom 15*. We turned the work over to her, who cleaned up our manuscript once again as we pushed toward publication.

On multiple occasions, our cohort expressed that, even if this book never saw the light of day, the entire process will have been worth it. From cold-calling people we aren't sure exist to turning around an entire chapter on a flight home from Russia, the journalistic lessons we learned have been formative in our graduation from *student-journalist* to *journalist*. And of course, no one wants to be a Starbucks slacker.

Reporting II Final Assignment, Winter 2020

Zack Demars

In an FBI office somewhere around the country, there's a letter. In fourth-grade class secretary handwriting, the letter instructs the recipient about the sender's hopes of "sharing our way of life." Accompanying the letter are other letters: some from other fourth graders, others from the federal government—and one from the government of Russia. In a file, these letters sit together, waiting to reveal the story they hold, the official account of an FBI inquiry into a fourth-grade class in the heat of the Cold War.

Or, at least, that's the hope.

That hope is based on a fluid set of facts. We think we know for a fact, based on our interviews, that the FBI came to the Riverside School in 1960 to collect those letters. We know, based on regular practice, that those letters are probably still in the possession of the FBI, sitting in a filing box, on a shelf, in a basement of some musty government building. We know—most critically—that the law allows us a window into the government's official narrative in the form of the Freedom of Information Act.

We have questions about what happened to Janice Boyle and her fellow fourth graders in Roseburg in January of 1960. The government has some answers to those questions through these letters and these files, and the law gives us theoretical free-rein to access those answers. So, in principle, that should be the end of it. But of course, it's not that simple.

The first complexity in obtaining these answers comes from the variety of characters involved in our story. There's a number of different people with whom the records we're looking to access might be associated, several agencies by which they might be held and countless complexities in prying them out of those agencies.

First, the characters. Janice Hall, the protagonist of our story, is the obvious first target of records searching. She brings some challenges in that she's got a variety of names (through marriage, and by way of misspellings in news-paper accounts), she was about nine years old at the time and might not have any records associated and (morbidly) that she's still alive so her records can't be released to a third party like us. That last challenge led to our ini-tial rejection by the FBI but, thankfully, we've been able to address it with her help. By having her sign and forward a letter to the custodian of the records we're interested in, we are anticipating that they will be able to release any records they might have about her to us. Her young age at the time, however, means we've had to widen our records search to include more characters: the adults.

The first and most obvious adult to look at is the adult in the classroom—the fourth-grade teacher, Ray McFetridge. If the FBI took something from his class, they might have put it under his name, and if he had some ulterior motive in encouraging his students to get in contact with communists, the FBI more than likely would've written it down. Thankfully—in the journalistically morbid sense—McFetridge's records should be a little easier to access than Janice's, in that he's already passed and therefore can't assert rights to privacy. The FBI has simply requested proof of his death in order to search for and return records related to him. An initial search of obituaries proved useless, but after prodding with some helpful librarians, fiche number 21 of the post-1981 Oregon Death Index in the Knight Library at the University of Oregon should prove to the FBI that Mr. McFetridge's records are free to be released. All that's left is to forward that document to the FBI in a new request.

Other adults we're interested in are Edward and Patricia Boyle, Janice's parents. In a letter from the FBI, the agency again rejected our request for their records because it lacked adequate foundation about their ability to assert rights to privacy—that is, whether or not they are still alive. With the help of the librarians at the University of Nevada, Las Vegas, we've been able to forward an obituary of Patricia's to the FBI in support of our request. Edward has proved trickier: he passed away in 2016 in a very small town in central Oregon, so an obituary isn't readily available in online or Knight Library sources. The next step is to inquire with county offices and local libraries in Jefferson County about the possibility of receiving a record of his death from one of them.

The final character is less of a character and more of a setting—Roseburg's Riverside School. Another one of our next steps will be to request records related to this location, as it is where the inquiry and (subversive?) activities took place. The FBI has confirmed that records about locations and events can, in fact, be requested, so the precise formulation of the request will prove critical.

As for the agencies holding these records, our efforts have been focused on the FBI, as that is the agency which allegedly took documents from the students and teachers involved. As such, the hope is that their archives would have the most texturally useful records. Also of interest is the State Department, as they had some degree of interaction when foreign governments got involved. They, however, have yet to acknowledge the request for their records, so a follow up with them is incumbent upon us at this stage.

Human memory is feeble, human sources fallible. These records will be the concrete foundation which underlies the remembered accounts of the events which took place in 1960. With these letters, we'll have, in their own words, what each of the characters in the story was hoping to gain or hoping to prevent with their actions. Pragmatically, they'll also offer our reader something textural, something interesting to engage with and immerse in. The struggle now is to find exactly where those concrete facts are and how to access them.

Demars finished his chapters on the long flight back to Oregon from Moscow. And the rest—to embrace a cliché Professor Laufer would abhor—is history.

AFTERWORD

by Scott McFetridge

There would be no Classroom 15 *book were it not for the lesson plan drawn up by teacher Ray (Bud) McFetridge. His son Scott works as a reporter and editor for the Associated Press. Journalism and journalists are a recurring theme throughout the* Classroom 15 *yarn—from Edward R. Murrow to Ann Curry and of course the student reporters at the University of Oregon who reported and wrote this book. Hence it is both an appropriate filial and professional role for Scott McFetridge to take pen (or keyboard) in hand and offer food for thought with the last words.*

I'm not sure what I find most intriguing about this story.

Is it the events 59 years ago in Roseburg that so starkly reflect the fear and paranoia of the Cold War? Or is it learning details about my father's role in this controversy and better understanding my own family thanks to the dogged and skilled efforts of University of Oregon students, none of whom I have met and none of whom had been born when dad died in 1978?

We can call it a tie, but personally, I'll always be grateful to the students and the professor who started this project for teaching me about my father's key role in this brief but illustrative series of events.

Of course, I knew my father had gained international attention when as a young teacher he asked his students to write to children in the Soviet Union. I knew reporters had called from throughout the country and that the effort was quickly dropped after my father's goal of helping his students learn about the lives of other children spiraled into Cold War politics in a way he never intended. But that was it. I don't believe my father mentioned the matter once to me.

While *Classroom 15* enabled me to learn about my father and unknown details from my mother and siblings—what other secrets do you have hidden in that cedar chest, Linda?—much of the description of my father also rang true. I was only 14 years old when dad died, but even then it was clear how devoted he was to his students.

I would ride along to the Oregon Coast on the weekend as dad took a few students to the beach and down a steep embankment to see the remnants of a shipwreck at Boiler Bay. I would accompany him to school on countless Sundays as he prepared for the coming week. And I'd see him spend night after night at the kitchen table, working on lesson plans and grading papers while the sound of classical music rose and fell from a clock radio pushed against the wall. His favorite hobby was shooting photos at school events and then developing the film and making prints in a makeshift darkroom in that same kitchen late into the night, all for the reward of giving the pictures to students and teachers.

Of course, none of this seemed out of the ordinary to me. It was only years later, after graduating with a journalism degree from the UO and working for a stint elsewhere that I returned to Salem to work as a reporter at the local newspaper. Time after time, I would introduce myself to a source to be met with a pause and then the question. Are you Ray McFetridge's son? I'd say yes and then hear a familiar description of how he was their favorite teacher because of his kindness and ability to make class interesting. He was a teacher who made a difference, they said. One they still think of.

So here we are, nearly 60 years after Bud McFetridge came up with an idea for making a difference to fourth graders at Riverside School in Roseburg. What dad may not have realized is that even as politicians and bureaucrats thwarted his attempt to help his students understand their world, and maybe break down barriers between so-called enemies, his work succeeded in spotlighting the government's puzzling attempts to build a wall between students—only a year before an actual wall was erected in Berlin. And now, many years later, the work of the UO students has put this simple effort into a historical context, letting us understand how a failed school project says so much about our country in an earlier era and today.

To those UO students, thank you for working to gather the information needed to finally tell this story. And thank you for letting me learn more about my father, who put so much value on teaching and had such care for his family and his students.

EDITORS, AUTHORS AND CONTRIBUTORS

Editors

Peter Laufer is the James Wallace Chair Professor of Journalism at the University of Oregon.

Julia Mueller is a writer and editor. She graduated magna cum laude from the University of Oregon's Clark Honors College and School of Journalism and Communication and was named one of her graduating class's Oregon Six top students for her interdisciplinary involvement, awarded research and honors thesis. She worked as a writing coach for the journalism school and as an editor for *The Daily Emerald*, and was brought on mid-way through the project as *Classroom 15*'s managing editor. She also authored a chapter and contributed to re-writes throughout the book. Mueller has written and published journalistic, nonfiction, fiction and academic writing.

Lead Reporter and Author

Zack Demars is an investigative journalist. Originally from Everett, Washington, Demars graduated summa cum laude from the University of Oregon with degrees in journalism and political science. He's reported for *The Daily Emerald*, The Catalyst Journalism Project, *The Bend Bulletin* for the Charles Snowden Program for Excellence in Journalism and more. Outside of reporting, Demars enjoys running, hiking and attempting new vegetarian recipes. As the lead reporter for *Classroom 15*, Demars spent a week of his last college winter break in Russia and spent months making his roommates nervous with the volume of correspondence he was receiving from the FBI.

Chapter Authors

Isabel Burton is a University of Oregon graduate with a degree in advertising and journalism. For the book, she dug through files of Oregon's Congressman Charles O. Porter.

Madie Eidam graduated the spring of 2019 from the University of Oregon School of Journalism and Communication. She was a photographer for the campus cannabis magazine *Green Eugene*. After graduating, Eidam returned home to Oakland, California, to work for a creative agency.

Hayley Hendrickson is a graduate of the University of Oregon with a B.A. in Journalism. For *Classroom 15,* Hayley spent an extensive amount of time tracking down sources for interviews, researching in the UO library, and compiling material for the development, writing and production of this book.

Vaughn Kness graduated from the University of Oregon's School of Journalism and Communication in the summer of 2020. Kness has won awards for his writing from the Oregon Newspaper Publishers Association, including first place in Best Writing and Best Editorial categories.

Carol Kress graduated from the University of Oregon School of Journalism and Communication in 2020 with a bachelor's degree in journalism. For *Classroom 15* she researched Roseburg history and the 1960 US presidential election.

Maddie Moore graduated from the University of Oregon in spring 2019 with degrees in political science and journalism. At the UO she devoted much of her time to her elected role on the Associated Students of the University of Oregon student senate. Now living and working in Sacramento, California, she is particularly interested in the intersection of politics and communications.

Amelia Salzman is a graduate from the University of Oregon with degrees in cinema and journalism. She is currently pursuing an MFA in writing. Living in London the fall of 2019, she worked for Transparent TV engaged in documentary production. She lives in Eugene, Oregon. She interviewed and researched the McFetridge family for the project.

Additional Contributors

Jennifer Mendez, Robert Kessler

The Original Cohort

Allison Barr, Isabel Burton, Bailey Cook, Zack Demars, Madie Eidam, Kaitlyn Jiminez, Elizabeth Kessel, Robert Kessler, Vaughn Kness, Ben Longeran, Jennifer Mendez, Ashley Price, Mitchell Riberal, Amelia Salzman, Hayley Hendrickson, Maddie Moore

The original cohort of students in Professor Peter Laufer's Reporting II course at the University of Oregon School of Journalism and Communication.

ACKNOWLEDGMENTS

Laurie Arellano, program manager at People to People International, for arranging contact with Mary Eisenhower.

Leslie Steeves, SOJC Senior Associate Dean, for her support of the project and her office's undergraduate research grant.

Josh Buetow, SOJC director of financial operations, for guidance through the university fiscal realities.

Julie Davie, for her assistance in connecting with former students from Ray McFetridge's classes.

The FBI Record Division's PIO and Beth Anne Steele, FBI public affairs officer, Portland Division, for guidance through the FOIA process and for information on FBI activities.

Priscilla Finley, humanities librarian, University Libraries, University of Nevada, Las Vegas, for her assistance in locating the obituary of Patricia A. Boyle.

Vartan Harabajahian, for his assistance in making preparations for reporting in Russia and work on translating materials throughout the book.

Brad Lowary, SOJC executive assistant, for his help arranging travel details.

Janet McFetridge, for providing copies of the Russian postcards sent to Roseburg.

Juan-Carlos Molleda, University of Oregon School of Journalism and Communication dean, for his early and continuing support of the project.

John Perusio, archivist, special access/FOIA staff at the National Archives & Records Administration, for his research assistance.

Terry Phillips, former CBS News Moscow correspondent, for his work in translating Russian materials, and for his assistance with fact-checking throughout the text.

The Chicago *Sun-Times* archive team and the library staff at University of Illinois Urbana-Champaign, for their assistance locating the obituary of LeRoy Wollins.

The University of Oregon Division of Global Engagement for its Global Oregon grant in support of reporting from Russia, and **Lori O'Hollaren** in that office for her assistance.

The University of Oregon Special Archives staff, for pulling over 40 boxes for us over the course of a year.

The University of Oregon Undergraduate Research Opportunity Program, for its grant in support of reporting from Russia, and **Karl Reasoner** in that office for his assistance.

The University of Oregon-UNESCO Crossings Institute for Conflict-sensitive Reporting and Intercultural Dialogue, for its financial support of the project.

Emma Wolf, SOJC graduate, for reviewing and editing early drafts of the manuscript.

INDEX

CPSIA information can be obtained
at www.ICGtesting.com
Printed in the USA
BVHW031814290321
603662BV00001B/17

9 781785 275975